WINE
ISN'T ROCKET SCIENCE

Ophélie Neiman

Illustrations by Yannis Varoutsikos

WINE ISN'T ROCKET SCIENCE

Translated by Nysa Kline

BLACK DOG
& LEVENTHAL
PUBLISHERS
NEW YORK

Black Dog & Leventhal Publishers
Hachette Book Group
1290 Avenue of the Americas
New York, NY 10104

www.hachettebookgroup.com
www.blackdogandleventhal.com

First English-language edition: April 2017

Black Dog & Leventhal Publishers is an imprint of Hachette Books, a division of
Hachette Book Group. The Black Dog & Leventhal Publishers name and logo are
trademarks of Hachette Book Group, Inc.

The publisher is not responsible for websites (or their content) that are not owned
by the publisher.

The Hachette Speakers Bureau provides a wide range of authors for speaking events.
To find out more, go to www.HachetteSpeakersBureau.com or call (866) 376-6591.

Library of Congress Cataloging-in-Publication Data has been applied for.

ISBNs: 978-0-316-43130-9 (hardcover); 978-0-316-43129-3 (ebook)

Printed in China

1010

10 9 8 7 6 5 4 3 2 1

CONTENTS

Tonight, Juliette is throwing a party. She has invited her friends Jack, Henry, Caroline, Elizabeth, and Paul. They love to talk about wine a lot, each bringing their own experience to the conversation: Elizabeth is obsessed with the proper etiquette for serving wine; Jack has learned about the flavors and aroma by tasting wine; Henry knows all about how wine is made; Caroline loves to travel and she understands what terroir means; and Paul is building a wine cellar.

Juliette is an amazing hostess. So before her friends arrive, she prepares carefully. She chooses the right glassware, selects the proper wines, and makes sure they are at the right temperature. It's not easy, and she does not want to disappoint her guests. She is not a sommelier who knows exactly how to choose wines to match the food and ambiance of the event. But she is using the information in this book to gain the knowledge she needs to feel like a pro.

She also makes a plan for after the party to clean up the dishes, the glasses, and any wine stains. And if a little bit of wine is left over, it's no big deal. She has some ideas for saving it and some recipes for using it. Most important, she won't forget what to do if she gets a hangover. But before the dinner party, she thinks maybe she should organize a blind tasting with games and some surprises.

This chapter is for all the Juliettes in the world who would like to throw a successful party with ease.

JULIETTE

PLANS A PARTY

Before the party • During the party
After the party

Which glasses ?

These are the glasses most commonly found on the table at a dinner party.

1. Water glass It's for serving water. Period. Only put wine in it if it's a cheap wine you don't care about. At any rate, if you use this type of glass for wine, you won't smell much. It is useful for serving just a taste.

2. Champagne coupe Pretty, but not very useful for discerning the aromas of Champagne. It was rumored to look like the breast of either Marie Antoinette or Madame Pompadour, Louis XV's mistress.

3. Champagne flute Perfect for tasting Champagne, of course. It could also be used for light and bubbly white wines or aperitifs, such as Kir, port, Madeira or sparkling cocktails.

4. All-purpose INAO/ISO wine tasting glass Although it is very well made, it's rarely preferred by wine judges or critics. They are used a lot in restaurants because they're cheap and great for tasting all types of wines.

5. Burgundy glass It has a big bowl but a smaller rim diameter. It's perfect for Burgundy but also shows off whites or other types of young red wines. It concentrates the aromas so you will have plenty to smell.

6. Grand Cru Burgundy glass This is for lovers of expensive and famous Burgundies. It concentrates the aromas, then disperses them at the rim to spread the bouquet.

7. Bordeaux glass This very tall, tulip-shaped glass works for all wines except delicate whites. It tapers in from the bowl yet the lip is open enough to spread the wine on the tongue, so it works for powerful wines.

8. All-purpose glass It's the same shape as the Bordeaux glass but smaller. It works for light, powerful whites and both young and old reds. It could also be used for powerful Champagnes. Basically, it works for everything and is not specialized for any type of wine.

9. The decorative glass This is generally colored or kitschy and is good for nothing—most definitely not for drinking good wine. It hides the colors and suffocates the aromas. Upcycle it into a little vase or candle holder. Unless it's got sentimental value, chuck it.

The reason for using a stemmed glass

A stemmed glass has two uses:

It keeps wine fresh. The stem gives your hand a place to hold the glass other than next to the wine. Warm fingers work like a hot water bottle on the liquid and warm the wine.

It liberates the aromas. A balloon glass allows the aromas to play about freely before concentrating to tickle your nostrils, so you can better smell the wine.

A regular glass without a stem lets the aromas escape, and *poof*, they're all gone. That's too bad, especially if you've bought a good wine. That would be a tragedy.

If you must choose just one over the other? Opt for a small Bordeaux glass or a big all-purpose glass—they work for every occasion and adapt to all wines. Avoid glasses that are too small. They inhibit powerful reds from expressing themselves. On the other hand, glasses that are too big can diminish enjoyment of delicate whites.

There are a number of other types of glasses. The wine glass has been the subject of much experimentation in efforts to enhance certain wine characteristics. Finnish glassmaker Chef & Sommelier makes one called Open Up that has a sharply angled bowl at the bottom, which allows the wine to "open up" and release the most aromas possible. Many other glass manufacturers make glasses in a similar style. If you like wines that are very aromatic, these glasses may be for you.

Glass or crystal?

What makes crystal so great?

Crystal can be very delicate, with a rim barely thicker than a sheet of paper. Drinking from crystal creates a light and elegant sensation in your mouth. Another advantage is that it keeps the wine fresh longer than would a regular glass because it conducts less heat. Crystal has a rougher surface than glass, so when you swirl to aerate the wine, more aromas are released. Crystal isn't recommended if you're clumsy. It's expensive and easy to break. If you find yourself buying more crystal glasses than bottles of wine, give it up. There are other materials that give the illusion of crystal, and they are much sturdier.

CORKSCREWS

What kind of corkscrew is in your drawer? The answer to this question depends on your tastes, your patience, your budget, and your habits—not so much on your muscles.

The principle of a corkscrew is simple: It combines a screw, often called a "worm," with a lever or lifter. To avoid shredding a cork, choose a model that has a spiral worm with no center post rather than an auger type that looks more like a screw. Be careful if the worm is very short, because you could break the cork.

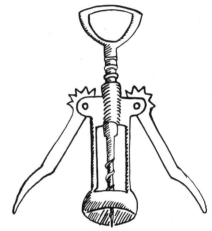

The classic winged corkscrew

It's easy to use, often cheap and stands up to lots of use. The only drawback is its tendency to pierce the cork and leave little bits of cork in the wine. Simply insert the screw into the cork and turn the key, which will raise the arms. Press the arms downward, which will lever the cork out of the bottle.

1 1 1

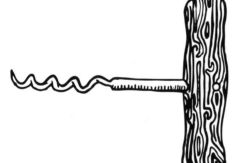

1 2 1

The simple corkscrew

This one doesn't have a lever; you just insert the screw and pull up on the handle with vigor. If you don't pull strongly enough, you won't be able to drink wine, and if you try to force it, you risk breaking the cork. In fact, this corkscrew is more useful for measuring the strength of your biceps than for anything else.

The lever-action corkscrew

This is the fastest, most efficient of the bunch, perfect for a ninety-year-old grandpa to use to open twenty bottles without risking a sprained wrist. On the flip side, it's heavy and expensive, and you can't adjust the position of the worm in the cork.

1 3 1

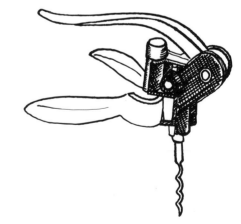

Juliette plans a party

The sommelier knife or waiter's friend

This is the one that you see used at restaurants. It's the most versatile because it allows for delicate removal depending on the state of the cork. This corkscrew also includes a knife to remove the foil that covers the neck of the bottle. It slides easily into a pocket (or handbag) and works in all sorts of situations. Choose carefully: Find one that's sturdy and has two positions on the fulcrum (the hinged part that braces against the neck of the bottle), which reduces the need for excessive pulling and avoids breaking the cork.

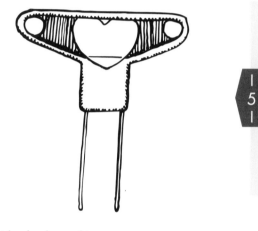

The two-prong cork extractor

This is the secret weapon of people who love old bottles. The two-prong cork puller or extractor is a rare tool and has the strange quality of not having a screw, so it doesn't pierce the cork. It requires a special technique, which is all about gliding the prongs between the neck of the bottle and the cork, then pulling while turning very carefully. When badly used, it pushes the cork into the bottle, but it's a useful opener for very old wines with corks that can break easily.

Ack! I broke the cork!

Don't panic. You have two choices. If you have a sommelier knife, screw it into the remaining cork at an angle to avoid making the hole bigger and creating cork crumbs. Wedge the piece of cork against the bottleneck and pull it up vertically.

Another option is to push the cork into the bottle and immediately pour the wine into a carafe to keep the cork from contaminating the wine.

Solution 1

Solution 2

HOW TO OPEN A BOTTLE OF WINE WITHOUT A CORKSCREW

Wait, nobody brought a corkscrew? There are several emergency methods you can use.

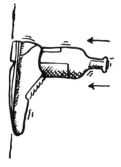

Force the cork into the bottle This works if you immediately pour all of the wine into a carafe so that the cork doesn't contaminate the liquid. This is a risky method, because it really can ruin the wine in less than three minutes.

Make an improvised corkscrew (like MacGyver) This is perfect for resourceful DIY-types and guaranteed to up your cool quotient at a party. The idea is to find something to hold on to the cork, then lift it. For example, a screw and pliers could work. One method tested and proven by yours truly in real life is to remove a screw from a microwave oven and use a pair of scissors: four bottles uncorked and a ton of happy new best friends.

Force out the cork using pressure For this you need a wall or a tree, and a shoe with a small wooden or rubber heel. Remove the foil from the top of the bottle. Stick the bottom of the bottle into the shoe and use it as a hammer, tapping the heel of the shoe against the wall or tree. The shockwave will move through the heel of the shoe and push the cork out after about seven or eight blows. Be careful, because under pressure a little of the wine will burst out of the bottle. And take care to protect your hands with a towel just in case of breakage. Aside from the dangerous nature of this method, it's not my favorite way to uncork a bottle of wine because it shakes the wine and can harm the quality. However, it's practical at picnics.

You are either lucky or psychic You have bought a bottle with a screw cap. No need to look for a corkscrew. Simply turn and open.

· HOW TO OPEN A BOTTLE OF CHAMPAGNE ·

Many people avoid drinking Champagne because they are afraid of putting an eye out or breaking Grandma's precious vase when they try to open a bottle.

1 Don't shake the bottle before opening it. If you have carried it in a bag and swung your arms around, let it rest at least an hour and a half in the fridge before opening it.

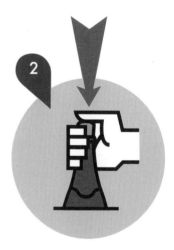

2 Once the wire cage that covers the cork is removed, put your thumb on the top and don't leave the bottle alone unsupervised.

3 Don't pull, turn! You have to hold onto the cork firmly, covering it with the palm of your hand so it doesn't fly away, then turn the bottle slowly. You will feel the cork slowly coming out and you'll be able to control how much pressure you use to release the cork and the gas inside the bottle.

4 Don't let go! Hold the cork and the bottle until they are completely apart. If you're doing this right you will hear a discreet and elegant pop.

5 Keep a glass within reach of the bottle. If you go too fast and the foam bubbles up, you will be ready to pour before the Champagne overflows out of the bottle.

Before the party

WHICH WINE FOR WHICH PARTY?

There is no strict rule here. It really just depends on your own tastes. Nevertheless, the choice of wine can influence the ambiance, for better or for worse, so here are some guidelines.

Date night
(dinner for two)

Good ideas
For an elegant ambiance: a red Burgundy (Côte de Nuits) or white Burgundy (Chablis)
For a relaxed evening: a Muscadet from France
For a sweet, "la dolce vita" ambiance: a Brunello di Montalcino from Tuscany
For a sensual ambiance: a white Loire (Chenin Blanc)
For a sexy ambiance: a red Côtes du Rhône
To melt a foodie's heart: an off-dry Riesling from Germany

Bad idea
A big red wine that stains: Purple teeth make a bad impression, guaranteed.

Big party

Good ideas
Bubbly: a Prosecco from Italy
Aromatic: an Albariño from Spain
White: a French Pays d'Oc Chardonnay
Red: from Languedoc or Chile (fruit, sweetness)

Bad idea
A big, delicate wine in a party cup. No one will be able to smell it.

Serious dinner party
(with family or your boss)

Good ideas for a white
To win points and gain respect: Meursault (Burgundy)
To impress: an Assyrtiko from Greece

Good ideaa for a red
Perfect son-in-law: a Saint-Émilion (Bordeaux)
Solid, can't-miss: a Rhône blend from France or California
Sensible, no-nonsense: a Barbera d'Alba from Italy
Authentic above all else: Morgon (Beaujolais)

A drink with a friend

Good ideas

A lesser-known appellation: a Jasnières from Touraine, a dry Sherry from Spain, or a Touriga Nacional from the Douro in Portugal

A forgotten vintage: white (Pinot Blanc from Alsace, France or Alto Adige, Italy) or red (Blaufränkisch from Austria).

A good wine with a bad reputation: Muscadet sur lie (from the Loire. Be sure to buy from a good wine store!) or Chiroubles (Beaujolais)

A wine for warm weather: a rosé from Provence

A glass of wine on the couch: Rioja (a red from Spain)

Bad idea

A cheap Bordeaux: You'll look simultaneously like a snob and a cheapskate.

Good ideas

Something to celebrate: Blanc de Blancs Champagne

The new baby is here: Puligny-Montrachet (a white from Burgundy)

I will always be there for you: Pommard (a red from Burgundy)

Will you marry me? Amarone della Valpolicella (a red from Veneto, Italy)

Toasting a special moment with friends: Bierzo (a red from Spain)

Watching time pass (birthdays): Pauillac (red from Bordeaux) or Napa Cabernet Sauvignon from California

The big moment

  All alone?

If you are alone, it's better to drink a bottle that's already open than to open a good bottle, because when the pleasure isn't shared you risk feeling more alone.

WHEN TO UNCORK?

Just before serving
Dry whites, fruity whites, light reds, sparkling wines, bubblies and Champagnes. It's enough to let them aerate in the glass to wake them up.

One hour before
Nearly all wines, reds as well as whites—except sparkling wines—will improve if you let them breathe an hour before serving. It's enough to remove the cork and let the bottle sit.

Three hours before
Young, intense red wines from France, Chile or Argentina as well as some from Italy, Spain, and Portugal. The more powerful ones, especially if they are very young, could even be opened six hours before the meal and poured into carafes for the last three hours.

Why let a wine breathe?

Oxygen is an indispensable friend to wine but can also be an enemy. When wine is exposed to oxygen, the wine evolves and grows, but eventually it gets old. Wine will age at an accelerated pace when exposed to oxygen.

Wine and air
Wine breathes in the bottle. The little air space between the wine and the cork maintains contact with oxygen.
In the glass, wine mixes with air, the aromas flourish, and the tannins soften. That's enough for light wines.

Old wines and air
An old or mature wine has a bouquet and tannins that have had time to age in the bottle, so it doesn't need to be aerated. Too much oxygen can ruin its very fragile aromas.

Wine and the carafe
Sometimes a wine needs to be aerated more fully to engage and awaken it, hence the need for a carafe. Wine will gain in intensity and complexity, and its structure will melt in your mouth. You can also aerate whites and Champagnes. A white wine is more sensitive to oxygen than a red wine. But fat and powerful white wines, made in oak barrels (like the big whites from California, Burgundy, the Rhône and certain exceptional Champagnes) will benefit from a short time in a carafe.

CARAFE OR DECANT?

The goal of using a carafe is to aerate the wine, while decanting permits the wine to separate from the deposits that accumulate in the bottle. You carafe a young wine; you decant an old wine.

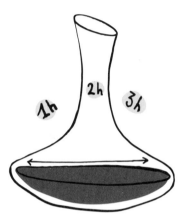

To aerate a young wine using a carafe

Why?
To wake up the aromas (the bouquet). This technique can also reduce and dissipate the aromas of young reds.

How?
At least an hour, or as many as two or three hours before bringing it to the table (depending on the intensity of the wine), pour the liquid from the bottle into the carafe. You can pour from high above, as some servers of tea do, to aerate the wine the most. You can also shake the carafe to aerate.

Which carafe?
Use a carafe with a large flat bowl, which allows a large area of contact between the wine and the air.

To decant an old wine

Why?
Decanting old wines is not mandatory, but when decanting, it requires great care because the tannins and coloring agents form a deposit in the bottle. Decanting helps separate the deposit from the wine so you don't pour it into the glass.

How?
First position the bottle upright on a table a few hours before the meal, so the deposits can drop to the bottom of the bottle. Then very carefully pour the wine into a clear decanter. Decant only a few minutes before serving. Oxygen can quickly deteriorate the quality of the wine.

Which carafe?
Choose an upright carafe, with a small, less-rounded bowl and a fairly small opening to limit the contact with the air.

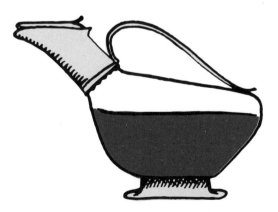

AT WHAT TEMPERATURE SHOULD WINE BE SERVED?

Wine temperature is important: It influences not only the perception of the aromas (bouquet) but also the sensation on the mouth (the mouthfeel). Here is a test: Taste a wine at 47°F/8°C and then the same wine at 65°F/18°C, and it will seem like you are tasting two completely different wines. A wine served at the wrong temperature could make the wine taste terrible—so be sure to be vigilant!

Heat
accentuates certain aromas, including the perception of fat and alcohol. A wine served too warm can seem nasty, heavy and pasty.

Why not serve all wines at the same temperature?
Because you have to adapt to their character, not the other way around. For a dry white wine with little bouquet, you're looking for acidity and freshness. Serve it chilled, even cold. For an intense, spicy red wine, you're looking for a softness of tannins and roundness of flavor. Serve it at nearly room temperature.

Cold
masks the bouquet and accentuates the perceptions of acidity and tannins. A wine served too cold can seem austere, hard and only somewhat aromatic.

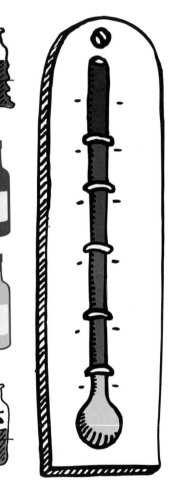

68°F (20°C) and above: nothing

61–64°F (16°–18°C): intense reds

57–61°F (14°–16°C): fruit-forward reds

52–55°F (11–13°C): intense whites, big Champagnes, light reds

46–52°F (8–11°C): sweet wines and muted wines, rosés and fruity whites

43–46°F (6–8°C): sparkling wines, champagnes, spicy and dry whites

 Better to be too cold than too warm

It is better to serve a wine a little too cold and allow it to slowly warm up in the glass (a wine can warm by 7°F (4°C) in about fifteen minutes once served) than to serve a wine too warm.

How to chill wine quickly

Normally, your wine would be stored in a room that is cool, even cold.
Normally your wine would not be stored at higher than 64°F (18°C).
Ideally it's kept at 59°F (15°C).
If that's not the case, what do you do?

3

You have less than one hour before the party

Use this speedy trick: Put the bottle into a large bowl or bucket half filled with cold water, half filled with ice cubes. Add a big pinch of salt to the water, which will help lower the temperature more quickly.

1

If you have two to three hours before the party

Put the wine in the fridge, adjusting the time according to the service temperature.

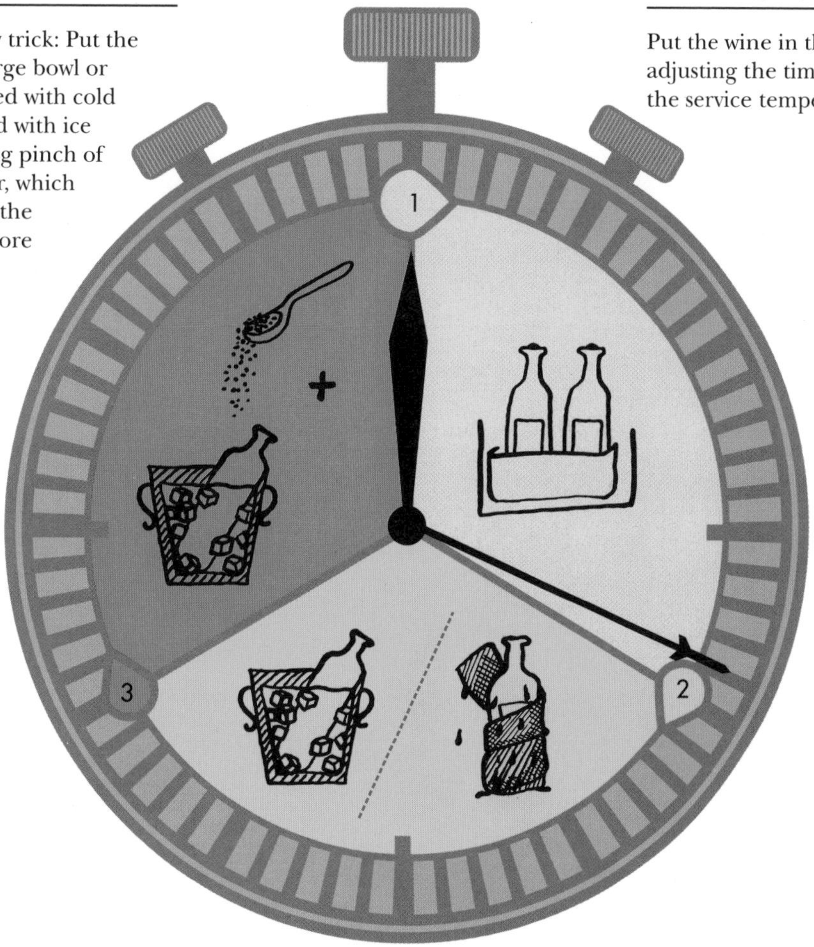

2

If you have one hour before the party

Put the bottle into a large bowl or bucket of cold water and add ice cubes. This method is as effective as putting the bottle in the freezer.

Another possibility: Soak a dishcloth in cold water, wrap it around the bottle and place it in the fridge. The damp cloth will accelerate the refrigeration.

Someone brought me bottle of wine. What should I do with it?

A guest arrives with a bottle of wine. What should you do? Thank the guest. If you feel that he wants to taste the wine that he brought, open the bottle. If the wine is not suited for the meal, put it aside and open the bottle that you planned to serve.

If the guest tells you that it's "a good bottle for aging," put it in the closet and promise to open it in a few years with him (and do it). If his intentions are not clear, it's up to you to decide if the wine is appropriate for the party or not.

The wine isn't appropriate

The wine doesn't go with the theme or mood of the party. It may be a better wine for a beach party, for example. Serve it later at a more appropriate occasion.

The wine doesn't go with the meal (a big red with fish or white with beef). Keep it for the next time and make a meal specially adapted to the wine.

The wine is appropriate

▲ A Champagne or other sparkling wine

If it is chilled, serve it with the appetizers.

If it is not chilled, tuck it away for next time.

If you are serving an entrée that goes with the wine, chill it using one of the express methods.

If, and only if, it is a sweet sparkling wine, keep it cool and serve during dessert.

▲ A dry white

If the wine is not cold, chill it using the express method and serve it during the first course as long as it's not a salad with vinaigrette.

You can also serve it with fish, a white meat like chicken or pork, or with a pasta that isn't in a tomato-based sauce.

 **A red**

Put it someplace cool, on a window ledge or in the fridge for half an hour, and serve with the meal if you are serving red meat or a pasta with red sauce.

 A sweet white

Put it in the fridge and serve it with dessert.

Bring good wine

A piece of advice for guests: If you want to bring a good bottle of wine suitable for the party, call your host the day before the dinner and find out what's on the menu. Then choose a wine that fits.

In what order should the bottles be served?

The order is important, because one wine shouldn't make you regret drinking the previous wine. To avoid this pitfall, take care not to offend, bore, stifle or divert your taste buds.

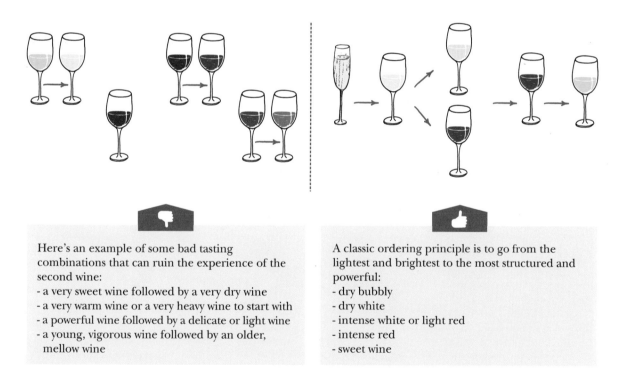

Here's an example of some bad tasting combinations that can ruin the experience of the second wine:
- a very sweet wine followed by a very dry wine
- a very warm wine or a very heavy wine to start with
- a powerful wine followed by a delicate or light wine
- a young, vigorous wine followed by an older, mellow wine

A classic ordering principle is to go from the lightest and brightest to the most structured and powerful:
- dry bubbly
- dry white
- intense white or light red
- intense red
- sweet wine

 In case the wines are similar

Go with the oldest to the youngest. The old wine normally has more finesse. During tastings, you often taste in this order, but in that case, don't eat. Eating can dull the taste buds.

HOW DO YOU SERVE WINE?

When you uncork a bottle, always pour yourself a glass from the bottle before serving your guests. This etiquette serves two functions: to catch any little particles from the cork that may have fallen into the bottle when you were opening it and, mainly, to taste the wine to verify that it doesn't have any defects.

When you're serving the meal, pour wine in the women's glasses first (from oldest to youngest), then move on to the men (in the same order).

Never fill a glass above one third. It's not about controlling how much your guests drink but to permit the wine to breathe so the aromas, or bouquet, can flourish. Your job is to let your guests taste the wine under the best conditions.

1/3

Before a guest's glass is empty, offer to refill it. If the guest refuses, don't insist.

Put a glass of water next to the wineglass if you have room on the table.

How to avoid drips

Most bottles have an annoying tendency to leak a drop or two during pouring, which drips along the bottle and, invariably, onto the tablecloth. To avoid tedious washing, try these three tips:

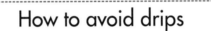

Plan ahead
Put a wine bottle coaster on the table. You can buy very pretty wine bottle coasters made out of stainless steel or silver. You could also use a saucer from a coffee cup or tea cup. Drops will happen without fear of staining the tablecloth. It's important to remember to put the bottle back onto the coaster.

Pouring tool
There are several gadgets you can buy that absorb or eliminate the annoying drip. For example, you can buy a ring that goes over the bottleneck. Usually made of steel, it has a velvet inner lining to catch the liquid. Another very useful tool is the Drop Stop, a little round piece of foil that you roll and slide into the neck. It cuts the flow of the liquid and stops the drop from forming.

Hand trick
This takes some practice. The technique consists of rotating the bottle slightly at the end of the pour. As you lift the bottle, the drip rolls around the rim of the bottle.

WHAT TO DO IF…

The wine tastes off

First, identify if it's just a bad or cheap wine, or if there's genuinely something wrong with it (see page 48).
Does it smell like vinegar? Then, use it as vinegar … or pour it down the drain.
Is it corked? Try aerating it and then taste it again a few minutes later. Sometimes the cork smell will fade and the wine becomes drinkable. Otherwise, pour it down the drain.
It is a cheap wine? Here are some solutions:

For a cheap white wine
Make a Kir by adding a fruit juice or syrup. The classic Kir recipe uses blackcurrant liqueur (crème de cassis), but a Kir can also be made with raspberry, peach, violet, chestnut or blackberry liqueur.
For a Kir Royal, use a sparkling wine.

For a Kir Soleil, use a rosé wine and grapefruit syrup. You can also make a quick cocktail by combining the white wine with grated orange peel, orange juice and Grand Marnier.

For a cheap red wine
In the summer, consider making a sangria with pieces of fruit and cinnamon. You can also add sugar, sparkling water or even port.
In the winter, you can make mulled wine by heating the wine in a saucepan with cinnamon, cloves, sugar and orange slices.
Other year-round options include:
- A Diabolo Plonk: Red wine with lemonade.
- A Calimucho: Half red wine and half cola.
- A Communard: Same as a Kir, but with red wine.

You don't know how many bottles to buy

A normal-size bottle (750 ml) fills six glasses (an average wineglass pour should be about 4 fluid ounces), or it can fill seven flutes. Assume three glasses per person over the course of an evening. Always plan to eat.

There are no wineglasses, only drinking glasses or paper cups

Opt for a fruity, round varietal wine, a sparkling wine, or a wine with "carbonic maceration" since this winemaking technique tends to bring out the fruit.

The wine isn't cold

Ask for a bowl of ice cubes. Put one or two cubes in an empty glass and swirl them around. When you see mist forming on the glass, discard the ice and pour the wine into the glass. The glass will transmit the cold to the liquid and lower its temperature by a few degrees in three minutes. If you've been served a wine by the glass, ask for an extra empty glass and perform the same operation.

The idea of a wine-tasting party is to compare the aromas and flavors of different wines ("the nose" and "the palate" in winespeak) and discuss among the group.

For a first-timers, it's best to start with comparing two wines that are completely different.
As you gain experience, you can work toward more specific tastings of wines that have more subtle differences. For each tasting, make sure you choose wines in the same price range. For about $15, you can find classic wines from many regions; big, complex bottles may run $30 or more (which may seem expensive but, if there are five of you, that makes it only about $9 each for the two bottles).

For beginners

Big red wines

$30 a bottle
A Bordeaux vs. a Burgundy or Washington State Bordeaux Blend vs. an Oregon Pinot Noir
They must be about the same age.
Normally, the difference is in the impact on the nose and on the palate. On the nose, the Burgundy (a Pinot Noir) smells of cherries, strawberries, prunes, even mushrooms, whereas the Bordeaux blend has aromas of black fruits like black currant and flowers like violet, tobacco, and leather. On the palate, the Bordeaux has more structure and is more tannic, while the Burgundy will be more acidic, more delicate, and airy.

Everyday reds

$15 a bottle
Bourgueil vs. Cairanne
The first comes from the Loire Valley, based on the Cabernet Franc grape. The second comes from the south of the Côtes du Rhône, mostly based on a blend of Syrah and Grenache. The first expresses notes of cherry, raspberry, licorice, and maybe even a little bell pepper. On the palate, there will be freshness, a kind of "crunch." The second will smell of black cherry, blackberry, pepper, and other spices. In the mouth, it will be warm, almost sweet, round, and more powerful.

Classic whites

$15–$20 a bottle
A Bordeaux vs. a Burgundy from the Côte de Beaune
The first, produced from a blend of Sauvignon Blanc and Sémillon (and sometimes Muscadelle), will have an intense aromatic expression of lemon, lime, and sometimes pineapple. Inversely, the Burgundy, made from Chardonnay, will be more discrete on the nose. It can release aromas of acacia, lemon meringue, and butter. On the palate, the first is bright and refreshing, while the second will be fatter, more ample and smooth on the tongue.

Across the ages

$15 for a young wine
$25 for an old wine
Young wine vs. old wine
Choose two wines that are from the same region and appellation, as close together as possible (a Bordeaux from the Pomerol appellation, a Burgundy from the Chablis appellation, a Nebbiolo d'Alba tasted against a Barbaresco, or even better, those two from the same winery. The two wines should be at least five vintages apart. The young wine will have fruity and floral aromas, with some notes of wood. The older wines should show less fruit and wood but should be richer in aromas of leather, tobacco, and mushrooms.

For experienced tasters

A leap from appellation to appellation

Compare several white Burgundies: a Chablis, a Meursault, a Saint-Véran. Note the differences: the precision of the Chablis; the richness and length of the Meursault; the good-naturedness of the Saint-Véran. Another idea is to explore the two sides of the Gironde River. Compare the elegant structure of a Médoc next to the soft, likable qualities of a Saint-Émilion.

A single varietal across the world

Taste Pinot Noirs from Burgundy, South Africa and Oregon, and you will discover it is sometimes dry, sometimes warm and sometimes expresses a hint of sugar.

For specialists

Organize a vertical tasting

Take the same wine from the same winery from three different vintages and try to identify the little differences year to year according to the wine's warmth, acidity and the maturity of the fruit.

Identify regions

Take three Rieslings from different regions, running from north to south. For example, try a range from Alsace—the Grands Crus of Kirchberg de Ribeauvillé, Sommerberg and Kitterlé.

A tasting of "pirate wines"

These are wines that don't seem to be what they really are.
For example: a Saint-Bris, the only Burgundy appellation where they make a wine with Sauvignon Blanc instead of Chardonnay; a Chardonnay from Limoux, in the Languedoc-Roussillon, where certain whites have a glowing freshness; a Crémant du Jura, a sparkling blanc de blancs; an old Bandol with power that makes you think of the South West of France; or a Cabernet Sauvignon from California that's been made in the Bordeaux style.

Talking about wine:
Phrases that work every time

Do you dream of standing out in society by commenting brilliantly on every wine you taste, but you don't know anything about the art of tasting?
Repeat one of these phrases at random and speak them with an air of conviction. After you've read this book, if you meet an expert who asks you to explain your thought, you'll be able to speak right up.

This one is beautifully vinified!

A very beautiful reflection of its appellation.

The nose is expressive, the mouthfeel is dense and the structure is long and deep.

The attack is smooth and the mouthfeel is admirable, with a superb persistence.

A wine that shows off its minerality.

A wine with character! The mouthfeel ravishes the palate. It is rich and harmonious, with a length you can appreciate.

An intense nose. On the palate, it has presence and a muscular, tannic texture.

This wine, with a beautiful and rich color, presents a sumptuous, expressive nose and expresses great maturity. The body is delicious, and the texture is silky.

A full-bodied and balanced wine!

The color is magnificent, the nose expressive and the mouthfeel straightforward and clean.

An expressive wine that will age wonderfully.

A dense wine with beautiful color. The attack is soft and refined. An assertive style!

The nose is still a bit closed but already reveals great concentration. It should open up nicely.

Wonderful deep color, with a fruit-forward nose. It has a mouthfilling fullness. What complexity!

Its varietal character is typical, but it still shows the signature of the winemaker.

What a magnificent expression of *terroir*!

AFTER THE PARTY

How to remove stains

Such drama! The party started off well, that is, before a drop of wine landed on your favorite shirt.

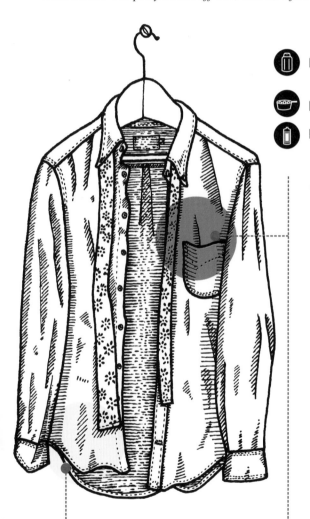

If it's a red or rosé, it is an especially annoying turn of events. If the stain is fresh (less than ten minutes), **forget the following:**

▶ Salt because it discolors the fabric, burns the fibers and fixes the stain rather than removing it.

▶ Boiling water, especially if the fabric is delicate.

▶ Bleach or baking soda, unless it's a white fabric.

Begin by sponging up the stain with an absorbent paper towel. Next, sacrifice a bottle of wine. If you think ahead, you should always have a bottle of acidic white wine in your cupboard, at room temperature and opened. Pour the wine in a basin and soak the stained clothing in it. Let it soak for one or two hours, or even more, and regularly rub the stained area. Then put it in the washing machine.

Try this home remedy: Keep a bottle with a mixture of one-third water, one-third rubbing alcohol and one-third distilled white vinegar. The idea is to always have a bottle of this mixture on hand. Proceed in the same way as with the wine solution above. Pour the liquid into a bowl and soak the clothing in it before putting it in the washing machine.

In both cases, the acidity and the alcohol dissolve the anthocyanins, or red coloring compounds, which are responsible for the tenacious staining.

If it's white wine or Champagne, it's not serious. They don't stain really. At worst they leave outlines on the clothes that come out in the wash.

If the stain is dry
Don't touch anything and take the clothing as quickly as possible to the dry cleaner.

Washing the glasses

When is a glass considered well cleaned? When it's clean, of course, without traces of smudges or wine, but also (and especially) without any odors!

Washing

Don't leave the glasses to soak in liquid dish soap. This will give the odor of soap to your next pour of wine.

NEVER

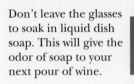

Don't put the glasses in the dishwasher with lots of rinsing agent. This gives a very unpleasant odor and a bitter taste to the wine.

YUCK

ALWAYS Do fill the glasses with very hot water right away after the end of the party. That way, you won't have to use soap. Simply wipe a sponge around the rim of the glass and let it dry on a dish rack or wipe it with a dishcloth, making sure to erase any traces left by lips. The hotter the water, the less likely there will be any traces when it dries.

Storage

When the glasses are dry, if you have a wineglass rack, hang the glasses upside down. If not, stand them upright in your cupboard.

👍

Avoid keeping glasses in the box. They will absorb the odor of the cardboard. If you can't put them anywhere else, rinse them with water before serving wine in them.

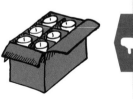

Never put your wine glasses upside down on a shelf: the ball of the glass will trap the odors of the shelf and transmit them to the wine at your next party.

SAVING WINE AFTER IT'S BEEN OPENED

Got some wine left at the end of the party? Don't force yourself to finish the bottle. A bottle of white wine half full can last two or three days in the refrigerator if it's carefully recapped. Reds can also last three days if they are kept in a cool spot away from light, or they will last four or five days in the fridge.

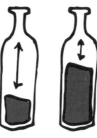

Notice how much wine is left and the amount of the airspace in the bottle. The more wine left in the bottle, the longer the wine will keep.

The air in the empty space left in the bottle will quickly attack the wine and kill it.

You can also extend the life of the bottle by three of four days with the help of a few commercially available tools.

Pressure plugs are very effective. You can also buy gas cylinders filled with a mix of nitrogen and carbon dioxide. These cylinders blow nonreactive gas into the bottle to expel the oxygen. For Champagne, there are special corks to keep it effervescent for at least twenty-four hours.

Cook with the rest of the wine

Leftover wine that's been in the fridge less than ten days can always be used in cooking. Here are some ideas.

With red wine, you can make:

- poached eggs
- any dish with a wine sauce, such as ribeye steaks with a red wine glaze, coq au vin, beef stew, a red wine and tomato pasta, red wine and mushroom sauce, salad dressings
- pears with wine and spices, strawberries with red wine, sugar and vanilla
- jams

With a dry white wine, you can make:

- sauteed veal or pork with mushrooms
- chicken with morel mushrooms
- osso buco
- steamed mussels
- scallops with beurre blanc
- risotto
- poached fish
- spaghetti with tuna
- cheese fondue

With a sweet white wine, you can make:

- eggnog
- a pear compote
- fruit salad
- a wine-infused apple cake
- chicken thighs in a sweet wine sauce
- foie gras

With Champagne, you can make:

- the same things you make with the dry or sweet white wine, depending upon the character of the Champagne

HANGOVER REMEDIES

The only truly effective cure for a hangover is, simply, to avoid getting one.

Where does a hangover come from?
Headache, nausea, cramps, intense fatigue
Did you drink a few bottles the night before? No doubt about it, you have a hangover.
The most common effect on the body of a hangover is dehydration. It's a classic consequence of alcohol metabolism in the liver. Dehydration is often compounded by the added effects of hypoglycemia, the result of another type of alcohol, mainly methanol, which breaks down into formaldehyde and formic acid, and certain polyphenols. Other substances present in alcoholic drinks of bad quality (whether wine or other alcoholic beverages) can aggravate a hangover. These include sulfites in high quantities or additives in the beverage.

What should you do on the night after drinking?
Drink water, lots of water before going to bed. Two glasses if possible, or even better, four. This is the most important rule and the most effective way to combat a headache. It's an easy method, but you need to have the presence of mind to remember to do it. Put a bottle of water on your bedside table. If you wake up, drink some water!

What should you do the day after?
Replenish your vitamins.
When you wake up, eat a banana or take some vitamin C. Bananas are jam-packed with vitamins, minerals, and sugar. It's also possible that you will have heartburn from the acidity of the drinks you had the night before. Avoid orange juice, which will never make heartburn go away.

Taking care of an upset stomach
If you have a stomachache:
Dilute a spoonful of baking soda in a glass of water and drink it down. This will neutralize the physical effects of the acidity.
Drink a detox tea or a chamomile tea.
Do not drink black teas or coffee. They are both diuretics and will worsen your dehydration, so stay away from them.
Eat rice. It lines the stomach and provides the carbohydrates that you will need throughout the day.

The last resort
Drink a Bloody Mary. Prepare this cocktail with a base of tomato juice, vodka (use a light hand), celery, and Tabasco. The vitamin C in the tomato helps and the vodka, which has a low concentration of methanol, allows the alcohol to be broken down more efficiently. But this solution is not a sure thing.

"I really like this wine! It's good. It's . . . the smell of . . . of wine! It's a good wine smell!"

Jack loves wine, but he doesn't have the knowledge or vocabulary to describe it, so he simply says, "This is good," which isn't bad. But Jack would like to know when he takes a sip what he should be thinking and what he should say. All he needs to do is learn how to use his other senses as he is tasting the wine: his sharp eyes, clear nose, clean palate, and his impatient tongue. He needs to focus on looking, smelling, tasting, and feeling. He can then describe each step with an adjective. In the beginning, one adjective is enough. Before each swallow, he takes a few seconds to pay attention to what's happening in his nose and mouth to monitor developments (getting a sense of the evolution of the wine). Jack isn't drinking more, but he is learning to taste better. He doesn't judge a wine by its appearance or its name. He simply gets to know the wine. He'll soon realize that tasting wine isn't complicated, it just takes practice.

This chapter is for all the Jacks out there who want to be able to taste wine better.

LEARNS TO TASTE WINE

The colors of wine • The aromas of wine
In the mouth • Finding the wine of your dreams

THE COLORS OF WINE

Why do wine lovers contemplate their glass before drinking? It's not to give a penetrating gaze. Nor is it to admire their reflection. You look at the color of the wine because it tells you a lot about the state of what you are about to drink. Before going into a clothing store, you look at the dress in the window. That's similar to what happens when you look at the wine's color. Through the color, the wine will tell you about its age.

Color and shade

How to do it like the pros

What are the shades?

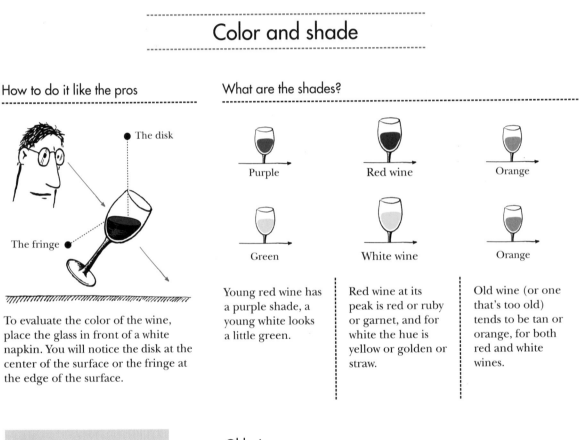

To evaluate the color of the wine, place the glass in front of a white napkin. You will notice the disk at the center of the surface or the fringe at the edge of the surface.

Young red wine has a purple shade, a young white looks a little green.

Red wine at its peak is red or ruby or garnet, and for white the hue is yellow or golden or straw.

Old wine (or one that's too old) tends to be tan or orange, for both red and white wines.

 Vocabulary

The colors of a white wine can be: green, gray, yellow, straw, golden, honey, coppery, amber, brown.

The colors of a red wine can be: violet, purple, ruby, garnet, cherry, mahogany, tan, orange, brown.

Old wines

To say a wine is old doesn't necessarily mean that it has to be ten years old or older. Depending upon its heritage or the life that it's led, a wine can age more or less rapidly. If it's been exposed to great temperature fluctuations, or if it's been exposed to air or light, it will age more quickly than the same wine that has rested comfortably in a cellar at 54°F (12°C). In addition, certain wines are born to live a long time. At ten years, such wines can still have a fresh complexion. Others will be at their peak during the first year.

Color and its intensity

The intensity and the age of the wine

Like the color itself, the intensity of the color shows more about the age of the wine. A red wine has a tendency to lose its pigment as it ages. The color descends and forms a deposit at the bottom of the bottle. Inversely, a white wine takes on color as it ages. So the colors of a red and white have a tendency to come closer together after more than a century of aging.

The intensity and the origin of the wine

Although there are wines that don't strictly follow this rule, the intensity of color often indicates the origin of the wine. Frequently, grapes that grow in cool latitudes give the wine a lighter color than those that grow under a blazing sun. Wine grape varieties vary according to regions and climates. Grapes grown in warmer climates resist heat and have a thicker skin, which is responsible for adding color to wine. Grapes that grow in the colder regions make for a lighter color.

RED WINE

Light, delicate wines generally come from a cool climate (for example, from Burgundy, New Zealand, Alto Adige and other parts of northern Italy, or Washington State).

Fruity wines generally come from a mild climate (for example, from Bordeaux, northern Spain, or Tuscany).

Powerful wines generally come from a sunny climate (for example, Malbec from South West France or Argentina, or wines from Napa Valley in California, southern Italy, and Australia).

WHITE WINE

Lively, crisp wines generally come from a cool or temperate climate (for example, Sauvignon from the Loire Valley).

Round and aromatic wines generally come from a temperate climate or have been barrel-aged (for example, Albariño from Spain, Torrontés from Argentina).

Powerful wine that's been barrel-aged a long time or sweet (for example, Sauternes, Tokaji)

ROSE WINE

The color of rosé doesn't indicate anything about the origin of the wine.

Vocabulary

The intensity of color in a wine can be: pale, light, strong, dark, deep, very dark.

The intensity of the color and the taste of the wine

A clear wine will often be more acidic and delicate than a dark wine. And most of the time a dark wine will be stronger in alcohol, fatter, more sugary, or more tannic.

What about the color of rosé?

It indicates nothing! Unlike white and red wines, the color of rosé depends on what the winemaker wants it to be. He or she has the ability to control coloration. To obtain a pink color, red grapes must be used (blending red wine with white wine to create a rosé is, with the exception of Champagne, illegal in the EU). It's the skin of the grape that gives the juice its color; the flesh of the grape is colorless.

The more skin used to infuse the grape juice, the more color there is in the rosé. To obtain a pale pink color, the winemaker separates the juice from the skins right away.

A very dark pink doesn't necessarily mean "stronger" in flavor or in alcohol than a pale pink.

Know that the color of a rosé obeys style. After a period when a very pronounced pink was the fashion, bottles today display tints that are more and more pale.

V Vocabulary

Rosé color can be: gray, apricot, onion skin, salmon, rosewood, flesh tone, peony, coral, cherry, currant, grenadine, raspberry, coppery.

BRILLIANCE (SHINE) AND CLARITY

Now that you have observed the color, including the shade and intensity, look at the reflections and clarity. Are there floating bits in the wine or a light veil?

The reflections in the wine

In rare cases, a microbial malady renders the wine very dull and unfit for consumption. But more often the brilliance is an aesthetic quality and doesn't indicate anything about the quality or flavor of the wine.

The deposit at the bottom of the bottle

It's not serious. These are unstable elements that precipitate as solid material. It can be a tarter crystal (for white wines), tannins, or coloring agents (for old red wines). In all cases, it doesn't spoil the wine and should not prevent you from drinking it. Of course, it isn't pleasant on your teeth, so avoid emptying the bottom of the bottle into your neighbor's glass.

The floating bits or cloudy wine

This is becoming more and more frequent, and paradoxically, less and less serious. In the past wines were filtered before being put into bottles, so cloudiness was rare. Today, an increasing number of "natural wine" producers don't filter their wines. The wines have a natural haze, which does not taint their taste. Often, winemakers who don't filter their wines state this right on the label, or they add a note that "a light haze may appear." On the other hand, if the wine is extremely cloudy, don't trust it.

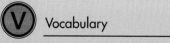

Ⓥ Vocabulary

Wine can be: crystalline, clear, hazy, cloudy.

TEARS, THE LEGS OF WINE

You can't love the "legs" of a wine without loving its "tears." Legs and tears are both terms that indicate the unique traces left by wine on the side of the glass. Just swirl your glass a couple times and admire the beautiful legs of your wine, if there are any.

Legs

Tears

What do the tears of wine signify?

The tears are an indicator of the alcohol percentage and sugar content in the wine. The more tears, the more alcohol or sugar in your glass of wine. A Muscadet doesn't leave any traces, while a Costières de Nîmes will cry its heart out. As a point of comparison, pour yourself a glass of water and a glass of rum. The difference is obvious.

The alcohol percentage

Although this technique gives you an idea of the level of alcohol in your wine, it doesn't really signify how it will feel in your mouth. In wines with higher than 14 percent alcohol, the best will offer equal amounts of strong acidity and beautiful tannic structure. The wines won't burn your mouth but instead will feel strangely balanced.

 ## Careful, the cleanliness of the glass can change everything

A dirty glass with traces of oil will cause more tears. Or, if there is a soapy residue, the wine will display legs all the way up to its neck!

EFFERVESCENCE

This concerns sparkling wines, of course! The bubbles are the star of this stage.

The size of the bubbles

The size of the bubbles gives you an indication of the quality of a sparkling wine that you are about to taste. Hold the glass at eye level and look at the way the bubbles interact. The more delicate the bubble, the better—it is the result of a slow and careful

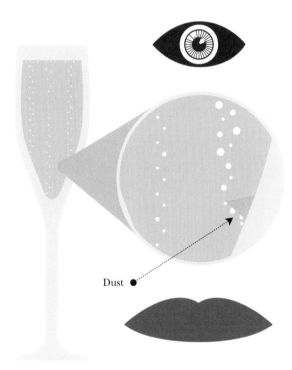

Dust ●

fermentation. If the bubble is coarse, it's a good bet that the flavor of the beverage will be as well. Ideally, the bubbles are tiny and equally bright while they float up the side or create a stream of bubbles that form a ribbon up to the surface.

The quantity of bubbles

The number of visible bubbles in the glass depends on the cleanliness of the glass. Surprising but true—the cleaner the glass, the fewer bubbles will escape. In a perfectly smooth glass, you won't see any bubbles at all. They show up in your mouth instead! Conversely, a glass that's a little bit dirty or just quickly cleaned with a rag will have lots of bubbles. The bubbles form thanks to the microscopic impurities on the wall of the glass. Because of this, sommeliers recommend drying your glasses with with a lint-free cloth, such as a microfiber towel.

The bubbles in the mouth

Don't waste time counting bubbles. It's better to judge by mouthfeel. Is it delicate, aggressive, or soft?

 Bubbles, where there should not be any

Have you felt bubbles in a wine that shouldn't have any? That's normal for very young wines. It's usually due to a small amount of unintentional residual sugar being left in the bottle, which re-ferments and causes a fizz or tiny bubbles. It will show up when you swirl the glass.

 Vocabulary

When a wine isn't effervescent, it's said to be calm. A calm wine that has a little perceptible CO_2 in the mouth is described as "beading."

THE AROMAS OF WINE

It's time for Jack to enter the fun house. Sometimes, smelling the wine is just as exciting as drinking it. One day you may even hesitate to wet your lips for fear of being disappointed with the flavor because the scent was so exquisite. To smell a wine is to accept an invitation to be seduced.

How to smell a wine

Free the aromas
Let the wine breathe to further liberate the aromas. Holding the base of the glass, swirl it in a little circle on the table (or in the air for the more skillful).

— 2 —

— 1 —

The initial nose
The initial nose is the aroma released from a resting wine. During a tasting, don't ever fill a glass to more than one-third full. The fuller the glass, the less space the aromas will have to express themselves. (Keep that in mind at a restaurant. A server should never fill the glass to the brim.)

The second nose
These are the aromas that can appear or change after the wine has had a chance to breathe. Normally the scents are clearer and more intense. If they remain unobtrusive, swirl more vigorously. The wine is without a doubt asleep, or "closed."

— 3 —

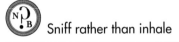 Sniff rather than inhale

For a very old or a very big wine
Avoid swirling the wine in the glass; you may risk exhausting it. Gently tilt the glass and smell the wine in different places—at the center of the glass or on the edges. That will be enough to perceive all of the complexity of the bouquet.

To smell a wine, don't inhale too deep or you will risk saturating your nose. Think more of a dog that sniffs along the ground: Gently inhale repeatedly, allowing your mind to open up as much as possible. Close your eyes if that helps you concentrate. Don't focus on a particular aroma. Just let them envelop you.

THE FAMILIES OF AROMAS

The big aroma families

There are hundreds of different smells in the world of wine. They aren't always easy to recognize. To make it easier, tasters group them into families.

Learning to smell

Are there scents that don't speak to you? For each aroma, try to think what it reminds you of. If you don't succeed, it's time to smell some fruit, flowers (either fresh flowers or perfumes), take a bite of chocolate, walk through the woods, lick pebbles if you have to! In the way a musician practices, a taster needs to practice using the nose. There are also special kits available that include vials of all the main wine aromas, which is a fun way to familiarize yourself with them.

Fruits

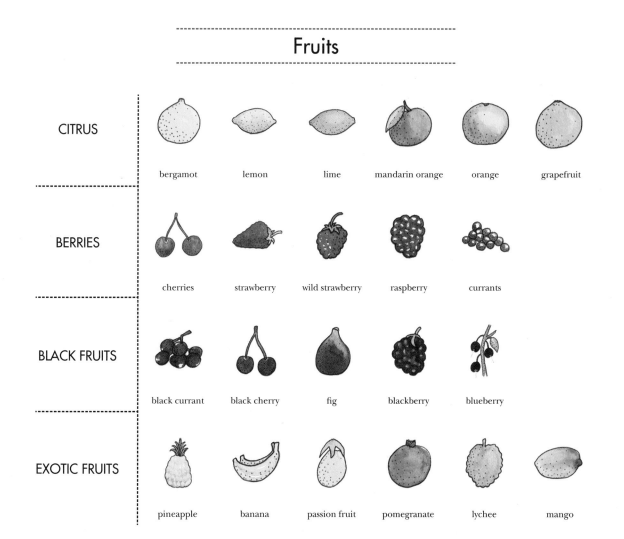

CITRUS	bergamot	lemon	lime	mandarin orange	orange	grapefruit
BERRIES	cherries	strawberry	wild strawberry	raspberry	currants	
BLACK FRUITS	black currant	black cherry	fig	blackberry	blueberry	
EXOTIC FRUITS	pineapple	banana	passion fruit	pomegranate	lychee	mango

Fruits

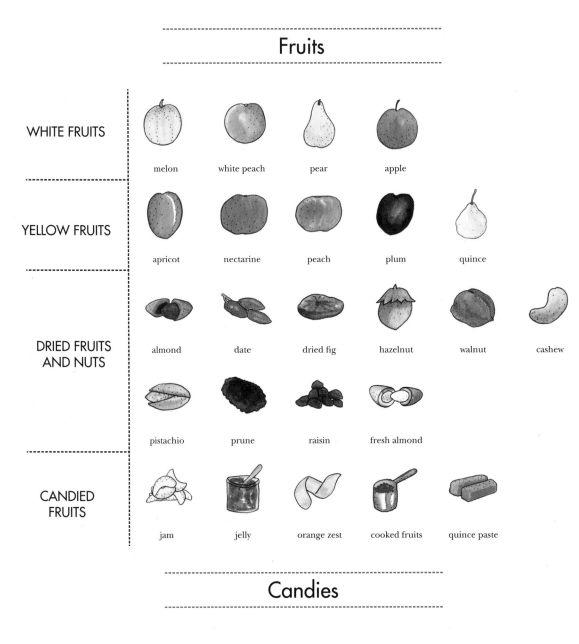

WHITE FRUITS	melon	white peach	pear	apple
YELLOW FRUITS	apricot	nectarine	peach	plum	quince
DRIED FRUITS AND NUTS	almond	date	dried fig	hazelnut	walnut	cashew
	pistachio	prune	raisin	fresh almond
CANDIED FRUITS	jam	jelly	orange zest	cooked fruits	quince paste

Candies

gummy bear   marshmallow

Jack learns to taste wine

Flowers

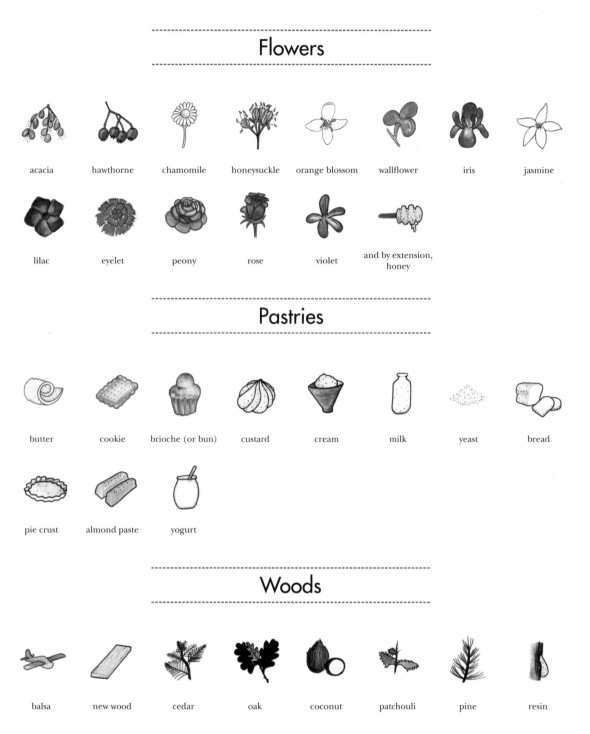

acacia · hawthorne · chamomile · honeysuckle · orange blossom · wallflower · iris · jasmine

lilac · eyelet · peony · rose · violet · and by extension, honey

Pastries

butter · cookie · brioche (or bun) · custard · cream · milk · yeast · bread

pie crust · almond paste · yogurt

Woods

balsa · new wood · cedar · oak · coconut · patchouli · pine · resin

sandalwood

Fresh and dried plants

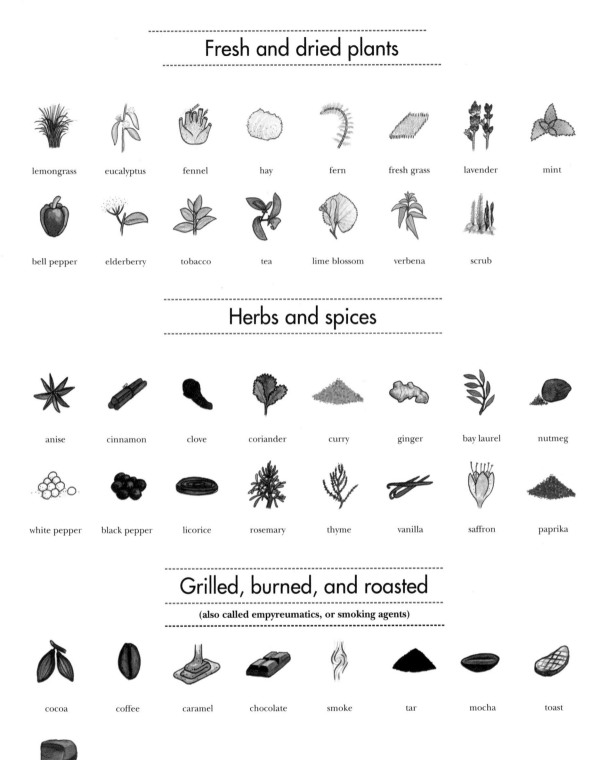

lemongrass   eucalyptus   fennel   hay   fern   fresh grass   lavender   mint

bell pepper   elderberry   tobacco   tea   lime blossom   verbena   scrub

Herbs and spices

anise   cinnamon   clove   coriander   curry   ginger   bay laurel   nutmeg

white pepper   black pepper   licorice   rosemary   thyme   vanilla   saffron   paprika

Grilled, burned, and roasted

(also called empyreumatics, or smoking agents)

cocoa   coffee   caramel   chocolate   smoke   tar   mocha   toast

praline

Jack learns to taste wine

Undergrowth (*Sous-bois* in French)

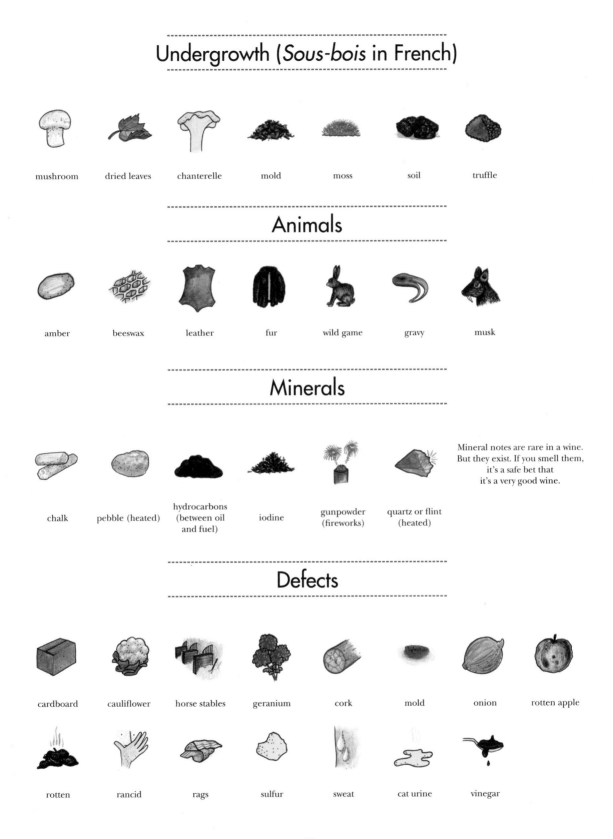

mushroom   dried leaves   chanterelle   mold   moss   soil   truffle

Animals

amber   beeswax   leather   fur   wild game   gravy   musk

Minerals

chalk   pebble (heated)   hydrocarbons (between oil and fuel)   iodine   gunpowder (fireworks)   quartz or flint (heated)

Mineral notes are rare in a wine. But they exist. If you smell them, it's a safe bet that it's a very good wine.

Defects

cardboard   cauliflower   horse stables   geranium   cork   mold   onion   rotten apple

rotten   rancid   rags   sulfur   sweat   cat urine   vinegar

The aromas of wine

The aromas of wine are never frozen in time. They evolve in the bottle, changing over the years.
They even change during the course of an evening, from the moment you serve the wine to the end of the meal.

The life cycle or seasons of wine

Wine follows a life cycle. It is young, it grows, attains adulthood, and after this peak phase, it begins its decline into old age before dying. The aromas evolving during the course of this life cycle reflect the cycle of the seasons.

During its peak and at the beginning of its decline, the wine will make you think of autumn, and then winter as it reaches the end of its life. This is a good way to identify where the wine is in its life cycle, with the hope that you've opened the bottle at its perfect level of maturity. This can vary greatly. At five years, some wine is still too young while another is already old.

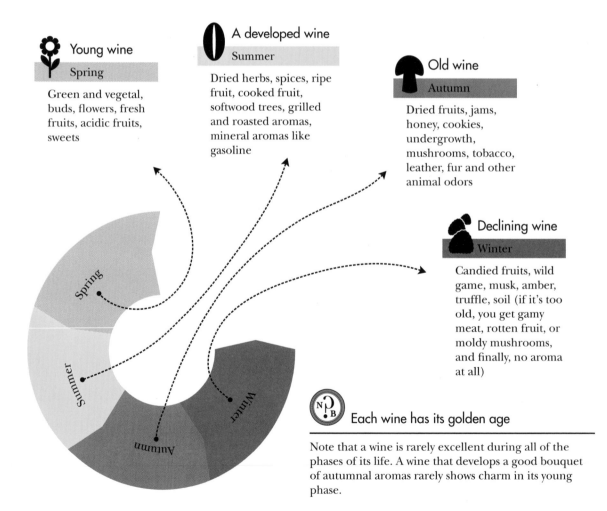

Young wine
Spring

Green and vegetal, buds, flowers, fresh fruits, acidic fruits, sweets

A developed wine
Summer

Dried herbs, spices, ripe fruit, cooked fruit, softwood trees, grilled and roasted aromas, mineral aromas like gasoline

Old wine
Autumn

Dried fruits, jams, honey, cookies, undergrowth, mushrooms, tobacco, leather, fur and other animal odors

Declining wine
Winter

Candied fruits, wild game, musk, amber, truffle, soil (if it's too old, you get gamy meat, rotten fruit, or moldy mushrooms, and finally, no aroma at all)

Each wine has its golden age

Note that a wine is rarely excellent during all of the phases of its life. A wine that develops a good bouquet of autumnal aromas rarely shows charm in its young phase.

PRIMARY, SECONDARY, AND TERTIARY AROMAS

Fermentation and aromas

Most of the aromas in wine show up while it's being made. Each type of grape carries a potential aroma, whether it's intense or discreet. But this potential doesn't express itself without fermentation, which gives birth to wines. Many other aromas appear during vinification and aging. To produce a wine, the goal is not just to make alcohol, it's also to create the aromas! Aromatic development in winemaking has three phases, which give rise to the primary, secondary, and tertiary aromas.

1 Primary aromas

The aromas contained in the grapes, which are freed during alcohol fermentation: **fruits, flowers, vegetal, mineral**

2 Secondary aromas

The aromas created by the yeast, according to their nature or during the malolactic fermentation: **sweets (confectionery), pastries**

3 Tertiary aromas

Aromas released by oak barrel-aging or bottle-aging: **wood, empyreumatic notes (grilled, toasted), undergrowth, animal odors**

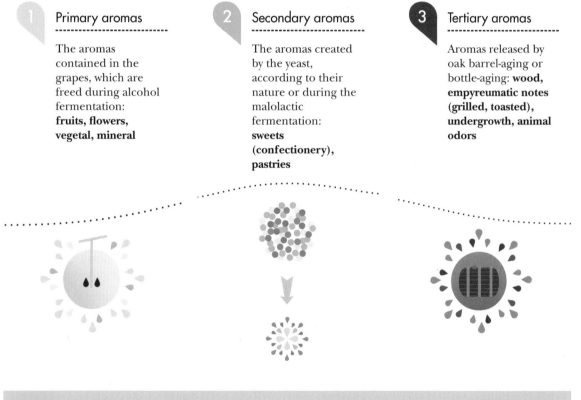

 Vocabulary

The "bouquet" means the aromas of a mature or old wine. It contains many of the tertiary aromas, but it also has some primary aromas, albeit a more advanced version. Like a trip to a good florist, the beauty of a great wine resides in the harmony of its bouquet.

THAT STINKS!

The wine doesn't smell good? There's not much you can do, apart from emptying your glass into the sink.

Unfixable defects

Several unpleasant odors can appear in wine for a variety of reasons.

 The grape isn't ripe enough: It smells like cat urine, grass, or green pepper.

 The wine has turned into vinegar: It smells like vinegar or nail polish remover.

 The wine is oxidized (except if it's a Madeira or another purposefully oxidized wine, in which case it's okay): It smells like Madeira (but isn't), walnuts, overripe apple, or rotten bell pepper.

 The wine is corked: It's been contaminated by a chemical in the cork (which happens in about 3 to 5 percent of all bottles). It smells mossy, dank, or rotten.

 The wine hasn't been stored well: This happens if the bottle is exposed to light or is stored too warm. It smells of dust or cardboard.

 The wine smells of *mercaptan*: This is a chemical compound that smells like rotten eggs or smelly socks. This happens when the yeast produce a sulfur compound because of a lack of air.

 **The wine is contaminated by *Brettanomyces*:** Also called simply "Brett" by wine tasters, it is an aroma caused by contamination with a wild yeast (genus *Brettanomyces*) on the skins of grapes. It smells like the sewer, a horse stable, dirty rags, or excrement.

Reduction in winemaking: an error in youth

The wine is reduced (by an oxidative process): It smells like cabbage, rotten onion, or even farts. It can be described as a less intense "*mercaptan*-like aroma." The odor, called "reductive aromas," is caused by a lack of oxygen in the wine during fermentation. This is the least serious of all the defects (even if sometimes it smells at least as awful as the others) because it is transient.

To rehabilitate a wine that is reduced:

 **Aerate the wine**
A vigorous decanting, even a serious shaking, and at worst several hours of waiting (yes, if it's not ready for dinner tonight, it should wait until tomorrow), the smell will go away.

 **Copper**
If you are in a hurry, you can plunge a piece of copper wire (a properly cleaned copper wire!) into the carafe. The copper precipitates out the sulfur molecules.

Jack learns to taste wine

Stuffy nose, closed wine

You have a cold. Your nasal passages are stuffed up, The tasting is damned. Yes, it's frustrating. Take care of yourself first. You can enjoy wines another day.

The wine is closed. It happens sometimes that the wine—some months after it's been bottled—cowers, angry from being enclosed. This grumpy phase can last several months. You must revive it by airing it in a carafe. Certain wines that have a particularly bad character need several hours to open up. If a wine rests closed for the entire evening, save it for lunch the next day.

It smells bad to you

Opening a bottle of wine can kick off a number of misadventures in tasting: a porous cork let air in and killed the wine, a cork contaminated by a chemical that leaves a "corked" wine, a wine that smells sour or of urine or smoke. When tasting a wine, you are always at risk of being disappointed, feeling you have wasted money for nothing. You should not make a fuss over encountering a bad wine. A good wine can make for a delightful evening, but a bad wine should not spoil it.

You can't smell what the others are smelling

You get a magnificent scent of rhubarb in your glass, but *wham!* the sommelier asks, "Do you smell that beautiful aroma of grapefruit?" You think, *Um, no.* Well, that doesn't matter. The perception of aromas varies from one individual to another. They depend on your gastronomic culture, and also on your genetic makeup. It's important not to be influenced by what your neighbor smells but to concentrate on what you smell. And if you are the only one to smell rhubarb, don't be embarrassed to say it. Curiously, if you don't like a particular aroma, you will detect it more easily.

IN THE MOUTH

How to taste wine

There are two ways to taste a wine. Note that in both cases you have to put the wine in your mouth.

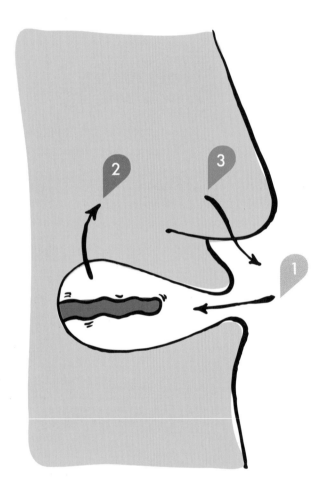

"Trill" the wine

When a taster makes a strange hissing sound (or whistling or slight gurgling) while tasting the wine, it's because he's "trilling" it. In fact, you have to make sure a little bit of air is in your mouth while the wine is still there. This is simple to do. With the wine in your mouth:

1. Purse your lips.

2. Breathe in some air. Then agitate the wine, warming it to help it express itself.

3. Sniff through the nose to let the air circulate between the mouth and the nasal passages, which sends the aromas toward the olfactory receptors.

"Chew" the wine

Yes, like one chews a steak! This method is even simpler than the first one, and serves the same purpose, to allow the beverage to express itself fully.

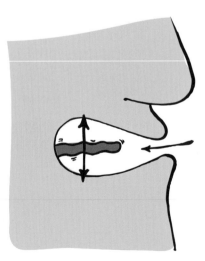

Use whichever method you prefer. You can also combine the two: "trill," then "chew" the wine (or the other way around). Or try clicking your tongue on your palate. The goal is to perceive all of the flavors of the wine, meaning the sweetness and acidity, for example, along with the aromatic aspects as perceived in the mouth, and the tactile sensations (such as any tingling or dryness).

Jack learns to taste wine

Bitterness, when it's gentle and not overbearing, is a sign of elegance. You can find a pleasing bitterness in certain white grapes: For example, in a white wine with a base of Marsanne (Côtes du Rhône), Mauzac (South West France), Rolle (southeast France), Pinot Grigio (Italy), and Gewürztraminer (Germany or Oregon). It becomes less pleasant if it's too present or accompanied by acidity. The bitterness often shows up in "the finish," several seconds after the other tastes dissipate. Those who don't eat endive, or don't drink beer, strong tea, or coffee are generally more sensitive to bitter flavors.

Sugar is present in wines, especially sweet wines! Soft white wines include sweet ones like Sauternes, intense examples like Vin Santo, soft or muted wines like a Muscat from Beaumes de Venise, Maury, or Banyuls. A wine can contain more than 200 grams of sugar per liter! The perception of sweetness is immediate. But the more sugar you eat, the less sweetness you will be able to perceive.

Saltiness occurs rarely, except in certain lively white wines like Muscat, Soave, and Prosecco. People talk about salty notes.

Acidity is the backbone of wine. A wine without acidity is a wine without a future. Good acidity in wine will make your mouth water; it will whet your appetite. But beware a wine that is too acidic: It will have an unpleasant mouthfeel and make your tongue and throat contract.

Very sweet

Sweet wines (with more than 45 grams of sugar per liter) include: Sélection de Grains Nobles from Alsace; Sauternes and Barsac from Bordeaux; Monbazillac and Jurançon from South West France; Bonnezeaux, Quarts de Chaume, and Vouvray from the Loire; Trockenbeerenauslese from Germany; German, Austrian, or Canadian Ice wines; Tokaji from Hungary.

Sweet

Soft white wines include: late harvests from Alsace; Coteaux du Layon, Montlouis, and Vouvray from the Loire; Jurançon, Pacherenc du Vic-Bilh, and Côte de Bergerac from South West France; Auslese from Germany.

Lightly sweet

These include: dry and semi-dry Champagnes; semi-dry wines from the Loire (from Montlouis and Savennières), and those from the New World; some red wines from the south of France and South Africa; some Mediterranean white wines.

Vocabulary

To categorize a wine according to its acidity, from weakest to strongest: flat, soft, fresh, lively, nervous, biting, aggressive.

DOES IT FATTEN OR DOES IT SING?

The tongue adjusts to different tactile sensations: metallic (unpleasant), spicy, fat, warm.

Fat

Alcohol, if it's too pronounced, heats the throat. Glycerol, formed during fermentation, gives an unctuous quality to the wine: It fattens the palate like butter. This "fat," or softness, characterizes the differences between several types of wine.

The structure of a wine

To imagine the structure of a wine, you evaluate two sensations—the acidity on one side and the "fatness" on the other. It's possible to represent the allure of a wine according to a little diagram. Below are four extreme examples:

The wine is fresh, lively, acidic and sharp, angular, or even aggressive. It can be perceived in very dry white wines or in easy-to-drink and refreshing reds, called *gouleyants* in French. The wine is too acidic if the grape isn't ripe or the flavors aren't concentrated.

Whites: Pinot Blanc from Alsace, Sauvignon Blanc from New Zealand, Riesling from Austria and Germany, Muscadet from the Loire, Petit Chablis, white Bordeaux, wines from Jura or Savoie.
Reds: Gamay from the Loire, Beaujolais, red Burgundy, Sangiovese from Italy

The wine is heady, warm, heavy, or even obese: These are powerful red wine charmers. If acidity is lacking, the wine feels like it's burning, and it tires the palate and becomes nasty. It can be found in wines whose grapes were overheated by the sun or also in sweet whites that lack acidity.

Reds from Languedoc, other regions in the south of France, South America, or California

acid

fat

The wine is small, light, thin, and watery: In all cases, it's not a good wine. You should not drink this one.

The wine is fleshy, full, and ample: These are powerful wines that have as much acidity as fat and are very pleasant to drink. They are often good candidates for aging. And they are often expensive.

Whites: Burgundy, Bordeaux, Loire, Languedoc, Riesling Beerenauslese from Germany, Ice wine from Germany or Canada, Australian Sémillon
Reds: Bordeaux, Côtes du Rhône, South West, Burgundy, Barolo, Barbaresco, California Cabernet Sauvignon, Washington State Bordeaux blend, Brunello di Montalcino, Amarone della Valpolicella

 Vocabulary

To classify a wine according to perception of "fatness," from weakest to strongest:
firm, full, round, fat, unctuous

WHERE ARE THE LEGS?

"Nice legs!"

This outdated description refers to a wine that is round, charming, and buxom, all while still keeping some nervousness. Tasters hardly ever say this anymore. Nevertheless, you can have some fun with these descriptions by stating, for example, that the legs of a Carignan from Languedoc are athletic and manly as hell, while the legs of a red Burgundy are more slender and delicate. It's up to you to see what you prefer to drink, depending on the occasion!

TANNINS IN WINE

Understanding tannins is fundamental knowledge for those who taste wine. Tannins belong mostly to the universe of red wines, though sometimes they occur in rosés too. They don't normally exist in white wines.

What are tannins?

Tannins dry the tongue, sometimes even the entire mouth. It's the same sensation that a tea steeped for too long can give you, because that beverage is also full of tannins. Certain red wines have just a little tannin, while others have a lot. Even those with a lot can be more or less elegant. Although they are astringent and can attack your tongue like a plank of wood, some can be more like a silky scarf. You must try to distinguish the amount of tannin in a glass of wine, but most of all focus on the quality of the tannins.

Where do tannins come from?

Tannins are contained in the grape's skin, seeds, and stem (the woody stalk that connects the cluster to the vine, which is often removed before pressing, precisely because it's too tannic).
To make red wine—in contrast to how white wine is made—you leave the grape juice in contact with the grape skins and the seeds. This gets the tannins into the wine.
Tannins give structure to the wine and assure a long life.

 Vocabulary

In the presence of tannins, one can say that wine is: flowing, supple, tannic, astringent, bitter.
According to their character, tannins are: rude, rough, fine, silky, velvety.
To summarize, we could show tannins like this:

Barely-there tannins	Aggressive, fat tannins	Astringent tannins	Fine tannins	Velvety, silky tannins

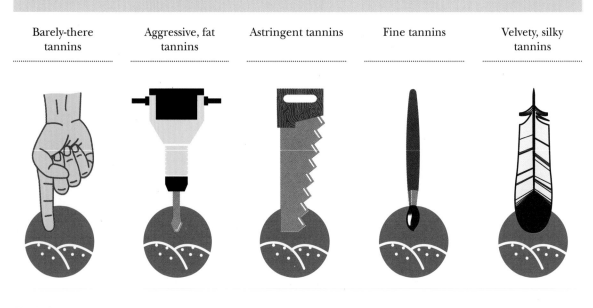

Jack learns to taste wine

SMELL WITH YOUR MOUTH

Did you know that you smell as much with your mouth as with your nose? This method of smelling relies on the retro-nasal passage. We also call it "retro-olfaction." We do it every day while eating!

There are two ways to tickle the olfactory mucosa: drawing aromas directly through the nose or by passing them through the mouth and up. It's the second pathway that allows us to perceive the flavor of foods. If you pinch your nose while eating, you will not know what you're tasting.

When it comes to wine, retro-olfaction can be weak or powerful. It confirms the aromas detected by the nose, or it can identify completely new aromas that were imperceptible until then. Some tasters find that this method of tasting is more sensitive than using just the nose, because it's used at every meal.

1   Air

2   Wine

3   Aromas

4   Inhale

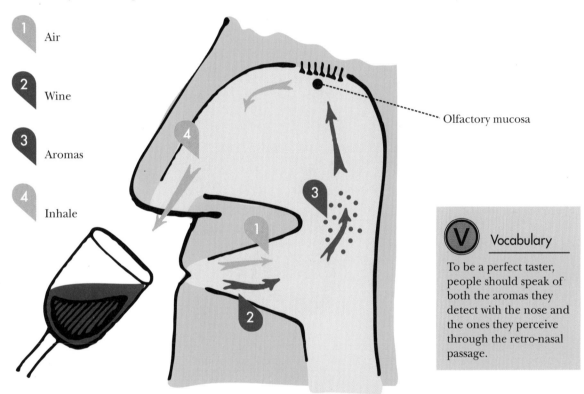

Olfactory mucosa

V   Vocabulary

To be a perfect taster, people should speak of both the aromas they detect with the nose and the ones they perceive through the retro-nasal passage.

When it's gone, it's there again

After having drunk a wine, it will sometimes rest on the palate for a few extra seconds, like it's been there forever. This persistence of wine applies to both the aroma and taste. The moment can be short or long: We call it the "length" of the wine. A persistent length is the sign of a good wine—one that is very pleasant, of course!

V   Vocabulary

The "caudalie" is a unit of measure of the length of a wine, or a measure of its duration on the tongue. It is, in fact, the number of seconds it lasts. A wine that lingers in the mouth 7 seconds after swallowing has a length of 7 caudalies.
Careful! This term isn't really used by casual tasters, who consider it a little snobby.

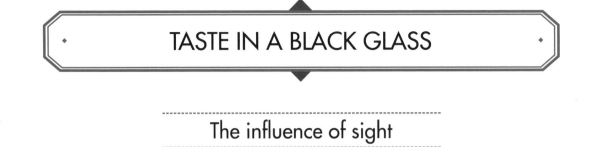

The influence of sight

Why is it interesting to taste wine in an opaque glass—in a black glass, specifically?

Because your eyes can play tricks on your other senses. In daily life, sight is the sense we rely on most. It dominates all others. It gives us an opinion on what we have in front of us. Even if it's delicious, a dish seems less appetizing if it's ugly. A bowl of sheep's brain or insect stew? The sight of it affects our judgment and even influences the other parts of the brain.

Numerous tests have been done on wine and the influence its color has on taste and smell. Most people are convinced that a glass of water dyed green tastes minty, or they say one that's tinted pink smells like strawberries. Similarly, tasters will perceive notes of red fruits in a white wine that's tinted red.

The influence of the label

The wine label can also influence a taster.

In a recent taste test conducted in Germany, a half dozen student sommeliers tasted a wine from two different Burgundy bottles. One didn't mention the name of the region, the other had a prestigious appellation. One hundred percent of the sommelier students declared that the second was better, finer, more complex, and very different. It turned out the same wine was served in both bottles.

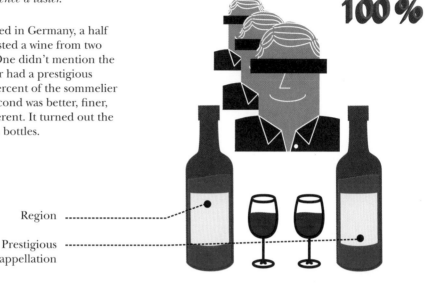

Region

Prestigious appellation

From white to red

Smell is a gullible sense. If it's not tested regularly, it is easily fooled by what the eyes see.

Red or white? It's the first question to ask if you are drinking in black glasses, and it's not that easy to discern.

The nose needs to figure it out: Citrus and brioche indicate a white wine; blackberries, leather, and tobacco are the signatures of a red wine. But between a barrel-aged white wine and a light red with crisp fruit, it's easy to make a mistake. If you don't trust your nose, the answer is in your mouth. The palate will help you determine if there are tannins in the wine, which will help you decide that it's a red. If the tongue contracts from the acidity, chances are it's a white.

BLIND TASTING

Invite some friends over and ask them to bring an anonymous bottle of wine (covered with a sock, for example). If possible, use black, opaque glasses. Give your friends a sheet of paper, taste the wines, and note your observations. It shouldn't last more than five minutes. Taste systematically. Begin with broad descriptions of what you're tasting, then refine your thoughts.

Taste

Taste and smell. Are the aromas evolved? What is the most striking taste? Is the wine sweet? Is your throat warming from the alcohol? Is your palate dried by tannins? Finally, what is the thing you notice most in this wine? What global impression does it give you? Do you have one word or expression to sum it up?

- 2 -

- 1 -

Smell

For the nose, start by identifying the most striking smell and determine its family of aromas. Make a choice within this family and note the possible degree of maturity. Put this smell out of your head and focus on capturing a second aroma, a third, and so on.

Deduce

Now, if you can, imagine a region, an appellation, or even a vintage. If you are super confident, try to name the producer, the château or the domaine.

- 3 -

Compare

Compare the results with your friends. And unveil the bottle! Note that your aromatic perception might be different than your neighbor's. Were you completely wrong? No big deal. You might have been tired, stuffed up, stressed, or simply blunted by the wines you had already tasted before that! Enjoy your evening. You'll do better next time.

- 4 -

Jack learns to taste wine

Sample tasting sheet

Nose	Aromatic family			Aromas
1st aroma	✕ Fruit ○ Pastry ○ Grilled ○ Mineral	○ Floral ○ Woody ○ Animal ○ Defects	○ Vegetal ○ Spicy ○ Undergrowth	Yellow fruit: apricot, very ripe apricot
2nd aroma	○ Fruit ○ Pastry ○ Grilled ○ Mineral	✕ Floral ○ Woody ○ Animal ○ Defects	○ Vegetal ○ Spicy ○ Undergrowth	White flower Intense: jasmine
3rd aroma	○ Fruit ✕ Pastry ○ Grilled ○ Mineral	✕ Floral ○ Woody ○ Animal ○ Defects	○ Vegetal ○ Spicy ○ Undergrowth	Between flowers and pastry: honey
Olfactory intensity	○ Weak	○ Medium	✕ Aromatic	○ Powerful

Mouth	Aromatic family			Aromas
Retro-olfaction	✕ Fruit ○ Pastry ○ Grilled ○ Mineral	○ Floral ○ Woody ○ Animal ○ Defects	○ Vegetal ○ Spicy ○ Undergrowth	Another fruit is appearing: quince
Aromatic persistance	Quince continues with honey			
Sugar	○ Imperceptible	○ Weak	✕ Present	○ Very present
Fatness	○ Barnyard	✕ Round	○ Fat	○ Unctuous
Acidity	○ Flat	○ Fresh	✕ Vivid	○ Nervous	○ Aggressive
Tannins (quantity/quality)	✕ Absent ○ Velvety	○ Melted ○ Silky	○ Supple ○ Fine	○ Present ○ Rough	○ Astringent ○ Coarse	○ Tart
Alcohol	○ Diluted	✕ Light	○ Generous	○ Warm	○ Hot
Taste intensity	○ Watery ○ Aggressive ○ Full	○ Thin ○ Heady ○ Severe	○ Small ○ Warm ○ Full-Bodied	○ Fresh ○ Pasty ○ Framed	○ Vivid ○ Ample	○ Acidic ✕ Rich
General impression	This is a soft, elegant, and harmonious wine.			

I conclude that: This wine is white, a little sweet, soft, from a Chenin Blanc grape. Therefore, it's from France, produced in the Loire. Given its elegance and vivacity, I'd say it's a Vouvray?

A QUESTION OF BALANCE

Once you master nearly all of the steps of the tasting, all that's missing is the conclusion. Compiling all of the characteristics of a wine does not give you a comprehensive description. Let's compare with humans: 5 foot 9 inches, 165 pounds, green eyes. That's not enough to describe your best friend. Is he handsome, especially nice, the funniest person you know?

If there is a dominant trait

Warm because of the alcohol, bright thanks to the acidity, austere because of the tannins. Wine is necessarily unbalanced. For all that, it can still be very pleasant.

If anything goes

As much acidity as fat for a white? As much acidity as alcohol as tannins for a red? It's balanced! Careful, a balanced wine isn't the Holy Grail. Some wines thrive on imbalances. Also, this notion varies according to region: Wines from southern France will lean more toward favoring the alcohol; from northern France, the wines will naturally have more acidity.

More than balance, pleasure

There's one fundamental question left to ask: Did you like this wine? Normally if you've enjoyed it, you must now know why. Was it for its aromas, for its texture, for its harmony? A wine can correspond well to all of the required criteria yet not please you that much. A wine without a major imbalance or defect can still be uninteresting to you simply because it's boring. The fact is, a little defect can be the most charming thing about a wine.

The categories of wines

At the end of your evaluation, you should be able to put each of the wines that you taste in one of these categories:

White wines

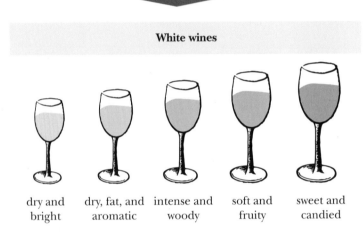

| dry and bright | dry, fat, and aromatic | intense and woody | soft and fruity | sweet and candied |

Red wines

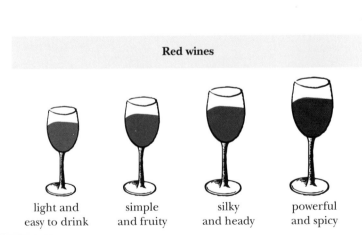

| light and easy to drink | simple and fruity | silky and heady | powerful and spicy |

SWALLOW OR SPIT?

You really need to swallow wine when you are at a dinner or a party:

- -

because if you are the only one who spits it out you will appear to be a snob;

because spitting is not very attractive;

because if you're eating at the same time, you risk confusing what you should and should not be spitting;

because wine, consumed in moderation, is one of life's pleasures and if you enjoy it, there is no reason to deprive yourself of it.

Exceptions to this rule: You are going to taste several wines, but you're also the designated driver. You are at a tasting party and there will be a lot of lovely wines to taste, but you're pregnant.

You should generally spit out the wine when you are at a winery tasting room, a tasting table, or touring a wine route:

- -

because a drunk taster can be embarrassing, and obviously, also dangerous while driving;

because alcohol diminishes your reaction time and you will have trouble commenting about the wine;

because alcohol blunts your sense of smell and taste—beyond a certain amount, you will have trouble distinguishing aromas and tasting the wine (is it hot or are you hot?);

because you'll lose your common sense and risk buying a wine you don't really like.

How to spit with elegance

Let gravity do the work.
Don't try to steer your spit anywhere but down.

Tilt your head to avoid dripping onto your chin.
Hold back your hair, scarf, or tie, which could get in the way of the spit.

Form an "O" with your lips as if to say, "Gooooood wine."

"GOOOOD WINE"

One more thing

Eject the wine with the same force it takes to whistle. If you simply let the wine flow toward the spittoon, it will sound like someone peeing—definitely not classy.

Jack learns to taste wine

FROM AMATEUR TO ALCOHOLIC

The benefits of wine, the harm of alcohol

Every wine amateur who wishes to taste must drink responsibly.

 "It's the dose that makes the poison," according to the principle of Paracelsus, a sixteenth-century doctor.

 Half glasses: These are preferred during a tasting. So if you drink three glasses (of a normal portion), you have actually tasted six different wines.

 Recommendations from the WHO (World Health Organization): Men shouldn't drink more than three glasses a day, two for women. Don't drink more than four glasses during a party, and completely abstain from drinking one day per week.

 A glass of water: Always have one in your hand. Respect the old French adage, "Water to quench his thirst, wine to quench his pleasure."

 Drinking in excess: Alcohol attacks the liver, the pancreas, the stomach, the esophagus, the throat, and the brain, and sometimes causes cirrhosis and cancers. Regular consumption causes addiction, then an extreme physical dependence takes hold.

The French Paradox

Why do the French, the top consumers of wine in the world per capita (50 liters per person per year), have a lower incidence of cardiovascular disease than people who live in other countries? It's called the French Paradox. Consumed in moderation, wine can have health benefits. An analysis published in 2011 showed the results of eighteen scientific studies that concluded drinking one to two glasses of wine a day can diminish the risk of cardiovascular death by 34 percent and help prevent Type 2 diabetes and neurodegenerative diseases (such as Alzheimer's and Parkinson's). In the southwest of France, where they eat fatty food but also drink tannic wines, which has surprising antioxidant properties, cardiovascular diseases are less prevalent than in the north of France.

liters

It is now time to identify what you like from your wine-tasting experiences.

From a tank or from a barrel?

Do you like?

First and foremost, you like the aromas of fruit, flowers, dried herbs, and aromatic infusions.
You also like to have the sensation of very crisp flavors, something airy and bright, with a little acid.
Then you are a follower of wines made in tanks.

Why?

Because a tank, whether it's concrete or stainless steel, doesn't impart any aromatic element or taste to the wine. It's neutral. It's therefore the grape that expresses itself, aided by the hand of the winemaker.

Do you like?

You like that fruit aromas blend with the woody aromas, giving you oak or whitewood, vanilla, coconut, clove, toast, praline, or caramel.
And you like a suave, round, velvety mouthfeel. Well, you like it when wood makes its mark on the wine.

Why?

Because barrels (or casks) interact with the wine. They transmit new aromas and create a different mouthfeel. The tannins evolve and polish it.

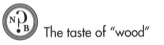 The taste of "wood"

For the past twenty years, very woody wines have been in vogue. At some point numerous wineries chose to vinify in tanks and add boards or wood chips to reproduce the effect of aging in barrels for a lower cost.

How a barrel is made has a lot of influence on the final taste of the wine.

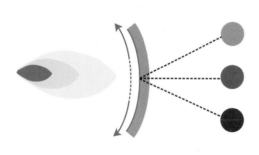

The choice of wood

Oak is the dominant wood used in making wine barrels. The use of chestnut is starting to disappear, but now you'll find rarer woods, like quebracho or acacia, being used for limited-production wines.

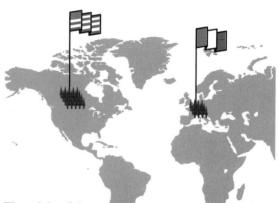

The origin of the wood

Oak's influence varies greatly between American oak (with its aromas of coconut, sweetness) and French oak (known for vanilla), especially when the oak comes from the prestigious forest of Tronçais in the Allier district.

The heating of the barrel

When barrels are made, the cooper heats the wood with a brazier. The aromas will vary from weak to strong according to intensity, with spicy, grilled, or burnt odors. The aromas range from vanilla to caramel to coffee to toast.

The age of the barrel

A new barrel is going to impart a lot more aromas and tannins to the wine. Sometimes it imparts too much if the wine doesn't have the power or the necessary structure to absorb the wood influence and melt into it. They say that the wood can mask the wines. Conversely, a barrel older than four years transfers hardly any aroma and is a nearly neutral container. For each style of wine, the winemaker will carefully choose the age of the barrels he uses.

Finding the wine of your dreams

Young or old?

It's a question of taste, but also your wallet. Buying an old wine is generally a lot more expensive. Don't feel obligated to like old wines on the pretext that they're more chic. The aromas of mold, earth, mushrooms, and wild game are very special, but they're not for everyone.

Young wine

Do you like bright colors, fields covered with flowers, crisp apples, juicy strawberries, a stroll in the orchard in summer, and picking fruit?
Bingo, you like wines in their youth, which are bright and bursting with aromas.

Old wine

Do you like autumn, walks through forests colored with fall foliage, the ambiance of an old club, wild boar stew, nuts, and truffles? Too bad for your bank account, but it's the old wines that your palate demands.

Varietal or *terroir*?

They say that a wine is varietal when it reflects the grape variety that it comes from. Conversely, a terroir *wine puts forth the soil, climate, and the winemaker.*

Varietal wine

Do you like inexpensive wines (but not bad ones), wines without swank or complication, a night on the couch watching a movie, and sharing a bag of chips with friends? Don't take yourself too seriously and buy a varietal wine. It won't be terribly refined, but if it's well made, it will go perfectly with your relaxed evening. If you must find a bargain at the supermarket, it's better to buy a modest varietal wine (a Sauvignon Blanc or a Syrah, for example) than a bottle trying to impersonate a wine from a famous winery.

Terroir wine

Do you seek emotion in wine, the smell of earth, the roundness of a warm year, the bitterness of a forgotten heirloom varietal, the mark of the winemaker? Without a doubt, you want a *terroir* wine, which demands attention and care. It's not necessarily expensive, but you will rarely find one in a supermarket. Try a little wine shop or go to the winery to find good *terroir* wines.

Jack learns to taste wine

Old World or New World?

Even if some wines from the New World (America and Australia) are now sometimes mistaken for European wines—and vice versa—you will normally notice differences in the aroma and taste profiles of these two categories.

New World Wine

Do you like to drink sweet, creamy, even fat wines? There's a strong likelihood that New World wines will seduce you. Easy to drink, extroverts in vanilla and cream, lots of roundness, sometimes a little obesity, whether white or red, they are charming and enticing. They can be jammy and lack complexity, but they are inherently pleasant. And they offer great quality for the price. Among the whites, you'll often find aromas of exotic fruits that are rare in the European latitudes. Shop around because there are more and more wineries that manage to get a lot of finesse, and they produce bright, fine wines that would just be wrong to ignore.

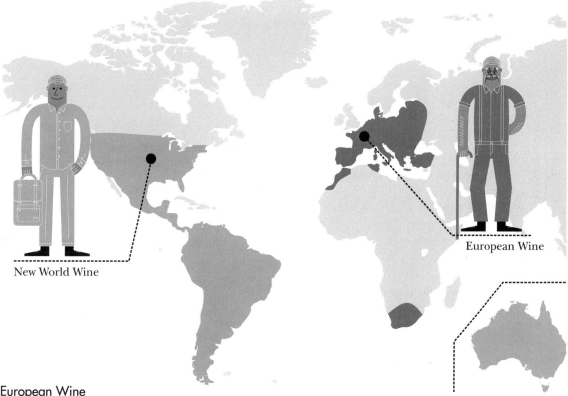

New World Wine

European Wine

European Wine

Do you like freshness and acidic tension? Do you prefer austere to outrageous? European wines will grab you immediately. Often criticized for the same reasons that they are acclaimed, these wines can lack suaveness, showing sharp acidity and severe tannins sometimes, but when they are successful they win in subtlety and elegance. Aging does not dim their character. Certain wines from Italy, Spain, or the south of France can be particularly lovely.

Finding the wine of your dreams

Technical, organic or sulfite free?

Technical wine

These are wines that, regardless of vintage, soil, and sometimes even their region, present a perfect balance. They are completely reliable and the ideal wine for business meals or other everyday occasions. Modern viticulture has allowed for the emergence of technical wines that are made with the goal of pleasing the greatest number of people.

Notes

These cookie-cutter wines are not terribly complex or interesting. In fact, they are so smooth they can be boring. However, they do have the advantage of not surprising or offending anyone. Wines from major brands are often made in this style.

Organic wine

It's almost impossible to distinguish the taste of an organic wine from a sustainable-agriculture wine (which include those that claim "reasonable" chemical use). It's only at the level of the soil where you'll find the difference. The soil of an organic wine contains more minerals and living organisms.

Notes

As soil becomes more and more depleted through the use of chemicals, we are left with vineyard soil that has lower concentrations of minerals. Drinking organically produced wine is doing a favor to our exhausted environment, provided of course, that the grapes are good and the work in the cellar follows the same principles as the viticulture. Fortunately today, there are more and more organic or biodynamic wines coming from the best areas of the world. Most in Europe have a seal on the label from ECOCERT, AB, Demeter, or Biodyvin.

Sulfite-free wine

What about a wine with no sulfur added? These wines, although quite individual, are increasingly popular in trendy wine bars. They are normally produced biodynamically (unless "sulfite-free" is just a marketing gimmick), and there is no addition of sulfur during winemaking or bottling. The wine is not stabilized or protected from oxygen. The result is the wine can be fragile and susceptible to evolving any which way in the bottle. It can oxidize quickly, or if it was over-protected from oxygen exposure, end up smelling like cabbage.

Some advice

Drinking sulfite-free wine is a little like playing slots in Vegas. But when you hit the jackpot, the result is rewarding. You just have to be willing to take the risk.

Depending on the season

Have you noticed, you prefer stews in winter and a green salad in summer? It's similar with wine. Don't choose a wine solely to suit your usual taste; choose a wine that matches the moment.

Tips for matching a wine with the moment

A warm wine will set the mood for seduction—great for a date, terrible for drinking with your mother-in-law.

Choose dry whites, rosés or light reds when it's warm outside. Open an ample white or a heady red in winter.

A full-bodied wine goes over well for a leisurely night with friend. An acidic wine is best saved for a professional conversation.

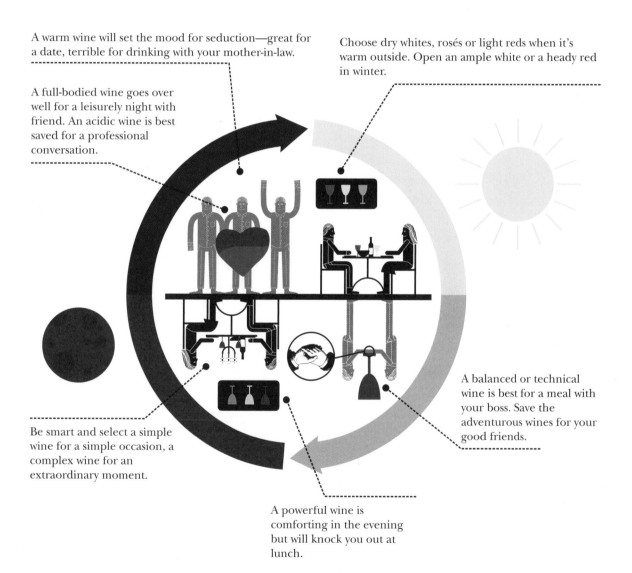

A balanced or technical wine is best for a meal with your boss. Save the adventurous wines for your good friends.

Be smart and select a simple wine for a simple occasion, a complex wine for an extraordinary moment.

A powerful wine is comforting in the evening but will knock you out at lunch.

Finding the wine of your dreams

It's the end of August, near the beginning of September. For kids and their parents, these days are synonymous with the end of summer and going back to school. But for the grape pickers, this time is a sign of achievement. And it's a moment of great joy.

Before starting his last year of school, Henry wanted to have a summer job in the open air. He's a strong and determined person, so he chose a job that demands both of these qualities—picking grapes. He hopped a plane for the south of France where he picked Syrah, Grenache, and Mourvèdre grapes. He learned the differences between them, and also about the age of the vine, its life cycle, and how it's cultivated. In the evening, he dined with the other grape pickers and toasted with wine from the winery. At the end of the season they had a big party.

Since he still had a few weeks before classes started, Henry asked to stay to help turn the grapes into wine, and the winery accepted. He discovered how they make wine, and the importance of vintage and barrel-aging.

He now has a much better understanding of how the wine he tastes was created, and why there are things like bubbles or sugar in the wine.

This chapter is for all of the Henrys in the world who want to know the origin of what they're drinking.

HENRY

PARTICIPATES IN
THE GRAPE HARVEST

The grape, from berry to harvest • White varieties
Red varieties • The life of the vine
Harvest time • Making wine • Aging

THE GRAPE, FROM BERRY TO HARVEST

Dissection of a berry

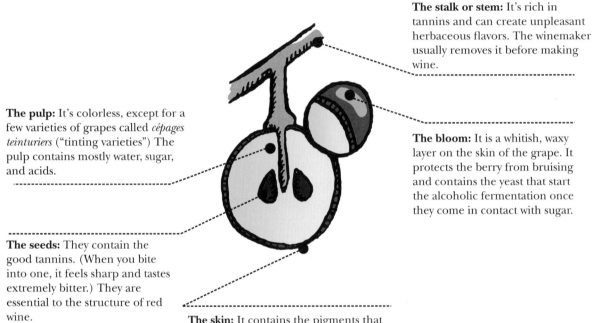

The stalk or stem: It's rich in tannins and can create unpleasant herbaceous flavors. The winemaker usually removes it before making wine.

The pulp: It's colorless, except for a few varieties of grapes called *cépages teinturiers* ("tinting varieties") The pulp contains mostly water, sugar, and acids.

The bloom: It is a whitish, waxy layer on the skin of the grape. It protects the berry from bruising and contains the yeast that start the alcoholic fermentation once they come in contact with sugar.

The seeds: They contain the good tannins. (When you bite into one, it feels sharp and tastes extremely bitter.) They are essential to the structure of red wine.

The skin: It contains the pigments that give color to the wine. It also contains aromatic substances.

Compared to table grapes

When choosing grapes for wine, you don't look for the same qualities as you do in table grapes. When you enjoy grapes as a snack, you want them to be juicy, with a thin skin and few or no seeds. But, when making wine, it's best to use a grape with a thick skin to extract the color and the aromas. You also want seeds that will give red wines the tannins that guarantee beautiful longevity.

The differences between berries

The berries differ in size and in character according to the type of grape. The same variety can be influenced differently by the weather, the soil, and the winemaker's work. If the vine gets too much water, the berry will be engorged and distended. The skin becomes thinner. During a drought, the grape will be the opposite—smaller, with a thick skin, which concentrates the aromas for the wine to come.

Henry participates in the grape harvest

A *vitis vinifera* varietal

The type of grape determines the different varietal wines that are produced in each region. Each varietal possesses its own characteristics.

There are about 10,000 grape varieties in the world. However, three-fourths of the world's wine comes from the use of only a dozen of them.

A quality wine uses varieties from the *Vitis vinifera* species. It's the species cultivated the most for wine, but there are other species, like the American *Vitis labrusca*. These belong to the genus *Vitis*, under the Vitaceae family. This large family includes all sorts of vines, including the virgin vine that decorates house walls.

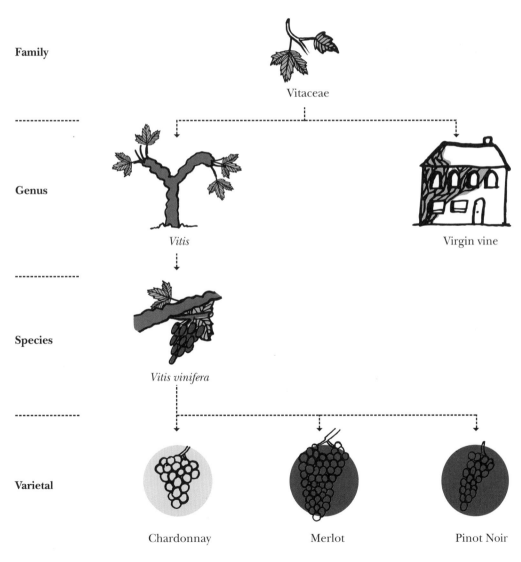

Family

Vitaceae

Genus

Vitis Virgin vine

Species

Vitis vinifera

Varietal

Chardonnay Merlot Pinot Noir

The grape, from berry to harvest

CHARDONNAY

FRUITS

 lemon   lime   apple   fresh almond   pear

FLOWERS

 lime blossom   acacia   honeysuckle   verbena   honey

BONUS

 butter   hazelnut   toasted almond   brioche   vanilla   toast

OVERVIEW

It is versatile and changes its character according to region, *terroir*, and the winemaker. It can be very floral or very fruity, and it can also reveal sharp, mineral flavors in the north of Burgundy, as a Chablis does, or it can be sensual and buttery like those from California. Because of its sponge-like personality, it doesn't have a singularly unique aromatic character, but generally it has aromas of lemon, acacia, and butter. It's often aged in oak barrels to develop notes of toast and brioche.

THE LOVE RATING

It's at the absolute top. It's the grape that produces the biggest dry white wines in the world—and the most expensive. It's also used to make Champagne.

HOT OR COLD CLIMATE?

Both hot and cold. This grape variety adapts to all climates, which is why it's so popular, but its personality changes. It will be dryer with mineral accents in cold climates, fatter with aromas of ripe fruits in hot climates.

WHERE DOES IT COME FROM?

France: Burgundy, Champagne, Jura, Languedoc, Provence; United States (mostly California), Canada, Chile, Argentina, South Africa, China, Australia

Henry participates in the grape harvest

SAUVIGNON BLANC

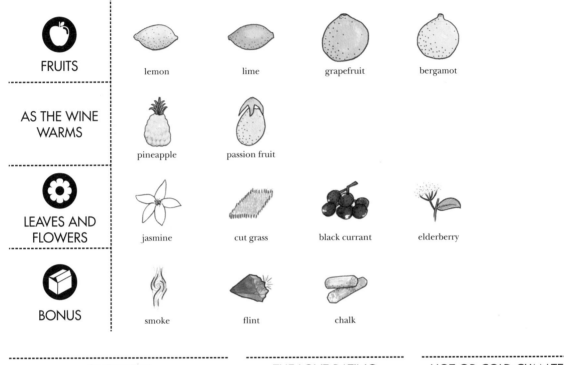

FRUITS

lemon   lime   grapefruit   bergamot

AS THE WINE WARMS

pineapple   passion fruit

LEAVES AND FLOWERS

jasmine   cut grass   black currant   elderberry

BONUS

smoke   flint   chalk

OVERVIEW

It's one of the most expressive varietals. It has refreshing aromas and notes of bright citrus, and can be reminiscent of tender grass that evokes springtime and the joy of living. With the aid of the winemaker and a good *terroir*, it can reveal aromas of smoke and pebbles. As frisky in the mouth as it is in the nose, it is sometimes nervous. During the winemaking process, it can be used alone or mixed with its friend from Bordeaux, Sémillon, to make dry or sweet wines that have a touch of lightness.

THE LOVE RATING

Sauvignon Blanc has become very popular thanks to the renown of Sancerres from the Loire and the white Bordeaux wines (both dry and sweet). It's exported to numerous countries. Very easy to drink and appreciate, it's the star of the white varietals. It consistently expresses the aromas of the grape variety.

HOT OR COLD CLIMATE?

Temperate. If it's too cold, it develops unpleasant aromas of greenness or even cat urine. If it's too hot, its fruit notes move from exotic to disgusting.

WHERE DOES IT COME FROM?

France: central Loire Valley, Bordeaux, South West; Spain, New Zealand, United States (California), Chile, South Africa

CHENIN BLANC

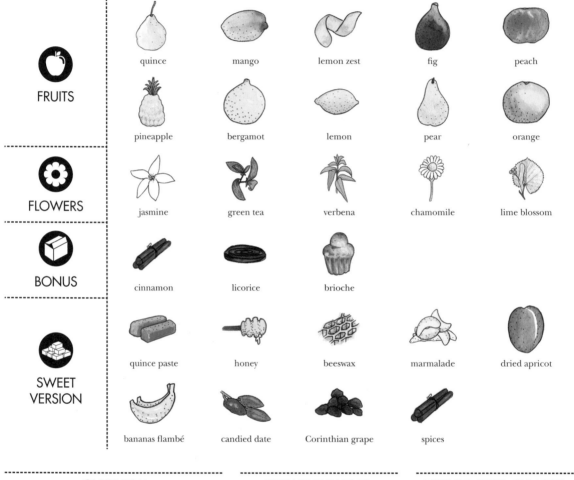

FRUITS

quince · mango · lemon zest · fig · peach

pineapple · bergamot · lemon · pear · orange

FLOWERS

jasmine · green tea · verbena · chamomile · lime blossom

BONUS

cinnamon · licorice · brioche

SWEET VERSION

quince paste · honey · beeswax · marmalade · dried apricot

bananas flambé · candied date · Corinthian grape · spices

OVERVIEW

This is a varietal of surprising sweetness and vivacity. Its acidity and its softness give this wine great versatility. It can be effervescent, dry, semi-dry, soft, or sweet. From quince to verbena, it can wear many masks, but it is good as a single varietal and does not need to be mixed with other grape varieties. Certain sweet versions of the wine can age for decades.

THE LOVE RATING

Confident and complicated, this variety is attracting increasingly more die-hard aficionados.

HOT OR COLD CLIMATE?

Temperate. It is too acidic to be good served cold, but it is drinkable at almost any other temperature.

WHERE DOES IT COME FROM?

France (Loire Valley), South Africa, United States (California)

Henry participates in the grape harvest

GEWÜRZTRAMINER

FRUITS

lychee · exotic fruits · passion fruit · orange zest

FLOWERS

rose · peony

SPICES

cinnamon · nutmeg · licorice

SWEET VERSION

caramel · leather · dried fruit · mango · honey

spice bread · praline · candied fruits

OVERVIEW

Easily recognizable for its unique aromas of rose and lychee, the variety also puts forth spicy scents. Indeed, its name comes from the German word *Gewürz*, which means "spice." It is so full-bodied in the mouth and so aromatic that the sweet versions of the wine can become cloying when they lack acidity. But it's delightful when it's made well. It's rarely mixed with other grapes.

THE LOVE RATING

It's either adored or hated according to personal taste, and it is generally reserved for aperitifs, desserts, Christmas dinners, or served with Asian foods (Chinese, Thai, or sushi).

HOT OR COLD CLIMATE?

Cold. It's a grape variety from the north of continental regions. It resists winter frosts well.

WHERE DOES IT COME FROM?

France (Alsace), Germany, Austria, the north of Italy

VIOGNIER

FRUITS

 apricot

 yellow peach

 white peach

 candied lemon zest

 pear

 melon

FLOWERS

 violet

 iris

 acacia

BONUS

 musk

 spices

beeswax

grilled hazelnut

tobacco

OVERVIEW

This grape variety produces a wine with aromas of apricot and peach, and they are often fat, full-bodied, and even heady. It has rare elegance when well made, but it can be cumbersome and pasty if made badly. Originating from the Rhône, this varietal is used on its own for the biggest wines, but it also blends well with other varietals from the region such as Marsanne and Roussane. In a red wine, a little Viognier can sometimes soften a Syrah.

THE LOVE RATING

Seductive as the devil in big white Rhône wines, which sell for the highest prices. It is lesser known among neophytes.

HOT OR COLD CLIMATE?

Mild to hot. It's very difficult to cultivate and produces grapes in small quantities. The challenge is to achieve a fragile balance between its inevitable roundness and the correctly balanced acidity.

WHERE DOES IT COME FROM?

France: Rhône Valley, Languedoc; United States (California), Australia

Henry participates in the grape harvest

SÉMILLON

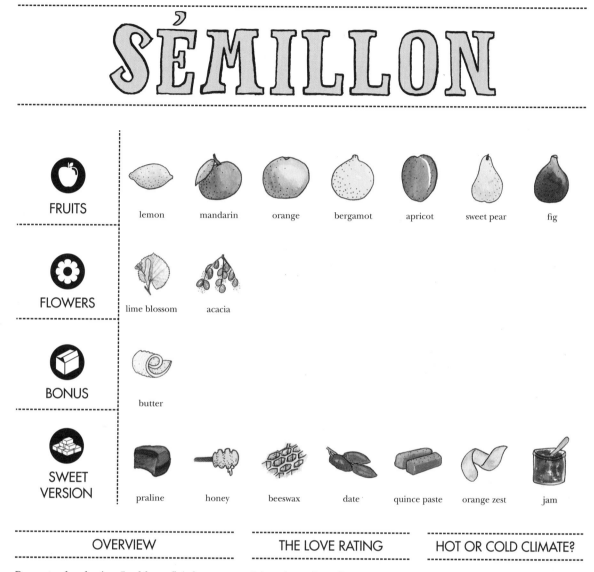

FRUITS

lemon   mandarin   orange   bergamot   apricot   sweet pear   fig

FLOWERS

lime blossom   acacia

BONUS

butter

SWEET VERSION

praline   honey   beeswax   date   quince paste   orange zest   jam

OVERVIEW

Prone to developing "noble rot" (when a fungus called *Botrytis cinerea* grows on the grapes), which concentrates the sugars in the grapes and gives birth to big sweet wines, Sémillon is the primary variety of the sumptuous, sweet white Bordeaux. Fat and a little too aromatic in a dry wine, it nevertheless assures a long life in the cellar, and it's truly the sweet version that shows off its potential. It is never used alone in a wine. Its favorite companion is Sauvignon Blanc, which can carry its roundness. Muscadelle sometimes completes the blend.

THE LOVE RATING

It's a champion. Great Sauternes sell for a fortune and are prized by wine aficionados all over the world.

HOT OR COLD CLIMATE?

Oceanic, temperate to mild. A powerful noble rot must develop in autumn to show this off to its fullest.

WHERE DOES IT COME FROM?

France: Bordeaux, South West; Australia, United States, South Africa

RIESLING

FRUITS

 lemon

 lime

 bergamot

 apple

 mirabelle plum

FLOWERS

honeysuckle

acacia

 mint

lime blossom

BONUS

hints of petroleum

mineral or flinty notes

OVERVIEW

This great German variety develops its flavors in the ground: It reflects the soil it comes from like no other variety. Its aromatic profile reflects the stone underground: More than any aromas of fruits and flowers, it's the aromas of minerals that surprise and delight in the big Rieslings. After a few years, the nose delivers a note of gasoline that is as much a mark of its character as anything. You'll also find notes of rock salt and overlays of citrus and delicate flowers. You'll find those in either dry or sweet versions of this variety. It is harvested late in autumn, though some are harvested even in winter and when very cold harvested as to make Ice wine.

THE LOVE RATING

It's a star. Along with Chardonnay it is considered by tasters to be one of the two best white varietals. Underestimated for most of the twentieth century, it is now pleases many more consumers, thanks to more rigorous production methods.

HOT OR COLD CLIMATE?

Cold, definitely. This is the quintessential northern varietal. Although it can certainly adapt to warmer climates, it loses a lot of complexity, elegance, and interest when it does.

WHERE DOES IT COME FROM?

France (Alsace), Germany, Luxembourg, Australia, New Zealand, Canada

Henry participates in the grape harvest

MARSANNE BLEND

FRUITS

 fresh almond   peach   apricot   apple   orange   dried fruit

FLOWERS

 jasmine   acacia

BONUS

walnut   truffle   almond paste   beeswax

OVERVIEW

This varietal brings power and roundness to a wine. It starts with its underlying almond aromas but also brings in jasmine and even beeswax. It's rarely the only varietal present in a wine. It blends harmoniously with other grape varieties, most notably Rousanne, which also comes from the Rhône Valley.

THE LOVE RATING

Although it's not very well known, it is very commonly blended into French wines with Rousanne. Marsanne also goes well with Rolle (the French name for Vermentino), Grenache Blanc or Viognier.

HOT OR COLD CLIMATE?

Hot. With pebbles at its feet.

WHERE DOES IT COME FROM?

France: the Rhône Valley, Languedoc, other regions of the south of France; Australia, United States (California)

VERMENTINO

FRUITS

 grapefruit

 pear

 golden apple

 peach

 pineapple

 green almond

FLOWERS

 hawthorn

 chamomile

 dill

 fennel

 anise

OVERVIEW

White Corsican wines are made with 100 percent Vermentino grapes. But in Provence, under the name Rolle, it also blends with a multitude of varietals such as Trebbiano (called Ugni Blanc in France), Marsanne, Grenache Blanc, Clairette, Chardonnay, or Sauvignon Blanc. Very fresh and very aromatic, it releases aromas of pear and also notes of anise seed or sometimes more like fennel. Finally, a fine bitterness comes through, which is delicious as long as it does not overpower.

THE LOVE RATING

It pairs very well with fish dishes in summer, but this variety is more difficult to pair with winter meals. But be sure to try it when you feel like going on vacation.

HOT OR COLD CLIMATE?

Hot! This variety appreciates hot sun and dry, infertile soils.

WHERE DOES IT COME FROM?

France: Languedoc-Roussillon, the southeast of France; Corsica, Sardinia, Tuscany

Henry participates in the grape harvest

MUSCAT

 FRUITS

 grape

 lemon

 apple

 FLOWERS

 lime blossom

rose

 SWEET VERSION

beeswax

quince paste

 jam

orange zest

raisin

OVERVIEW

A grape variety originating in Greece, Muscat has been cultivated since antiquity, Muscat Blanc à Petits Grains (also called Moscato) is found all over Europe. Frontignan is famous for its Muscat de Frontignan wine. Dry and floral, it is the only varietal to deliver aromas of real, crisp grape. Vinified fine and sparkling in Italy, it often makes a fortified wine in the south of France and in Greece. It is a sweet wine, almost candied, and perfect for dessert. Think Muscat de Beaumes de Venise or Muscat de Rivesaltes. Do not confuse it with other varieties, such as the Muscat of Alexandria (which has big berries), the Muscat Ottonel, and especially not Muscadet (which is a dry wine from the Loire made with the Melon de Bourgogne variety)!

THE LOVE RATING

Very popular and sells like candy to grandparents, it is less popular with young people.

HOT OR COLD CLIMATE?

Mild. But it adapts easily.

WHERE DOES IT COME FROM?

France: Alsace (as a dry wine), the south of France (as a fortified wine); Corsica, Italy (both dry and sparkling Moscato), Greece (soft Muscat from Samos), Spain, Portugal, Australia (especially from Rutherglen), Austria, Eastern Europe, South Africa

PINOT GRIGIO/ PINOT GRIS

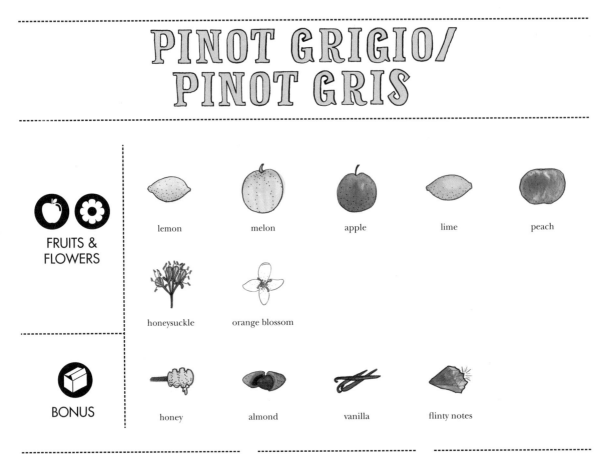

FRUITS & FLOWERS

lemon   melon   apple   lime   peach

honeysuckle   orange blossom

BONUS

honey   almond   vanilla   flinty notes

OVERVIEW

Pinot Grigio is the same grape as Pinot Gris, but you wouldn't know it by tasting it. The styles of Pinot Grigio (the Italian name) and Pinot Gris (French) are so distinct that you couldn't fault anyone for thinking they were separate varieties. The lighter, more citrusy Pinot Grigio style is achieved by picking the grapes early in an attempt to salvage the brightness in this low-acid grape. Pinot Gris (originally from Burgundy but now better known in Alsace) is picked later, leading to more peachy, stone-fruit flavors. And it's often aged in neutral oak or on the lees (the dead yeast cells at the bottom of the tank) to add richness and texture.

THE LOVE RATING

Love is in the air for both styles! Pinot Grigio flies off store shelves and is consumed in great quantities by "ladies who lunch" and those looking to drink something alcoholic that is wholly inoffensive. Pinot Gris, on the other hand, is revered and adored by wine geeks everywhere. A win-win for Pinot Grigio/Pinot Gris.

HOT OR COLD CLIMATE?

The cooler the better. Low temperatures help retain some natural acidity in this low-acid grape.

WHERE DOES IT COME FROM?

France (Alsace); Italy: Trentino, Alto Adige, Veneto; Germany and Austria: Rheinhessen, Pfalz, Baden, Burgenland, Styria; United States: California, Oregon; Australia, New Zealand, Hungary, Romania

Henry participates in the grape harvest

PINOT BLANC

FRUITS

apple   white peach   citrus   melon

BONUS

almond   smoke   mineral   honey

OVERVIEW

Mild-mannered Pinot Blanc (known as Pinot Bianco in Italy and Weissburgunder in Austria and Germany) is a white grape with round, fleshy apple flavors and low acidity. The grape is sometimes compared with Chardonnay but the flavors are much milder and the body not as full. Pinot Blanc is a bit of a chameleon: It's made in light, crisp styles to smokier oaked styles to sweet styles. It even makes sparkling wines.

THE LOVE RATING

Pinot Blanc rarely generates excitement but some examples from Austria and northern Italy will turn the heads of enthusiastic wine lovers searching for something different. If you're looking for a party pleaser, look no further than Pinot Blanc. It's a great value and a safe bet for its freshness and drinkability.

HOT OR COLD CLIMATE?

Cool temperatures are preferred.

WHERE DOES IT COME FROM?

France: Alsace, Burgundy, Champagne; Germany, Austria, Italy (Northern), United States: California, New York, Oregon; Canada, Slovenia, Croatia, Hungary, Spain

MUSCADET

FRUITS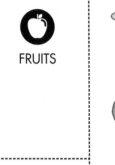

 lemon

lime

 green apple

 pear

 peach

quince

BONUS

chalk

 flint

black pepper

OVERVIEW

Muscadet is made from the Melon de Bourgogne grape and is produced in the Loire Valley of France. The wine's delicate, refreshing citrus flavors and faint briny scent, reminiscent of the ocean, make it a no-brainer to match with oysters and other types of seafood. To add flavor and texture to the wine, many Muscadet producers leave the wine on the lees (yeast settled at the bottom of the tank) for several weeks or months. This is called *sur lie* and it adds a yeasty flavor and more body to the wine.

THE LOVE RATING

Like a gentle squeeze of lemon on your oysters or a burst of acidity to offset a decadent plate of fish and chips. Muscadet is an often overlooked wine that deserves some attention. There are a lot of bland examples out on the market, so be sure to ask your wine merchant or sommelier to point you in the right direction.

HOT OR COLD CLIMATE?

Cold and wet. The Loire Valley has one of the coldest growing seasons in all of France.

WHERE DOES IT COME FROM?

France: Loire Valley
United States: Washington State, Oregon

Henry participates in the grape harvest

SOAVE

FRUITS

peach

melon

lemon

orange zest

BONUS

honey

apricot

fennel

chalk

almond

mineral

OVERVIEW

Soave is a white wine made from the Garganega grape in the northeast Italian region of Veneto. Soave is an important white grape for Italy (ranking right up there with Pinot Grigio), and you will find it in two different styles. The leaner, simpler styles are fermented in steel tanks, and those with a slightly fuller body and a nutty character are aged in old wooden barrels. The best Soaves come from vineyards in the volcanic hills around the village of Soave.

THE LOVE RATING

Great deals abound for those willing to give Soave a chance. At one time, producers in Soave were going for quantity over quality, and the wine developed a well-deserved reputation for being diluted and bland. Quality-conscious winemakers are now producing delightful, even complex, examples, and since the wine is still underappreciated, you can snag one for less than $15.

HOT OR COLD CLIMATE?

Cool temperatures though summer and winter.

WHERE DOES IT COME FROM?

Italy: Veneto, Friuli, Lombardy, Umbria

ALBARIÑO

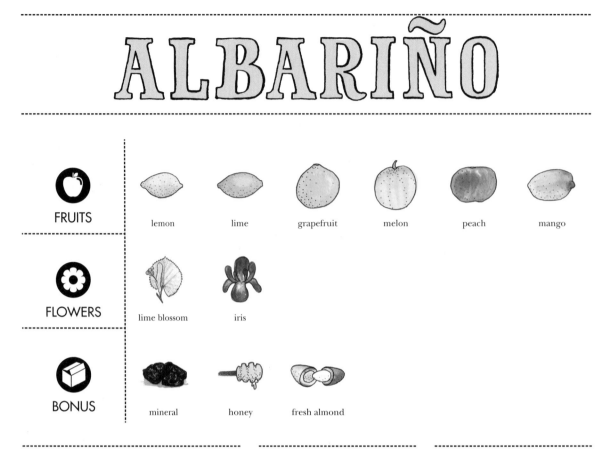

FRUITS

lemon   lime   grapefruit   melon   peach   mango

FLOWERS

lime blossom   iris

BONUS

mineral   honey   fresh almond

OVERVIEW

Albariño hails from northern Portugal (where it is called Alvarinho) but has made more of an impact right across the border in Spain, in the Rías Baixas region. The predominant characteristic is citrus, but wines from the Albariño grape can also tend toward tropical fruits. The refreshing acidity and notable briny character make the wines easy to drink and an effortless match with food, especially seafood. The best Vinho Verdes from the Minho region of Portugal are made from the Albariño grape.

THE LOVE RATING

Unassuming Albariño has suddenly become synonymous with white wine from Spain, much as Pinot Grigio has long been associated with white wine from Italy. Whether this is a good thing or not remains to be seen, but the wines provide a light, refreshing alternative to Pinot Grigio and Sauvignon Blanc, and those from the hands of enthusiastic winemakers have the potential to get noticed at pool parties and dinner parties alike.

HOT OR COLD CLIMATE?

Cool and wet. This grape loves the rain, as well as the fog and mist spray off the ocean in the leading Albariño-producing regions.

WHERE DOES IT COME FROM?

Spain: Rías Baixas
Portugal: Minho
United States (California)

Henry participates in the grape harvest

TORRONTÉS

FRUITS

 peach

 tangerine

 grapefruit

 lemon

 pineapple

FLOWERS

 rose

geranium

BONUS

chalk

cut grass

fennel

jasmine

OVERVIEW

The Torrontés grape originated in Argentina, and most of the Torrentés in the world comes from that country. Although it is grown across Argentina, the finest examples come from the high-altitude vineyards of the Salta region. Often compared with Albariño from Spain and Sauvignon Blanc from France, this zesty wine is bright and bursting with fascinating floral aromas. Wines made from the Torrontés grape are almost always produced in a dry style.

THE LOVE RATING

Torrontés has risen to fame on the coattails of the red grape darling of Argentina, Malbec. It's conceivable that this fresh and fruity white could become the next big thing.

HOT OR COLD CLIMATE?

Cool, with big day-to-night temperature swings and high altitudes.

WHERE DOES IT COME FROM?

Argentina: La Rioja, Salta, San Juan, Rio Negro
Chile, United States (California)

GRÜNER VELTLINER

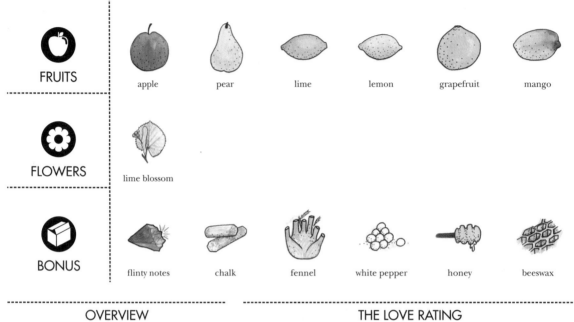

FRUITS
apple   pear   lime   lemon   grapefruit   mango

FLOWERS
lime blossom

BONUS
flinty notes   chalk   fennel   white pepper   honey   beeswax

OVERVIEW

Grüner Veltliner is Austria's most popular white grape variety. The vast majority of plantings are in Austria, though a small percentage of acres are planted in nearby Eastern European countries. It is a refreshing white wine with a perceptible spicy, peppery note. There are light and zesty Grüners from the cooler Austrian regions, which are meant to be drunk young and fresh, and there are richer, spicier styles from the slightly warmer areas that can age longer and feature more tropical fruit flavors.

THE LOVE RATING

Grüner Veltliner has had a bit of a roller-coaster ride when it comes to popularity. The easy, refreshing wine, often in a liter-size screwcap bottle, became a trendy summertime party sipper—a spicy alternative to Sauvignon Blanc or Pinot Grigio. As sometimes happens when a wine gets too trendy, instead of remaining loyal, people started looking for the next cool thing, and Grüner fell by the wayside. Happily, it is making a comeback of sorts, and not just with the cheap and easy liter bottles. There's growing interest in some of the richer, more serious bottlings as well.

HOT OR COLD CLIMATE?

Cool to warm. Different temperatures produce different styles of Grüner Veltliner, but if the weather is too cold, the grapes do not fully ripen and lack character.

WHERE DOES IT COME FROM?

Austria: Niederösterreich, Burgenland
Slovenia, Czech Republic, Northern Italy, New Zealand, Australia, United States

Henry participates in the grape harvest

ASSYRTIKO

FRUITS

 citrus

 lemon zest

peach

apple

FLOWERS

 acacia

BONUS

mineral

stone

earth

SWEET VERSION

apricots

brioche

dried fig

honey

OVERVIEW

Cultivated on the island of Santorini, Assyrtiko comes from some of the world's oldest vineyards. Assyrtiko vines can reach nearly seventy years of age, even in the excessively dry and windy conditions on the island. The grape is able to maintain its bright acidity, despite the heat, to produce wines with structure and body while also offering freshness and minerality. Assyrtiko is also planted on mainland Greece, where the wines are more round and fruity. When combined with other indigenous Greek grapes, Assyrtiko becomes part of the blend that makes up the traditional Greek sweet wine called Vinsanto (wine from Santorini).

THE LOVE RATING

Assyrtiko may well be the only Greek grape variety that some folks know by name, and even then it's only likely because they once vacationed on the beautiful island of Santorini. Just a few short years ago, it was practically unknown even among sommeliers and others in the know about wine, and the grape was obscure and difficult to find. If you see it on a wine menu pronounce it out loud (ah-SEER-tiko), and order a bottle of this unique wine.

HOT OR COLD CLIMATE?

Hot! Assyrtiko thrives in extreme conditions and challenging *terroirs*.

WHERE DOES IT COME FROM?

Greece: Santorini, Paros, Naxos, Crete, Macedonia, Attica
United States (California)

CHAMPAGNE

FRUITS
lemon   peach   melon   pear   apple   cherry   strawberry

FLOWERS
honeysuckle

BONUS
chalk   ginger   honey   smoke   hazelnut   almond   toast

BARREL-AGED
vanilla   coconut   brioche   cream

OVERVIEW

Champagne is sparkling wine from the Champagne region of France. No other sparkling wine can legally be called Champagne, although people often mistakenly refer to all sparkling wines as Champagne. Champagne is made in both white and rosé styles, and the three grapes used to produce the wines are Pinot Noir and Pinot Meunier (both red grapes) and Chardonnay (a white grape). The bubbles come from a second fermentation of the wine in the bottle, which is called *méthode champenoise* in France, and referred to as the classic or traditional method elsewhere.

THE LOVE RATING

Champagne is all about love, holidays, and celebration. Famous quotes about Champagne abound, with references to drinking stars, zest, elegance, diamonds, truth, love, and sparking, smiling eyes. The only downfall to all this Champagne adoration is that people tend to save it for special occasions. Champagne can really be enjoyed more often. After all, Champagne is versatile with all types of foods, you can find great Champagne at various price points, it's sparkly and refreshing, and it comes in a variety of styles, from white to rosé to sweet to ultra-dry.

HOT OR COLD CLIMATE?

Cold. The Champagne region's average temperatures are lower than any other French winegrowing area.

WHERE DOES IT COME FROM?

France: Champagne

Henry participates in the grape harvest

CAVA

FRUITS

lime   apple   pear   quince

FLOWERS

honeysuckle

BONUS

almond   anise   chalk

BARREL-AGED

smoke   toast   cream

OVERVIEW

Cava is the sparkling wine of Spain and is produced mostly in the Catalan region of Penedès, near Barcelona. Three traditional grapes make up Cava—Macabeo, Xarel-lo, and Parellada—although other grapes, such as Chardonnay and Pinot Noir, can be used. The wines are made by the same method as Champagne from France, where the secondary fermentation (which causes the bubbles) happens right in the bottle. The best Cavas have similar flavors and aromas to Champagne and pair well with all types of food.

THE LOVE RATING

If Prosecco is a sparkling wine fan's first love, Cava steals the heart with a little more substance and a touch of the unexpected. It's closer to Champagne, not only in the way it is produced but also in the fine quality of the bubbles, the dryness on the palate, and the toasty, biscuity flavors that make it more complex. With reasonable price points on a par with Prosecco, Cava may just sweep you off your feet.

HOT OR COLD CLIMATE?

The traditional Cava grapes thrive in cool temperatures with moderate rainfall.

WHERE DOES IT COME FROM?

Spain: Penedès (Catalonia), Aragón, Castilla y León, Extremadura, Rioja, the Basque Country, Navarre, Valencia

PROSECCO

 FRUITS

 melon

 lemon

 green apple

 grapefruit

 peach

 **FLOWERS**

 honeysuckle

 **BONUS**

 honey

 chalk

 cream

 hazelnut

OVERVIEW

Prosecco is an affordable sparkling wine from Italy produced in the northern Italian regions of Veneto and Friuli. Although the official name of the grape used to make Prosecco is Glera, most people still informally refer to the grape as Prosecco. Other grapes are allowed to be added, but the main grape is always Glera. One distinction from Champagne is that the second fermentation, which creates the bubbles, is done in a large tank instead of the bottle. This is a more affordable method, which means that Prosecco is less expensive and also has softer, frothier bubbles.

THE LOVE RATING

There is enormous love for Prosecco, especially now that quality has gone up across the board. Fun, affordable celebrations everywhere include popping a bottle of this bubbly stuff. And it makes a mean Mimosa too.

HOT OR COLD CLIMATE?

Cool temperatures though summer and winter.

WHERE DOES IT COME FROM?

Italy: Veneto, Friuli

Henry participates in the grape harvest

PINOT NOIR

AROMAS

cherry · raspberry · strawberry · black currant · iris · violet

BARREL-AGED

wood · vanilla · cinnamon · tobacco

WITH BOTTLE AGE

fur · leather · undergrowth · moss · truffle · musk

OVERVIEW

This king of Burgundies shows as much finesse as power. The wine is a brilliant ruby color, with bewitching aromas of red fruit, and in the mouth, its texture is fine and silky with low tannins. But it's much affected with aging, as you may discover when it loses its allure after a few years. It will develop very desirable bouquets of autumn forest, leather, and truffle. It is mostly vinified on its own and sometimes blended with another variety.

THE LOVE RATING

Immense! It's one of the most appreciated (and most cultivated) varietals in the world. The prices of the really big Burgundies can be astronomical. Happily, you can also find a nice drinkable Pinot Noir for a nice drinkable price for any occasion.

HOT OR COLD CLIMATE?

Cool. Its skin is thin, and in a hot climate, the grape will ripen too quickly and the aromas will not be as interesting.

WHERE DOES IT COME FROM?

Everywhere wine is made—Europe, North America, South America, and South Africa. The most interesting *terroirs* are in Burgundy, Champagne, Oregon, New Zealand, and Australia.

Less tannic · Very tannic

CABERNET SAUVIGNON

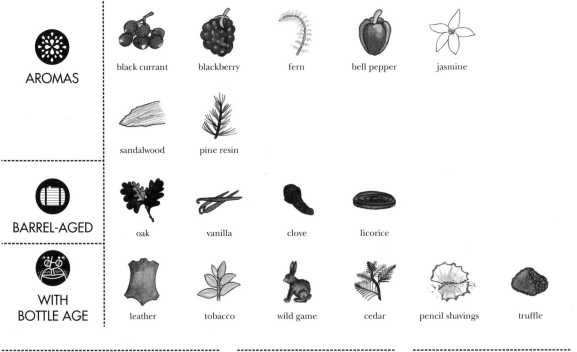

AROMAS

black currant · blackberry · fern · bell pepper · jasmine

sandalwood · pine resin

BARREL-AGED

oak · vanilla · clove · licorice

WITH BOTTLE AGE

leather · tobacco · wild game · cedar · pencil shavings · truffle

OVERVIEW

This is another monarch variety, this time from Bordeaux. This grape is the marathon runner of the wine world. Wine made from these grapes is made to last. Its abundant tannins are an invitation to wait decades for the wine to develop a powerful bouquet and extremely complex aromas of cassis, tobacco, wild game, and cedar. Cabernet Sauvignon produces powerful wines that are structured, serious, and slightly exuberant. In its youth, this wine can seem austere, even surly. That's why you'll often see it blended with its debonair companion, Merlot.

Less tannic — Very tannic

THE LOVE RATING

Gigantic, like a Pinot Noir. It's the most widespread red grape varietal in the world. And its wines are among the most sought after (and the most expensive).

HOT OR COLD CLIMATE?

Fairly warm. The skin of the little berries is very thick and it ripens slowly, so it needs a lot of sun.

WHERE DOES IT COME FROM?

All over, from France to China. It's best known from Bordeaux and the south of France.
Italy, Chile, United States, and elsewhere

Henry participates in the grape harvest

MERLOT

AROMAS

prune

blackberry

blueberry

black cherry

violet

mint

WITH BOTTLE AGE

leather

wild game

meat juice

OVERVIEW

This is the ideal companion for Cabernet Sauvignon, (in which Cabernet plays Laurel to Merlot's Hardy). It can also be bottled without blending because it is immediately likable, opulent, and soft on the palate. It can cozy up equally to Cabernet Franc, which prolongs its life span.

THE LOVE RATING

This is a very popular everyday wine. It's fruity and easy to drink while young and pleases many palates.

HOT OR COLD CLIMATE?

Temperate to hot. It is easy to cultivate, and its big berries with thin skin ripen easily.

WHERE DOES IT COME FROM?

France: Bordeaux, South West, Languedoc-Roussillon
Italy, South Africa, Chile, Argentina, United States (California)

Less tannic   Very tannic

CABERNET FRANC

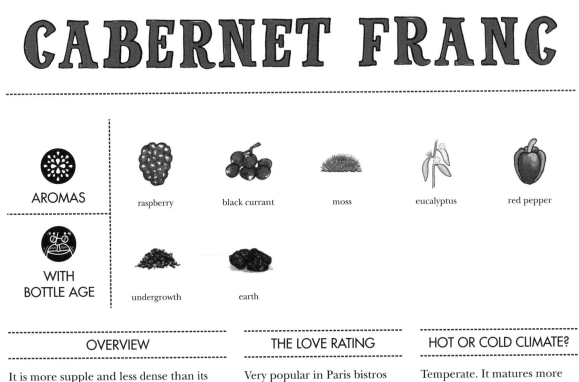

AROMAS

raspberry black currant moss eucalyptus red pepper

WITH BOTTLE AGE

undergrowth earth

OVERVIEW

It is more supple and less dense than its ancestor, Cabernet Sauvignon. In varietal wines, it gives silky wines aromas of black currant and leaves. If it's picked too early, a touch of bell pepper can be detected. On the right bank of Bordeaux, it is also often blended with Merlot, which gives these wines both roundness and a refreshing quality.

THE LOVE RATING

Very popular in Paris bistros when the wines come from the Loire. They also like it in Bordeaux because it can be drunk young.

HOT OR COLD CLIMATE?

Temperate. It matures more rapidly than Cabernet Sauvignon.

WHERE DOES IT COME FROM?

France: Bordeaux, Loire, South West
Italy, Chile, Australia, United States

Less tannic   Very tannic

Henry participates in the grape harvest

MALBEC

FRUITS

 black cherry

 blueberry

 plum

BONUS

 cedar

 leather

OVERVIEW

An essential varietal in Argentina. This grape variety gives red wines both richness and velvety characteristics, but it can take on more rustic and tannic characteristics in South West, in France. It can be vinified as a rosé or a red, alone or in a blend.

THE LOVE RATING

Once widespread in France, its popularity has waned there, though it has become smoking hot in the Americas.

HOT OR COLD CLIMATE?

Rather hot. It is sensitive to frost.

WHERE DOES IT COME FROM?

France: Bordeaux, South West
Argentina, Chile, Italy, United States (California), Australia, South Africa

Less tannic

Very tannic

PETIT VERDOT

 FRUITS

 blueberry

 blackberry

 cherry

 plum

 FLOWERS

 lavender

 violet

 BONUS

 thyme

 clove

 wild game

 smoke

 BARREL-AGED

 nutmeg

dark chocolate

vanilla

hazelnut

OVERVIEW

Petit Verdot's traditional role is as a blending grape in the red wines of Bordeaux. The grape adds color, tannin, and floral aromas to blends, even in small amounts of 3 percent or less. The grape needs a lot of sun to fully ripen, which Bordeaux doesn't have, but sunnier wine regions in California, Washington State, Spain, and Australia, have had success with Petit Verdot as a single-variety wine. Oak-aging is often used to soften the tannins and add a little spice.

Less tannic ——————— Very tannic

THE LOVE RATING

Petit Verdot is an acquired taste, and the grape's strong flavors and grippy tannins are not for everyone. If you are the type who's always reaching for the peppermill or looking to the spice cabinet to liven up your food, Petit Verdot may be the wine for you.

HOT OR COLD CLIMATE?

Hot. Warm temperatures and plenty of sunshine will ensure that the grape ripens completely and does not produce undesirable green flavors.

WHERE DOES IT COME FROM?

France: Bordeaux, Languedoc-Roussillon
United States: California, Washington State
Spain, Australia, Italy, South Africa, Chile, Argentina, Portugal, Canada, Turkey, Brazil, Uruguay

Henry participates in the grape harvest

BORDEAUX BLEND

FRUITS

black currant   plum   blueberry   pomegranate

HERBS & SPICES

cola   bay laurel   tobacco   black pepper   menthol

BARREL-AGED

vanilla   cedar   smoke   dark chocolate

BONUS

leather   pencil shavings   tar

OVERVIEW

Bordeaux blend is the term used for wines made up of two or more of the grapes used to produce the classic red wines of the Bordeaux region of France. These grapes include, predominantly, Cabernet Sauvignon, Merlot, and Cabernet Franc, but smaller percentages of Petit Verdot, Malbec, and sometimes Carménère can be in there. You'll taste a notable difference between wines depending on whether Cabernet Sauvignon or Merlot is the lead grape. Cabernet-dominated blends are more herbal and tannic, Merlot blends smoother and fruitier. The term Bordeaux blend is now used ubiquitously for this type of red wine blend all over the world.

Less tannic   Very tannic

THE LOVE RATING

The classic Bordeaux blends from the Bordeaux region of France have always been, rather unromantically, associated with high prices, luxury, and wealth. But Americans are crushing on the affordable Bordeaux Blends coming out of places like California and Washington State, as well as those from Argentina and South Africa.

HOT OR COLD CLIMATE?

Bordeaux blends can be successful in both hot and cold climates because there are five to six grape varieties to choose from. Blends from warmer climates will be lusher, while blends from cooler climates more structured.

WHERE DOES IT COME FROM?

France: Bordeaux, South West
United States: California, Washington State
Italy: Tuscany, Veneto
Australia, Argentina, South Africa, Spain, Chile

SYRAH

 FRUITS

 blackberry　　 black cherry　　 black currant

 HERBS & SPICES

 black pepper　　 white pepper　　nutmeg　　dark chocolate　　violet　　 licorice

 BARREL-AGED

cinnamon　　coffee　　smoke

 WITH BOTTLE AGE

wild game　　fig　　tobacco　　truffle

OVERVIEW

Syrah is like an evening gown in rich, dark purple. Bewitching, it delivers powerful aromas of pepper, nutmeg, and licorice. And it is associated with the softness of violet. It produces wines that keep well, are dense and strong when they are vinified alone, and are more fruity and easy when married with Grenache.
(It's called Shiraz when it's cultivated in Australia, New Zealand, and Chile.)

THE LOVE RATING

It's the celebrity of the appellations in the Rhône—Hermitage, Côte-Rôtie, Saint-Joseph—where it's only appreciated after being cellared for a few years. It's the most planted red grape variety in Australia.

HOT OR COLD CLIMATE?

Temperate to hot.

WHERE DOES IT COME FROM?

France; Rhône, south of France
United States (California), Italy, South Africa

Less tannic　　　　　　Very tannic

Henry participates in the grape harvest

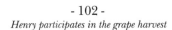

GRENACHE

AROMAS

 fig

strawberry

 blueberry

 nutmeg

 garrigue (thyme, bay laurel, rosemary)

 cocoa

 cinnamon

 eau-de-vie (Calvados)

BARREL-AGED

vanilla

coffee

licorice

caramel

WITH BOTTLE AGE

dried fig

prune

mocha

leather

OVERVIEW

This grape originates from Spain and produces gourmet wines with forward aromas of prunes, chocolate and *garrigue* (the fragrant, herbal vegetation of the Mediterranean coast). It tends to be sweet on the tongue, and sometimes these wines have a very high percentage of alcohol. It's often used in rosé and in natural soft (sweetened) wines and, of course, in red blends and single-variety wines. In the Rhône, it likes to flirt with the big, powerful Syrah, softening the tannins of the latter with its roundness.

THE LOVE RATING

This is the most-planted red grape variety in the world. Very prized for its presence in big wines like Châteauneuf-du-Pape but also in muted wines like Banyuls and Maury. It goes very well with chocolate.

HOT OR COLD CLIMATE?

Hot. It fears cold spring rains but has no fear of drought.

WHERE DOES IT COME FROM?

France: Rhône, Roussillon
Spain, Australia, Morocco, United States (California)

Less tannic

Very tannic

MOURVÈDRE

AROMAS

blackberry

licorice

garrigue (thyme, bay laurel, rosemary)

cinnamon

pepper

musk

WITH BOTTLE AGE

leather   wild game   truffle

OVERVIEW

Mourvèdre produces wines that are almost black, very powerful, and often high in alcohol. If it displays hard and earthy characteristics when it's young, it develops softer aromas of leather and truffle with age. It is often blended with other grapes to give structure to wines from the south of France, both reds and rosés.

THE LOVE RATING

Not as well known to the general public, this varietal requires patience from the winemaker. It results in magnificent Bandols from Provence.

HOT OR COLD CLIMATE?

Hot! Its skin is thick, and it needs a lot of sun to ripen.

WHERE DOES IT COME FROM?

France: Rhône, Languedoc-Roussillon, Bandol
United States (California), Australia, Spain

Less tannic   Very tannic

Henry participates in the grape harvest

CARIGNAN

FRUITS

blackberry   banana   prune

BONUS

garrigue (thyme, bay laurel, rosemary)   licorice   mineral notes

OVERVIEW

Sometimes used for mass production, Carignan is not generally very interesting. It can be acidic and not very aromatic. But when winegrowers reduce the yields of the crop, it allows the vines to age, and then it produces a wine of strong character that is powerful, deeply colored, and generous. It is certainly rustic, but it possesses inimitable aromas of *garrigue* and mineral notes. It is widely used in blends.

THE LOVE RATING

Despite its presence in a lot of red and rosé wines from the south of France, it is still not very well known to the general public. Because it's difficult to cultivate, only some die-hard winemakers work it as a single-varietal wine, specifically to appeal to those in the know.

HOT OR COLD CLIMATE?

Hot. It loves the sun, dry weather and the wind.

WHERE DOES IT COME FROM?

France: Rhône: Languedoc, Provence
Spain, Maghreb, United States (California), Argentina, Chile

Less tannic   Very tannic

RHÔNE BLEND/GSM

FRUITS & FLOWERS

raspberry   cherry   red plum   blackberry   orange zest   lavender

HERBS & SPICES

black pepper   white pepper   black tea   thyme

BONUS

leather   smoke   earth   clove   coffee

OVERVIEW

Rhône blends originated in the Rhône region of France, but the GSM blend (which stands for the grapes Grenache, Syrah, and Mourvèdre) has become popular the world over. All three grapes blended together result in a powerful, full-bodied wine with concentrated fruit and secondary flavors of spice, leather, and even bacon. The most prominent wines from the Rhône that use the GSM blend are Châteauneuf-du-Pape (which actually allows for up to thirteen different grape varieties), Côtes du Rhône, and Vacqueyras.

THE LOVE RATING

Everyone is crazy for red blends! For years, blends were thought to be inferior to single-variety wines, but people have finally caught on that blending certain grapes together balances the wine and makes for some pretty delicious combinations of flavors. There is a reason this traditional blend works, and it's catching on.

HOT OR COLD CLIMATE?

All three of these grapes like it hot.

WHERE DOES IT COME FROM?

France: Rhône, Languedoc-Roussillon
Spain: Catalonia, Aragon, La Mancha, Madrid
United States: California, Washington State; South Australia, South Africa

Less tannic   Very tannic

Henry participates in the grape harvest

GAMAY

FRUITS

 red cherry   strawberry   raspberry   red currant   blackberry   banana

FLOWERS

 jasmine

BONUS

chocolate

OVERVIEW

Gamay is synonymous with Beaujolais, the region where this grape occupies 99 percent of the vineyards. It is a variety that could not be more fruity and charming. Numerous aromas of gourmet red fruits, a fresh mouthfeel, and a supple and not too tannic body—that's what makes this wine easy to drink and suitable for all occasions. Although sometimes manhandled in making the fashionable Beaujolais Nouveau (with a fermentation process that provokes a nose of banana and bourbon), it can also, when it's well made, age like a great beauty.

THE LOVE RATING

Poor Gamay has fallen into disgrace because of too much high-volume, forced production, but it is coming back to the table thanks to interested wineries that are making wines that combine intense flavors and high quality.

HOT OR COLD CLIMATE?

Cool to temperate. It's a varietal as precocious as it is productive.

WHERE DOES IT COME FROM?

France: Beaujoloais, Loire, Ardeche, Burgundy
Switzerland, Chile, Argentina

Less tannic   Very tannic

NEBBIOLO

FRUITS: cherry · strawberry · raspberry · cranberry · fig

FLOWERS: rose · violet

HERBS & SPICES: licorice · anise · white pepper · black tea

BONUS: cedar · tobacco · cola · leather · smoke · tar

OVERVIEW

Nebbiolo is one of Italy's most esteemed grapes, and it's used to make the famous wines of Barolo and Barbaresco in the northern Italian Piedmont region. These wines have monster tannins when young and require aging to truly enjoy the myriad of complex aromas and flavors they have to offer. Although they are both intense wines, Barolo is generally the more masculine and powerful, while Barbaresco has an elegant, feminine side. There are other regions in Piedmont, such as Roero, Gattinara, and Ghemme, which produce more approachable wines from the Nebbiolo grape. Next door, in the Italian region of Lombardy, Nebbiolo makes the less famous, but still distinct, wines of Valtellina. The most common descriptors you will hear to portray Nebbiolo are tar, roses, violet, and cherry.

THE LOVE RATING

Longing for something you can't have is how many people feel about Nebbiolo—Barolo and Barbaresco in particular. Arguably among the world's most beautiful and intense wines, they are also expensive and require patience, something that many of us just don't have. You can find a nice, drinkable Nebbiolo for a decent price, so see what you think before graduating to the "Big B's."

Less tannic ———— Very tannic

HOT OR COLD CLIMATE?

Cool and foggy. *Nebbia* means "fog" in Italian, and the Nebbiolo vineyards are blanketed by it during harvest mornings.

WHERE DOES IT COME FROM?

Italy: Piedmont, Lombardy United States, Mexico, Chile, Argentina, Brazil, Uruguay, South Africa, Australia, New Zealand

Henry participates in the grape harvest

SANGIOVESE

FRUITS

cherry   raspberry   red currant   plum   mushroom

BONUS

black pepper   thyme   almond   rosemary   leather   bay laurel

BARREL-AGED

clove   tobacco   espresso   sandalwood

OVERVIEW

Most Sangiovese can be found in its home region of Tuscany, Italy. There, Sangiovese plays a leading role in the area's most significant wines, including Brunello di Montalcino, Vino Nobile di Montepulciano, Chianti, and the Super Tuscans. The most notable characteristics of the grape are the mouthwatering acidity (which matches well with the tomato-based dishes of the region), the cherry-focused fruit flavors, and the unmistakable notes of herbs and savory spices.

THE LOVE RATING

Who doesn't love to be transported to Tuscany? Sangiovese wines will have you dreaming of romance among the vines and olive groves and late-night visits to the Uffizi. The range of styles of Sangiovese, from charmingly rustic to thoroughly polished, means there is something for everyone to love.

HOT OR COLD CLIMATE?

Warm daytime temperatures that cool down at night suit the Sangiovese grape well.

WHERE DOES IT COME FROM?

Italy: Tuscany, Umbria, Campania;
United States: California, Washington State;
Argentina, Chile, France (Corsica), Australia

Less tannic   Very tannic

BARBERA

 **FRUITS**

red cherry

blackberry

strawberry

plum

 HERBS & SPICES

fennel

rosemary

black pepper

licorice

BARREL-AGED

chocolate

coffee

vanilla

BONUS

wild game

black tea

tobacco

OVERVIEW

Indigenous to northern Italy, Barbera flourishes in Piedmont, but it is also grown as far south as Sicily and Sardinia. In the best Barbera wines, ripe fruit, high acidity, full body, and low tannins combine to produce a round, juicy, zesty, powerful wine. There is a distinct difference between the two main Barbera regions in Piedmont, Barbera d'Alba and Barbera d'Asti. The examples from Alba are generally bolder and more flavorful, whereas the wines from Asti are lighter and zippier. Traditionally, Barbera did not see a lot of oak-aging, but this has been changing as some winemakers aim for richer wines with more fruit and less spice.

Less tannic ←——————→ Very tannic

THE LOVE RATING

Overshadowed in its own home region of Piedmont by the royalty that is Nebbiolo, Barbera has adopted a reputation as the rustic, friendly red of the north. Some higher-end examples, aged in oak and from specific vineyard sites, are available, but there is just something about the delicious simplicity of traditional Barbera with pizza and pasta. What's not to love?

HOT OR COLD CLIMATE?

Hot, but not too hot. Excessive heat produces flabby wines with baked-fruit flavors.

WHERE DOES IT COME FROM?

Italy: Piedmont, Emilia-Romagna, Puglia, Campania, Sicily, Sardinia
United States (California), Australia, Argentina

Henry participates in the grape harvest

VALPOLICELLA BLEND

FRUITS

 red currant cherry plum strawberry raisin

BONUS

 cinnamon almond black tea hazelnut

 leather smoke

BARREL-AGED

 tobacco clove nutmeg

OVERVIEW

The grapes that make up wines from Valpolicella in the Veneto region of northern Italy wear many hats. The indigenous grapes Corvina, Rondinella, and Molinara are the basis for everyday Valpolicella wines. But the same varieties are also responsible for the slightly richer Valpolicella Ripasso wines and one of Italy's most celebrated wines, Amarone della Valpolicella. Amarone is a dry red wine made using the unique process of drying the grapes to concentrate the sugars before pressing and fermenting the juice. This makes for a powerful and ageworthy wine with raisin, fig, and brown sugar flavors. You get a little taste of Amarone in the more affordable Valpolicella Ripasso because the Amarone skins are infused into the fresh wine to add body and layers of flavor.

THE LOVE RATING

The public's fascination with big, powerful wines comes and goes, and so it goes with the adulation of Amarone. There will always be those who are ready to put on their velvet gown or three-piece suit and indulge in a rich, expensive Amarone. The good news for the rest of us is that we can don our jeans and kick our feet up while sipping a Ripasso for less than half the price.

Less tannic | Very tannic

HOT OR COLD CLIMATE?

Cool climate, with breezes coming off the Italian lakes and the Alps.

WHERE DOES IT COME FROM?

Italy: Veneto

AGLIANICO

 FRUITS

black currant   plum blackberry   wild strawberry red currant

SPICES

white pepper nutmeg cinnamon licorice

BARREL-AGED

cocoa cedar leather smoke

BONUS

truffle earth

OVERVIEW

Aglianico is the primary grape of the Campania and Basilicata regions on the Mediterranean coast of southern Italy. The grape is known for producing bold, structured wines with high tannin and ample acidity, which have the potential to soften and improve with age. The most famous and ageworthy wines made from the Aglianico grape are from the Taurasi appellation, where the vineyards are located high above sea level in the hills of Avellino. Aglianico del Vulture, Aglianico del Taburno, and Irpinia are other appellations that produce excellent examples of wines from the Aglianico grape. Many southern Italian winemakers are now producing Aglianico wines that are more approachable when young to introduce more wine drinkers to the grape.

THE LOVE RATING

Aglianico is considered one of the noble grapes of Italy, although it is rarely invited to sit at the table with the king of Italian wines, northern Italy's Barolo, made from the Nebbiolo grape. Aglianico and Nebbiolo both boast high tannins, powerful structure, and excellent aging potential, but Aglianico's fruit profile is distinctly darker and more intense. Too humble and classy to resort to bullying, Aglianico quietly accepts praise from those who know the grape is indeed worthy of its noble status.

HOT OR COLD CLIMATE?

This late-ripening grape thrives in warm, dry climates and reaches its top potential in volcanic soils at high elevations.

WHERE DOES IT COME FROM?

Italy: Campania, Basilicata
United States: California, Texas; Australia

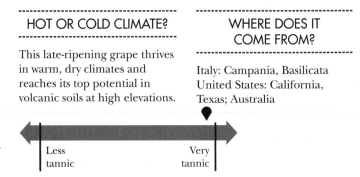

Less tannic

Very tannic

Henry participates in the grape harvest

MONTEPULCIANO

FRUITS

 plum

 strawberry

 cherry

 blueberry

 black currant

HERBS & SPICES

 black pepper

 clove

BARREL-AGED

coffee

 cocoa

OVERVIEW

Montepulciano is one of the most widely planted grapes in Italy and the most famous examples come from the region of Abruzzo, where it is labeled Montepulciano d'Abruzzo. The grape is a relatively easy one to grow and mainly produces plump, juicy wines with soft tannins, which generally appeal to new wine drinkers. The red fruits and gentle spices make it an easy choice to pair with pizza and simple pasta dishes.

THE LOVE RATING

There is a bit of a love-hate relationship between wine drinkers and Montepulciano. Many confuse it with Vino Nobile de Montepulciano, which is from Tuscany and made from the Sangiovese grape. Some critical wine drinkers cast it aside as a cheap and cheerful wine with no substance. Still others recognize the beauty in its chugability and also realize that some producers, including the renowned Emidio Pepe, are producing high-quality, ageworthy wines from the grape.

HOT OR COLD CLIMATE?

Montepulciano likes it hot in the summer and cold in the winter, and it appreciates high altitudes.

WHERE DOES IT COME FROM?

Italy: Abruzzo, Marche, Molise, Puglia
New Zealand, Australia, United States

Less tannic — Very tannic

NERO D'AVOLA

FRUITS

 blueberry
 blackberry
 plum
 black cherry
raspberry

 dried strawberry
 orange zest

HERBS & SPICES

bay laurel
eucalyptus
 licorice
mint
black pepper

BARREL-AGED

cedar
 smoke
 vanilla
tobacco
 leather

OVERVIEW

The most widely-planted grape on the Italian island of Sicily, Nero d'Avola makes bold, fruity wines with lots of body. The style that the grape produces differs based on oak treatment. When aged in barrel, Nero d'Avola makes richer wines with darker fruit and barrel-spice flavors. Outside the barrel, the grape tends to show more red fruits and fresh acidity. Whichever style you prefer, this is overall a hearty wine built for flavorful foods like burgers and barbecue.

THE LOVE RATING

Nero d'Avola got very used to winning the Sicilian popularity contest, but now that wine drinkers have become wise to Sicilian wines made from the charming and mineral-driven Nerello Mascalese grape, and the light and lively Frappato grape, Nero d'Avola seems to have taken a back seat.

HOT OR COLD CLIMATE?

Hot, although tannins are tamed at higher elevations where things cool down a bit.

WHERE DOES IT COME FROM?

Italy: Sicily
United States (California), Australia

Less tannic

Very tannic

Henry participates in the grape harvest

NEGROAMARO

FRUITS

black cherry

plum

blackberry

black currant

HERBS & SPICES

cinnamon

clove

ginger

BARREL-AGED

chocolate

tobacco

vanilla

smoke

OVERVIEW

Native to the Italian region of Puglia, on the "heel of the boot," Negroamaro is the most-planted grape in that region. The wine is dark and fruity, with some earth notes and silky-smooth tannins. The grape is often blended with other grapes, including Sangiovese, Montepulciano, Primitivo, and Malvasia Nera. The best examples of Negroamaro come from the Salice Salentino region of Puglia; some other regions that are making tasty wines from the grape include Squinzano, Copertino, and Nardo.

THE LOVE RATING

Not a grape that people generally seek out, Negroamaro is like a gregarious and boisterous friend. Overtly fruity, with a soft body and an alcohol kick, some people find the grape eminently charming, whereas others find it too tedious and overbearing.

HOT OR COLD CLIMATE?

Warm, and dry. Negroamaro can prosper with very little rainfall.

WHERE DOES IT COME FROM?

Italy: Puglia
United States (California), Australia

Less tannic

Very tannic

Red varieties

ZINFANDEL

FRUITS

 raspberry

 strawberry

 plum

blueberry

 blackberry

 raisin

SPICES

white pepper

clove

cinnamon

BARREL-AGED

 tobacco

 vanilla

 nutmeg

 caramel

OVERVIEW

Although Zinfandel is known as California's red grape, it has origins in Italy and Croatia. Italy's Primitivo grape and an ancient Croatian variety have both been found to be genetically identical to the Zinfandel grown in California. Zinfandel is peppery and jammy with super-smooth tannins. Alcohol levels can be high, so it's best to pair a red Zinfandel with bold, flavorful foods.

THE LOVE RATING

Red Zinfandel is getting some much-deserved respect lately, but there is still some confusion because of the happy accident that became White Zinfandel. White Zinfandel, which is actually pink in color and generally slightly sweet, was wildly popular in the 1970s. It helped Americans, who were used to drinking soda and syrupy fruit juices, slowly graduate to the world of fine wine.

HOT OR COLD CLIMATE?

Cool climates with high elevations produce the most interesting Zinfandels, but the grape still thrives in warmer areas.

Less tannic   Very tannic

WHERE DOES IT COME FROM?

United States: California
Italy (Puglia)

Henry participates in the grape harvest

PETITE SIRAH

 FRUITS

 blueberry

 black currant

 blackberry

 black cherry

 HERBS & SPICES

 rosemary

black tea

 menthol

licorice

BARREL-AGED

 tobacco

 mocha

 nutmeg

 chocolate

coffee

OVERVIEW

Petite Sirah, also called Petit Syrah or Durif, has origins in France and is a cross of the Syrah grape and the little-known Peloursin variety. Petite Sirah makes inky, teeth-staining wines, and more is produced in California than anywhere else in the world. The wine gets its name from the small, tight clusters of berries that give the grape a high ratio of skin to juice, resulting in high tannin levels and a deep, dark color. The grape also has high acidity, which sometimes comes across as a tangy flavor on the palate.

THE LOVE RATING

Petite Sirah is still waiting to have its moment. Some mistake it for the same grape as Syrah, but the flavors of the two grapes are distinct. Petite Sirah is very often a great value, so for lovers of full-bodied wines, it's a worthy alternative to Cabernet Sauvignon or Zinfandel.

HOT OR COLD CLIMATE?

Warm to hot. In particularly hot climates, alcohol levels escalate.

WHERE DOES IT COME FROM?

United States: California
Australia, Israel, Mexico, Chile, South Africa, Brazil

Less tannic — Very tannic

CARMÉNÈRE

FRUITS
- raspberry
- blackberry
- red plum

BONUS
- bell pepper
- white pepper
- flint

BARREL-AGED
- tobacco
- vanilla
- cocoa

OVERVIEW

Carménère is originally from the Bordeaux region of France but is now mostly grown and produced in Chile. The grape was almost entirely destroyed in the late nineteenth century by phylloxera, an insect that attacks the roots of grapevines. What saved Carménère's existence is that winemakers from Chile took cuttings from Bordeaux vineyards before the phylloxera epidemic broke out, thinking they were taking Merlot vines. They brought the cuttings back to Chile, which has never had an outbreak of phylloxera, and years later they discovered the vines were Carménère. The grape is similar in body and flavor to Merlot, but with a distinct bite of green peppercorn.

Less tannic ← → Very tannic

THE LOVE RATING

"It's complicated" might be the relationship status for Carménère. It's a fussy grape, and if not completely ripened, the pleasant green-peppercorn flavors can come across as vegetal and bitter. Fully ripe, however, Carménère brings together all the things that people love about Merlot and Cabernet Sauvignon in one smooth, crowd-pleasing package.

HOT OR COLD CLIMATE?

Hot! Carménère needs lots of sunshine and warm weather.

WHERE DOES IT COME FROM?

France: Bordeaux
Chile: Maipo Valley, Colchagua, Apalta, Rapel
United States: Washington State, California
Italy (northern), New Zealand, China

Henry participates in the grape harvest

TEMPRANILLO

FRUITS

cherry   plum   strawberry   black currant

BONUS

chocolate   tobacco   vanilla   clove   leather

OVERVIEW

Tempranillo originates from southern Spain and is today a mainstay of some of the top wines from Spain and Portugal, including the wines from Rioja and Port wines from Portugal. Tempranillo is full of complex flavors, and depending on where it grows, features charming red fruit flavors (in cooler climates) or dried fruit and tobacco flavors (in warmer climates). Tempranillo also plays well with oak, and when aged in barrel, demonstrates warm spice notes while still allowing the fruit to take center stage. Tempranillo has the power to age: Good examples are Vega-Sicilia Unico and Dominio de Pingus from Ribera del Duero in Spain.

THE LOVE RATING

Although Tempranillo is almost wholly responsible for the hauntingly savory reds of the Rioja and Ribera del Duero regions in Spain and the Douro region in Portugal, it rarely gets any of the attention. Fans only began to take notice when New World wine regions, such as the United States and Australia, started to bottle the grape as a single-varietal wine with its name front and center on the label.

HOT OR COLD CLIMATE?

Warm days and cool nights allow the Tempranillo grape to take a break from the heat and retain some acidity.

WHERE DOES IT COME FROM?

Spain: Rioja, Ribera del Duero, Penedès, Navarra and Valdepeñas
Portugal: Douro, Alentejo;
United States, Australia, Argentina, Chile

Less tannic   Very tannic

MENCIA

 FRUITS

 black cherry

 blackberry

 strawberry

 plum

 blueberry

 black currant

 red currant

 **BONUS**

licorice

 wild game

 pencil shavings

 smoke

 vanilla

OVERVIEW

Mencia grows in Spain and Portugal and is most associated with red wines from the region of Bierzo in Castilla y León, Spain. As accomplished winemakers have taken notice of the grape, the world has been introduced to more interesting, high-quality examples of Mencia. The wines appeal to many palates, combining the pure fruitiness of a Gamay, the complexity of a Loire Cabernet Franc, the medium body of a Merlot, the fragrant aromatics of a Pinot Noir, and a balanced acidity that makes the wine sing.

THE LOVE RATING

Mencia is still relatively unknown, but it's certainly worth making its acquaintance. There should be more wines made from Mencia available in the United States as popularity grows. It is a wonderfully versatile food wine and works with all types of meats, sauces, and even difficult-to-pair vegetables such as artichokes and cabbage.

HOT OR COLD CLIMATE?

Mencia prefers a mild climate, and the areas where the grape excels tend to be cooler than other wine regions in Spain and Portugal.

WHERE DOES IT COME FROM?

Spain: Bierzo, Valdeorras, Ribiera Sacra
Portugal: Dão

Less tannic ← → Very tannic

Henry participates in the grape harvest

TOURIGA NACIONAL

FRUITS & FLOWERS

 blackberry

blueberry

 plum

 black currant

violet

BONUS

 mint

flint

pencil shavings

 black tea

 leather

BARREL-AGED

 dark chocolate

vanilla

nutmeg

OVERVIEW

Marketed as Portugal's best red grape variety, Touriga Nacional is dark and full-bodied, with the potential to last as long in the cellar as proven ageworthy grapes like Cabernet Sauvignon and Nebbiolo. Wines made from Touriga Nacional will coat your palate and stain you tongue, enticing your senses with complex berry aromas and flavors of black tea and mint.

THE LOVE RATING

The grape that was once known as just one of the blending grapes in the production of Portugal's famous dessert wine, Port, has only recently come out of the shadows and proclaimed itself one of the world's great grapes. It remains to be seen if this catches on, but with flavors that intense and prices that low, no one would be surprised to see Touriga Nacional appear before cheering crowds.

HOT OR COLD CLIMATE?

Temperate, with warm days, cool nights, and high elevations.

WHERE DOES IT COME FROM?

Portugal: Douro, Dão, Alentejo, Beira, Lisboa
South Africa, United States, Australia, Argentina, Brazil

Less tannic — Very tannic

PINOTAGE

 FRUITS

 blackberry

 black currant

 plum

 cherry

 fig

 HERBS & SPICES

 menthol

pepper

licorice

 BONUS

 wild game

 sweet tobacco

 black tea

mushroom

 earth

OVERVIEW

Pinotage is the signature grape of South Africa and has had little success in any other winegrowing region. The grape was actually created by a scientist who thought it was a good idea to cross Cinsaut (a French blending grape) with Pinot Noir. Oddly, the wine is reminiscent of neither of those grapes, instead tasting of dark, black fruits with strong notes of earth and tobacco. The scientist who created it was looking to produce a hearty grape, but Pinotage is fickle and things can easily go wrong during the grape-growing and winemaking process.

THE LOVE RATING

Pinotage has a few fanatical supporters, but it also has its share of haters out there in the wine world. Don't be surprised when you ask someone about the grape and they crinkle their nose. There are certainly good examples of high-quality Pinotage on the market, but you have to navigate your way through a minefield of bad Pinotage to get there.

HOT OR COLD CLIMATE?

Warm and sunny sites are best, but if it's too hot the wines will develop a burnt character.

WHERE DOES IT COME FROM?

South Africa: Stellenbosch, Western Cape; New Zealand, United States (California), Israel

Less tannic — Very tannic

Henry participates in the grape harvest

BLAUFRÄNKISCH

 FRUITS

 black cherry

 blackberry

 plum

 pomegranate

 mandarin orange

 HERBS & SPICES

 black pepper

 clove

 bay laurel

 eucalyptus

BONUS

cocoa

smoke

mineral

OVERVIEW

One of Austria's signature red grape varieties, Blaufränkisch is grown throughout the country but is most prominent in Burgenland. The variety is versatile and the wine comes in many styles, including elegant, spicy, medium- and full-bodied. The characteristic that rings true across all styles is freshness; freshness of fruit, juicy acidity, and clean flavors. Traditionally it is aged in large oak casks to give the wine structure, but winemakers must be careful not to overdo it as the grape is highly susceptible to tasting over-oaked.

THE LOVE RATING

Blaufränkisch has not received much love outside of Austrian restaurants, but critics and bloggers are now starting to spread the word about this charming and versatile grape. If you want to add a little spice to your life, get to know this zesty grape and share the love by serving it up at your next backyard barbecue.

HOT OR COLD CLIMATE?

Hot. The grape ripens late and needs the warmth to fully mature.

WHERE DOES IT COME FROM?

Austria: Burgenland, Südburgenland, Neusiedlersee, Neusiedlersee-Hügelland, Carnuntum
Hungary, Croatia, Czech Republic, Slovakia, Romania, Bulgaria,
United States: New York (Finger Lakes), Washington State
Canada

Less tannic — Very tannic

LAMBRUSCO

FRUITS & FLOWERS

cherry strawberry red currant blackberry

rose violet

BONUS

earth thyme bitter almond

OVERVIEW

Lambrusco, which is also the name of the grape, produces red sparkling wines, mainly from the Emilia-Romagna and Lombardy regions in northern Italy. There are many different varieties of Lambrusco grapes, the three most popular being Lambrusco Salamino, Lambrusco di Sorbara, and Lambrusco Grasparossa. The resulting wines are bright and fizzy and come in various sweetness levels, including dry, off-dry, and sweet (*secco, amabile,* and *dolce* in Italian). The gentle bubbles come from a second fermentation that takes place in a big tank, unlike Champagne, in which this second fermentation takes place in the bottle.

THE LOVE RATING

Much like clothing styles and hair trends, Lambrusco has gone in and out of fashion. It was hot in the 1970s and 1980s, when the United States imported mostly the sweeter styles that taste like wine soda. It then fell out of favor with wine lovers until Lambrusco's more serious side was popularized by sommeliers and wine writers in the 2010s. Bright red, fruity, and refreshing, Lambrusco pairs well with salty, savory meats and cheeses, lasagna, and even fried foods. Drink it chilled!

HOT OR COLD CLIMATE?

Lambrusco grapes grow best in dry climates with hot days and cool nights.

Less tannic — Very tannic

WHERE DOES IT COME FROM?

Italy: Emilia-Romagna, Lombardy, Piedmont, Basilicata
Argentina, Australia

Henry participates in the grape harvest

ROSÉ

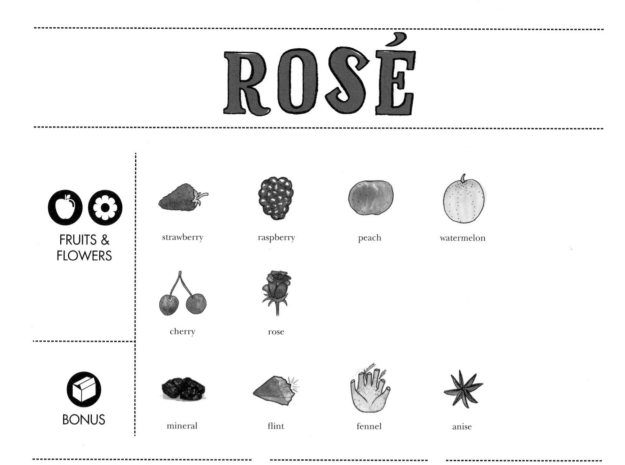

FRUITS & FLOWERS

strawberry   raspberry   peach   watermelon

cherry   rose

BONUS

mineral   flint   fennel   anise

OVERVIEW

Rosé wine is a category of wines that are made by pressing red grapes that spend time on the red skins for only a short period of time, which results in pink juice. They are not made, at least by reputable producers, by blending white wine with red wine, which is a common misperception. Rosé wines are made all over the world and can range from dry to sweet, still to bubbly.

THE LOVE RATING

There is finally a rosé craze happening in the United States. Immensely popular in Europe, the pink color of rosé scared away the most macho among us, and White Zinfandel (which was actually pink in color and strongly associated with the groovy 1970s) scared away the rest. But today, rosé is back with a vengeance, especially in the spring and summer months, when picnic-goers and fashionable party-seekers can't get enough of it.

HOT OR COLD CLIMATE?

Rosé can be made from a wide variety of grapes that thrive in both hot and cold climates.

WHERE DOES IT COME FROM?

France, Italy, United States, Spain, and many other parts of the world

PORT

SHERRY

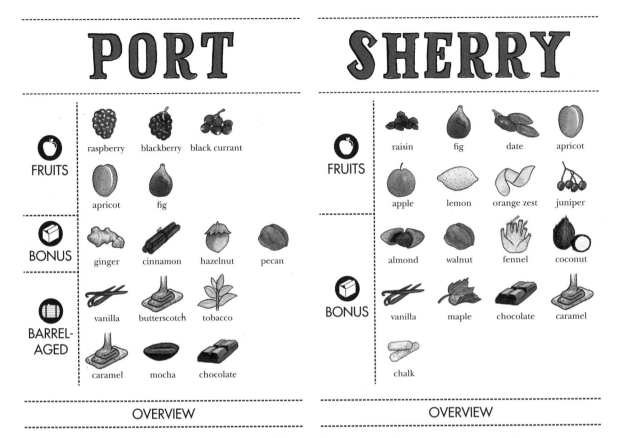

FRUITS

raspberry · blackberry · black currant
apricot · fig

BONUS

ginger · cinnamon · hazelnut · pecan

BARREL-AGED

vanilla · butterscotch · tobacco
caramel · mocha · chocolate

FRUITS

raisin · fig · date · apricot
apple · lemon · orange zest · juniper

BONUS

almond · walnut · fennel · coconut
vanilla · maple · chocolate · caramel
chalk

OVERVIEW

Port is a sweet, fortified wine produced in the Douro Valley in Portugal from a blend of local Portuguese grapes. Ruby Port is affordable; it's a young Port with fresh, fruit-forward flavors. LBV (late bottled vintage) has been aged in barrels and has a vintage year on the label. The flavors of spice and mocha come through in addition to the fruit. Tawny Port spends even more time in barrels (ten to forty years) so the wine begins to oxidize, creating a palate of dried fruits, nuts, and caramel. Vintage Port is the top tier, made only in the best vintages, and is matured in bottle for twenty or more years. It's a powerful wine with concentrated flavors that often include chocolate, spices, and tobacco. Finally, there's White Port, which you won't run into very often, but it makes a delicious substitute for gin in a Port Tonic.

OVERVIEW

Sherry is a fortified wine from southern Spain, specifically Andalusia. Contrary to popular belief, most Sherry is made dry and pairs extremely well with food. A fortified wine, Sherry is made using the solera system, a process where younger wine is used to top off barrels of older wines, and consequently, there is no vintage dating. This process results in consistency of the final product. The three white grapes that are used to make Sherry are Palomino, Pedro Ximénez, and Moscatel. Dry, salty, nutty Sherry is made in different styles: Fino and Manzanilla are the lightest styles; Amontillado is nuttier; Palo Cortado is richer; and Oloroso is the most oxidized style. The sweet style of Sherry you will come across most is Pedro Ximénez (often called PX), which is luscious, sweet, and nutty.

THE LOVE RATING

A glass of port is a wonderful way to end a meal, whether with richly flavored cheeses or chocolate-based desserts. The term "Port" can only officially be used for wine from Porto.

HOT OR COLD CLIMATE?

Warm and dry.

WHERE DOES IT COME FROM?

Portugal: Porto

THE LOVE RATING

With the help of enthusiastic wine professionals and creative mixologists, Sherry is slowly making its way back into the hearts of younger consumers and it is creating curiosity about this versatile wine.

HOT OR COLD CLIMATE?

Warm and sunny.

WHERE DOES IT COME FROM?

Spain: Andalusia

Henry participates in the grape harvest

MARSALA MADEIRA

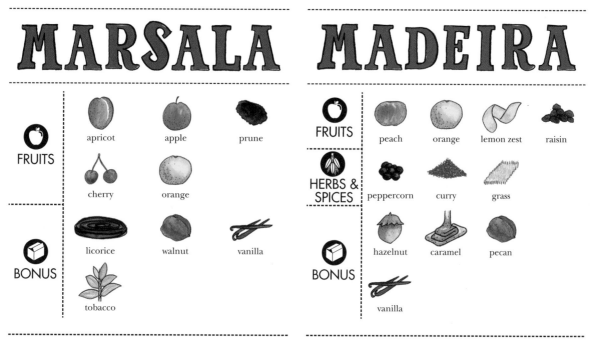

MARSALA

FRUITS
- apricot
- apple
- prune
- cherry
- orange

BONUS
- licorice
- walnut
- vanilla
- tobacco

MADEIRA

FRUITS
- peach
- orange
- lemon zest
- raisin

HERBS & SPICES
- peppercorn
- curry
- grass

BONUS
- hazelnut
- caramel
- pecan
- vanilla

OVERVIEW

Marsala is a fortified wine from the Italian island of Sicily. There are many grapes that go into the production of Marsala, both white and red, including Grillo, Catarratto, Inzolia, Damaschino, Pignatello, Calabrese, Nerello Mascalese, and Nero d'Avola. Marsala, like Sherry from Spain, is made using the solera system. This is where younger wine is used to top off older wines resulting in consistency and no vintage association.

OVERVIEW

Madeira is a fortified wine made in Portugal, on the island of Madeira in the Atlantic, near Lisbon. The key to making Madeira is heat, which deliberately oxidizes the wine and creates the desired flavors of nuts, burnt sugar, and caramel. The grapes used to make Madeira include Sercial, Verdelho, Bual, Bastardo, Folgasão, and Tinta Negra. Madeira can be made dry for drinking at the beginning of a meal, or sweet to be enjoyed as an after-dinner drink.

THE LOVE RATING

If you type *Marsala* in to your web search, you will likely be met with hundreds of recipes for Chicken Marsala and not find much about the fortified wine. Marsala is indeed used in recipes, in both sweet and dry versions, but it's also is a wonderful treat to have as a drink, chilled, with Parmesan, Gorgonzola, or other flavorful cheeses.

HOT OR COLD CLIMATE?

Marsala is made in a hot, Mediterranean climate.

WHERE DOES IT COME FROM?

Italy: Sicily

THE LOVE RATING

Poor Madeira is extremely misunderstood. In fact, most people associate it with the cheap styles used for cooking. It is indeed a lovely cooking wine, but there is much more to it than that. Madeira can stay fresh for up to hundreds of years and is made in various quality levels. There is much to explore with Madeira, and the rewards can be very satisfying.

HOT OR COLD CLIMATE?

Madeira has a hot, humid, subtropical climate.

WHERE DOES IT COME FROM?

Portugal: Island of Madeira

VIN SANTO

SAUTERNES

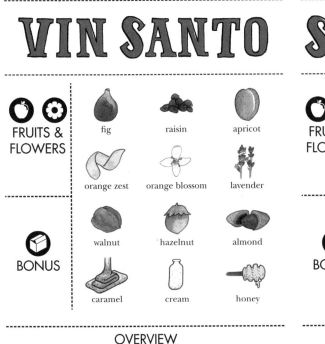

FRUITS & FLOWERS

fig · raisin · apricot

orange zest · orange blossom · lavender

BONUS

walnut · hazelnut · almond

caramel · cream · honey

FRUITS & FLOWERS

apricot · apple · pear · peach

pineapple · orange zest · quince · honeysuckle

BONUS

honey · chalk · butter

smoke · toast

OVERVIEW

Vin Santo's traditional home is Tuscany, in central Italy, although it is made and served all across the country. The sweet dessert wine has a long history, dating back to at least the Middle Ages. The grapes used for making Vin Santo, customarily Trebbiano, Malvasia, and sometimes Grechetto, are laid out to dry on straw mats after they are harvested. They are left in the sun to dry out for four to six months, until the sugars are concentrated. The raisinated grapes are fermented in small oak barrels, and ultimately produce a sweet, golden wine with flavors of nuts and caramel.

THE LOVE RATING

The traditions that come with Vin Santo, much like the wine, will leave you with a warm, fuzzy feeling. In Tuscany, the wines are offered to guests along with almond-flavored biscotti to welcome them into the home. It's the perfect wine to sip slowly at the end of the day and contemplate your next vacation.

HOT OR COLD CLIMATE?

Warm and mild, with cooler temperatures closer to the sea.

WHERE DOES IT COME FROM?

Italy: Tuscany, Trentino, Veneto, Umbria, Marche

OVERVIEW

Sauternes are the classic sweet wines of Bordeaux made from the white grapes Sémillon, Sauvignon Blanc, and sometimes Muscadelle. The wines are the result of grapes affected by "noble rot" (*Botrytis*), which dries the grapes out and naturally concentrates the sugars. The best Sauternes wines balance out the sugary sweetness with high natural acidity to make the wines taste fresh and not syrupy.

THE LOVE RATING

Not many people drink sweet wine after a meal anymore, so this Old World wine has gone the way of old traditions. The price of Sauternes, which is rarely inexpensive, doesn't help its reputation as something reserved only for the rich and conservative.

HOT OR COLD CLIMATE?

Warm, with morning mists that promote the growth of "noble rot."

WHERE DOES IT COME FROM?

France: Bordeaux

Henry participates in the grape harvest

TOKAJI

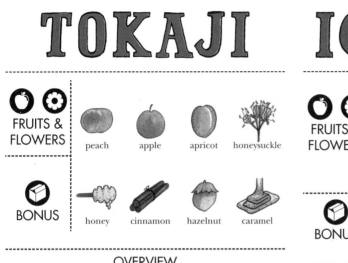

FRUITS & FLOWERS

peach · apple · apricot · honeysuckle

BONUS

honey · cinnamon · hazelnut · caramel

OVERVIEW

Tokaji is Hungary's most famous wine region, dating back to the seventeenth and eighteenth centuries. The eponymous sweet wines are made from a blend of grapes including Furmint, Hárslevelü, and Muscat Blanc. The wines are made from grapes affected by "noble rot" (*Botrytis*), which dries the grapes out and naturally concentrates the sugars. Tokaji wines are lusciously sweet, and you can drink them on their own as an aperitif. However the balanced acidity makes them fresh enough to enjoy with rich dishes such as foie gras and cheeses, or with fruit or chocolate-based desserts.

THE LOVE RATING

Tokaji isn't well known enough to get people excited. Additionally, as with other rare dessert wines, the price point keeps people from experimenting with this luscious treat. In fact, Tokaji comes in different grades, called Puttonyos, which is related to the amount of sugar in the wines. As you climb the Puttonyos scale, the price goes up. Hungary just abolished the lower grades, which makes it even more difficult for the masses to get on board.

HOT OR COLD CLIMATE?

Cool to cold, and dry.

WHERE DOES IT COME FROM?

Hungary: Tokaji

ICE WINE

FRUITS & FLOWERS

lychee · passion fruit · pineapple

mango · apricot · orange blossom

BONUS

honey · vanilla · cinnamon

OVERVIEW

Ice wine is made from the juice of grapes that have frozen on the vine, and can only be produced if the weather allows. The grapes hang on the vine until at least December, and sometimes as late as February, before they are ready to be picked in the freezing-cold evening hours. For comparison, harvests for most wines in Eastern Hemisphere wine regions occurs between August and October. Ice wine originated in Germany (where it is called Eiswein) and is now a big part of the Canadian wine scene (where it is called Icewine). Whereas other dessert wines rely on "noble rot" to concentrate the sugar in the grapes, Ice wine relies on the water freezing inside the grapes to concentrate the sweet, fresh flavors of the remaining juice.

THE LOVE RATING

Ice wine isn't cloyingly sweet but rather fresh and luscious, with a bit of tartness as well. It is, however, very expensive to make. The longer the grapes stay on the vine, the smaller the harvest becomes, due to weather, pests, and predators. In addition, because the frozen water in the grapes is squeezed out, it takes up to seven times as many grapes to make a bottle of Ice wine than a bottle of regular table wine.

HOT OR COLD CLIMATE?

As you may have guessed, Ice wine can only be produced in cold climates.

WHERE DOES IT COME FROM?

Austria, Germany, Canada, Switzerland, United States (Michigan, Finger Lakes NY)

Red varieties

THE LIFE OF THE VINE

Wine is the result of two very different types of labor. First comes the work on the vine, or viticulture. Then comes the work in the cellar that transforms the grape into wine: that's vinification.

Over the years: Birth, size, maturation

Winter
Hibernation: The vine sleeps. The colder it gets, the better it will be for the next harvest (so long as the sap is not frozen in the roots).

Pruning: The sap does not circulate anymore. The vines benefit from pruning because it inhibits the growth of too many branches. The more fertile the vine, the shorter it should be cut.

Beginning of spring
The vine starts to "cry." It's the sap that rises and peaks after pruning.

Labor: It's time to cultivate the earth between the rows to aerate the soil, promote the life of the soil, and allow water to better penetrate it. There's a saying, "Lots of tillage is worth several rains."

Bud: The bud forms, opens up, and leaves a little crown. Be careful of a late frost, which can kill a bud instantly.

End of spring, beginning of summer
Foliation: One by one, leaves appear, unfold and spread.

Flowering: The amount of sunlight and temperatures increase; tiny little white flowers appear, already in the form of a cluster.

Fruit: The grapes form in the fertilized flowers. The winegrower makes an initial guess at when to harvest.

Henry participates in the grape harvest

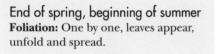

Topping: The winegrower cuts the top branches so that the vine doesn't grow too much and can concentrate its growth in the grapes.

Stripping: The winegrower cuts the leaves that cover the grape clusters from the rising sun. Depending on the region where the grapes are grown, the winegrower will leave just enough so that the clusters receive an optimal amount of sun without getting burned.

N.B. Risks during the life of the vine

Fertilization might not go well because there isn't enough wind, or there's too much rain or heat. "Running" means the sap doesn't flow toward the fruit, which then can fall off the plant. Millerandage is a condition in which the berries don't grow larger in the bunch. There is also a risk of hail destroying the grapes.

Summer
The vine follows a growth phase during which, if all goes well, the grape clusters grow.

Green harvesting: In some vineyards, when the vine is too fertile, winegrowers will cut the grape clusters to limit yields and facilitate the maturation of the remaining grape clusters. Weak yields are often a gauge of better wine quality.

Veraison (ripening): At this point, the grape is green, opaque, and hard. During this period, the berry finally changes color, turning pale yellow for white varietals and red to dark blue for red varietals.

Maturation: This lasts until the harvest. It's a momentous period, because it plays a fundamental role in the character of the vintage. During maturation, the grape gains sugar and loses acidity, and its skin becomes thinner. If the weather becomes erratic during this phase, it will have a direct effect on the wine.

sugar

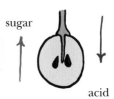

acid

Harvest: At about a hundred days after flowering, the grapes are ready to be picked! The winegrower waits for optimal maturity before picking the perfect grape, which is ripe but not too ripe.

Autumn
The leaves change color and fall. The vine enters hibernation.

THE DIFFERENT LOOKS OF A VINE

Depending on region, climate, and vintage, the winegrower chooses the pruning technique best suited to his vine. He should not forget that vines are creepers. Without a good pruning in winter, the vines will produce more wood to the detriment of the fruit.

There are different systems for pruning a vine:

Shoot

Foot of the vine

Rod

Goblet Pruning

This method is especially common in Mediterranean vineyards (the south of France, Spain, Portugal, and Italy) because the leaves protect the grapes from the sun. The base of the vine is very short and each arm carries a branch, like fingers on a hand. No trellising is necessary, but it's impossible to mechanize the work.

Guyot Pruning (single or double)

This pruning technique is very widespread. The single method is usually used in Burgundy, while in Bordeaux they often use the double (which means there's a long arm on each side). This very practical system allows you to have good yields during vintages that aren't very fertile and allows a tractor to pass between the vines. Because this pruning technique can fatigue the vine very quickly, you use a different rod each year.

The Royat Cord (also called Cordon Training)

This method is easy to maintain with machines (both in pruning and harvesting) because the grape clusters are spread out and aerated. It is a pruning technique that's preferred for vigorous vintages.

The young vine and the old vine

A vine can live a very long time, fifty years on average, while some are hundreds of years old. The older the vine is, the fewer grapes it produces, but that creates a better wine. A parcel of old vines is therefore a valuable asset to which the winemaker pays special attention. As the vine develops during the first three years, the grapes it produces aren't good enough to be turned into wine. When it reaches between ten and thirty years, it is at the top of its form for producing big quantities. After that, it settles down and concentrates more juice in the berries. Its life isn't so different from ours: birth, gaining strength, then finally wisdom.

Henry participates in the grape harvest

THE HISTORY OF THE ROOTSTOCK

Today, 99.9 percent of French vines grow from roots that were grafted before they were planted. And the vines of nearly all countries on the planet that grow wine grapes use the same method. When winegrowers are in need of vines, they buy a varietal that is attached with wax to a rootstock.

To understand where this practice comes from, you have to go back in time, to 1863 and the appearance of phylloxera. Until that time, European winemaking had been trouble-free, but suddenly the vines got sick. The sickness spread, destroying a significant part of the French vineyards, and within twenty years there was a serious grape and wine crisis across the continent.

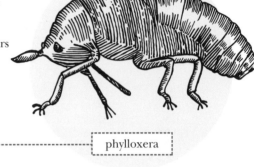

phylloxera

The culprit? A tiny aphid from North America known as phylloxera. In just a few weeks, phylloxera attacks the roots of the vine, weakening and then killing it.

The discovery in the United States of an indigenous vine immune to phylloxera gave birth to the technique that revolutionized modern viticulture. The American strain serves as a rootstock for European grapevines, which are then grafted onto it. The technique became the norm beginning in 1880 and it revitalized the vineyards, but it took another fifty years before winemaking recovered.

Today, nearly all vines around the world are grafted. With few exceptions, local grape varieties are either resistant or the vines grow in a sandy soil, where the parasite can't survive.

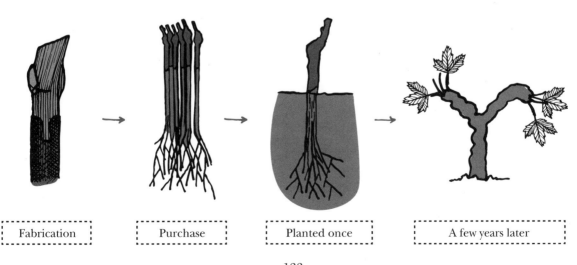

Fabrication   Purchase   Planted once   A few years later

WEATHER AND ITS EFFECT ON VINTAGE

Climate and weather are two different things. The first consists of a geographic location. France, for example, is affected by an oceanic climate in Bordeaux vineyards, but the wines of Burgundy are affected by a semi-continental climate. Looking to the climate provides guidance to the winemaker for preferred grapevines, selection of pruning technique, and possible harvest dates. Weather predicts the vintage. A hot, dry year will result in a very different character of wine than a cold, rainy year. It's especially true with weather in the last weeks before harvest.

The influence of the weather

A good vintage happens when the weather has been mild. The grape easily reaches its full ripeness, and it's filled with sugar and acidity without significant loss or decay in the crop.

If the weather isn't cooperative, the winegrower can lose a part of his harvest, either to a late frost, developing rot (driven by rains along with heat), sunburn, hail, or other conditions. The grape harvest will be profoundly affected by what it has lived through.

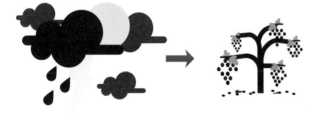

A heat wave can result in a poor vintage, making wines low in acidity and strong in alcohol, because the grapes have been overheated by the sun.
On the other hand, a rainy year has a tendency to engorge the grapes with water, making a wine that is diluted and weaker.

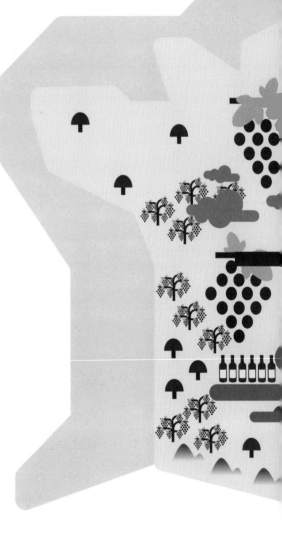

Henry participates in the grape harvest

The effect of vintage

Depending on the weather, a vintage can be excellent in one winegrowing region and mediocre in another. To get a better understanding of how weather influences vintage, conduct a vertical tasting. Taste several vintages of the same wine, starting with the youngest and going to the oldest. You will find that the wine, in addition to showing age, changes character depending on the year.

A case study:
Non-vintage Champagnes and sparkling wines

Have you noticed that most Champagnes don't have a date on their label? That is because the harvest of one vintage is blended with older wines to balance out their different characteristics. The goal is to produce a sparkling wine that is identical from one year to the next. Vintage champagnes reflect the character of one special, favorable year.

Oldest wine

Harvest from one year

The effects of global warming

Over the last thirty years, observations show a small evolution in the maturation of grapes: They ripen earlier, sometimes much too early than was historically seen as optimal in particular grape-growing regions. As a consequence, the grapes are producing higher sugar content, which in turn produces wines that have a higher alcohol content. At the same time, grapes grown on the coast of England are producing new wine regions. What will a map of winemaking regions look like fifty years from now?

TENDING THE VINE

Throughout the year, the winegrower must protect the vine against insects, fungi, viruses or rot that threaten it.

Treatments

The winegrower uses an arsenal of treatments, either chemically based or more natural, including fertilizers, pesticides, insecticides, sulfur, nettle slurry, and what's known as a "Bordeaux mixture" (a mix of copper sulfate and lime). He chooses products depending on the type of agriculture he practices: intensive, reasoned, organic, or biodynamic.

Intensive agriculture

This is the old-school treatment. It is an abusive use of chemical products that exhausts the soil, not to mention the health risks it poses to farmers and consumers.

Reasoned agriculture

This is the most common treatment today. The use of chemicals is authorized, but they are used in far lower quantities. Instead of employing a preventative treatment, the grower waits to reach a certain threshold of tolerance before resorting to treatments.

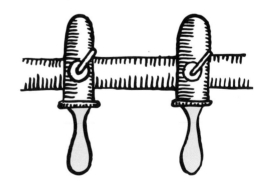

Henry participates in the grape harvest

Organic agriculture

Wines labeled "Organic" come from grapes cultivated using organic farming methods.

Winegrowing

To obtain an organic label, the winegrower cannot use any chemical fertilizers, herbicides, or pesticides. Instead, they must use natural fertilizers such as manure. Only a small amount of sulfites can be added to preserve the wine, and it must be stated on the label. In Europe these wines are labeled "Organic Wine" and in the United States these wines are labeled "Made from Organic Grapes."

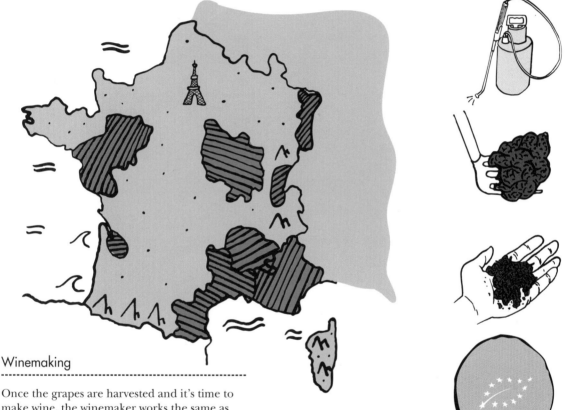

Winemaking

Once the grapes are harvested and it's time to make wine, the winemaker works the same as any other winemaker—organic or not. A wine labeled "Organic" is not necessarily a better wine. It's simply better for the environment and your health.

Organic farming demands more attention, more work, more hands, and more money. It's complicated to manage on difficult terroirs. But it is used to ensure a perennial crop and a healthy soil, rich in nutrients and microorganisms.

Regions

Organic vineyard farming is in full swing in France, Italy, and Spain. It is now also thriving in Germany and Austria. The United States is moving forward quickly, with a good percentage of new vineyards being planted in Oregon and California that are following organic farming practices from the start. New Zealand promptly adapted to organic viticulture and Australia and South Africa are catching up. Organic practices are on the rise in Argentina and Chile and gradually developing in Portugal.

Biodynamic agriculture

Biodynamics goes much farther than organic farming. It seeks to enhance the energy from the soil and natural elements to promote the development of the vine. Though less practiced than even organic agriculture, it's seeing a growing demand from consumers.

The origin of biodynamics

Biodynamic farming builds on the sometimes contested work of Austrian philosopher Rudolf Steiner, who was noted for a series of conferences given to farmers in 1924. This method considers the whole field of agriculture as a living organism—a diversified and autonomous entity, the function of which you must understand and respect. Instead of treating an illness, the winegrower strives to correct the imbalance that created this illness.

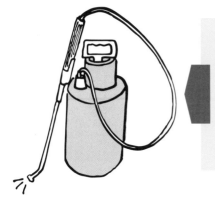

The method

This type of production uses all the principles of organic farming, but it then takes into account lunar and planetary rhythms. A biodynamic viticulturist uses natural preparations that are pulverized with a homeopathic treatment to reinforce the vines, invigorate the soil, and limit the development of parasites. Just as in organic farming, a Bordeaux mixture can be used to fight mildew. Lastly, the vine cuttings are plowed into the soil.

The Demeter label

The international biodynamic farming label is the Demeter label. It follows a set of very precise instructions, adding to practices of organic farming a specific calendar for the treatment and care of the vine according to the influence of the moon, the sun, and the planets.

The Biodyvin label

Since 1996, the Biodyvin label, created by the International Union of Biodynamic Winemakers, also adorns biodynamic wines certified by ECOCERT.

Henry participates in the grape harvest

Examples of biodynamic treatments

Horn manure
This preparation, although comical, is one of the most famous and widely used in biodynamics. Its goal is to promote the healthy soil and the growth of the roots. To prepare it, you must fill a horn with cow dung and bury it during the winter to mature. Its contents are then diluted in water and stirred vigorously before being sprayed in the vineyard.

The ascending and descending moon
The influence of the moon on water and vegetation is primordial in viticultural biodynamic practices. You need to consider which are the prosperous periods for developing roots, and which for leaves, flowers, or fruits. It's considered advantageous, for example, to plow and spread compost in the descending phase and to harvest fruits in the ascending phase. You must not confuse the phases with those of the moon's waxing and waning, which follow a different cycle.

Lunar calendars
Biodynamic winegrowers use a lunar calendar detailing all of the phases and the symbol of the day: root, leaf, flower, or fruit. These last are sometimes used to choose the best days for tasting.

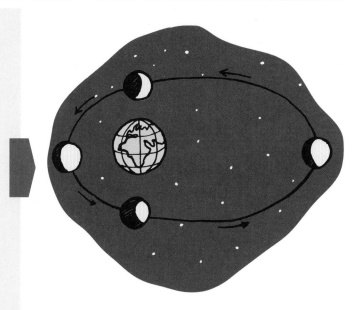

The effectiveness of biodynamics

Biodynamics stirs up big questions about its true effectiveness on winegrowing, and there is even some skepticism. It is nevertheless practiced with success by a smattering of winemakers of international fame who produce wines of great quality. Nicolas Joly, of La Coulée de Serrant in the Loire, is one of the pioneers of biodynamics in viticulture. The winery Domaine de la Romanée-Conti, the most reputed in Burgundy, is another.

Its acceptance

Although it is becoming more and more prized by consumers who are unhappy with the use of pesticides, it still represents a very small segment of the wine industry, likely under 10 percent. It is difficult to estimate the exact percentage of vineyards worldwide that are using biodynamic methods. There are many different biodynamic certification organizations, and some wineries are simply experimenting with the biodynamic approach.

98%

2%

Biodynamic   Other

HARVEST TIME

When to harvest?

Choosing the date to harvest the grapes is crucial

If the winegrower picks the grapes too early, they will not have enough sugar and be too acidic. If he picks too late, the grape will be too ripe, too rich in sugar, and too poor in acidity, and the wine will be heavy and pasty. The whims of the weather complicate the task even further. Abundant rains will rot the grape; a heat wave will dehydrate it.

Not all grapes ripen at the same rate

This depends on the vintage, of course, but also on the terrain. The type of soil, the altitudes of different parcels of land, and their geographic location can hasten or delay maturity. To harvest the grapes at their optimal level, the winegrower must adapt to each of these parameters. In the Languedoc region, for example, where they cultivate Grenache, Syrah, Carignan, Mourvèdre, or Cinsaut, the harvest time can last two to three weeks. They pick the early-ripening varieties first, parcel by parcel, then harvest the rest of the vines a little later.

Quite a few days to play around

A violent shower can fill the ready-to-pick grapes with water and ruin them. So the winegrower must be particularly vigilant in watching the weather and the state of the grapes a few days before the intended harvest.

MONTH					
1	2	3	4	5	6
7	8	9	10		

Henry participates in the grape harvest

Yields

Depending on the method the winegrower has used during the season, and taking into consideration the soil, vintage, and grape variety, he will harvest larger or smaller quantities on a given surface. In most of the world, he will measure yields in hectoliters per hectare; in the United States, he will talk of tons per acre. Vineyards growing grapes for table wines or sparkling wines may generally yield 80 to 90 hectoliters per hectare, or about 6 tons per acre. Growing for a classic Appellation d'Origine Contrôlée region in France will restrict yields to around 45 hectoliters per hectare (about 3 tons per acre). Vineyards for the highest-quality wines rarely surpass 30 hectoliters per hectare (about 2 tons per acre).

Late harvests

These grapes are reserved for sweet wines that are particularly complex. The best dessert wines come from grapes affected by "noble rot" (*Botrytis*). It affects the berries in a wonderful way, by drawing water from the grape and concentrating its sugars and aromas. Because this fungus doesn't form on all the grape clusters at once, the harvest must be spread over the course of several months (from September to November in Northern Hemisphere vineyards, such as in France and the United States, and February to April in Southern Hemisphere regions, including Australia and Argentina). This ensures that at each harvest date pickers can focus on the perfect berries, those resembling raisins.

Ice harvests

To make an Ice wine, the winegrower waits for colder temperatures, below 20°F (below -7°C), when a film starts to surround the grapes. The grapes are even more concentrated in sugars than in the grapes for Late Harvests and barely contain any water. In addition to being more exhausting work, the losses are enormous and the yields frightfully low (10 hectoliters per hectare, 0.7 tons per acre), which explains the high prices of these bottles. This harvest is only possible in countries with climatic conditions that permit it, such as Germany or Canada, but even those countries are now being affected by global warming.

HARVESTING BY HAND

How does it work?

Depending on the size of the operation, the grower calls on his family, friends, or seasonal hired hands to help with the harvest. They cut the grape clusters and place them carefully into a basket. Carriers collect the baskets and transfer the grapes carefully into crates to avoid damaging the fruit.

Pros

The work of cutting and sorting performed by the harvesters is detail oriented and great care must be taken with the vine. Some harvests require sorting and several passes of picking over a few weeks. This is generally needed for grapes that are turned into wines of high quality.

Cons

A lot of people are needed to harvest the grapes before they begin to rot in the hot sun. It's imperative that the berries stay intact when they arrive at the press, otherwise, the juice could oxidize and begin to deteriorate. This handwork is expensive but may be worth the cost for the winegrower.

Henry participates in the grape harvest

MACHINE HARVESTING

How does it work?

The harvester moves between the rows of vines and shakes the base of each vine. The ripe grapes fall off the clusters. A rolling conveyor belt collects the fallen grapes. The operator must adjust the machine correctly and drive it skillfully to make sure the berries are removed from the stems and are not crushed. This method requires precise machinery and adjustments. One false move and the grapes will be ruined.

Pros

This is the fastest and most cost-effective way to harvest. It doesn't require much handwork and very little intervention is needed throughout the harvest.

Cons

Too much shaking could cause the vines to die prematurely. If the grapes don't ripen at the same time, you need to sort through them first before harvesting to make sure to keep only the good clusters. It is still complicated, and sometimes impossible, to use machinery in vineyards on a steep slope or are otherwise difficult to access. Lastly, in some appellations, such as Champagne or Beaujolais, machine harvesting is forbidden.

MAKING RED WINE

After the harvest, the grape clusters are sent to the cellar to be transformed into wine as quickly as possible. The grapes are placed on a sorting table to remove the stems and any bad berries.

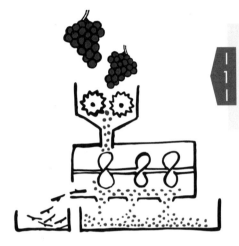

Stalking (de-stemming) and crushing
The winemaker separates the berries from the grape clusters. He throws away the stems (the rod), which contain herbaceous flavors (however, in Burgundy the grapes are only partially de-stemmed to keep the tannic structure). The berries are crushed to liberate the juice.

1

Maceration
The berries and the juice are transferred into casks for two to three weeks. The skins color the juice.

2

Punchdown or pumpover
During maceration, the skins, the pulp, and the seeds rise to the surface and form a solid layer called the *marc*, or the pomace. To put aromas, color, and tannins into the juice, the winemaker breaks the layer and pushes the solids into the juice (called "punchdown"), or he pumps the juice from the bottom of the tank and pours it over the pomace (called "pumpover").

3

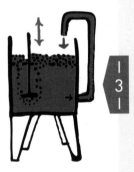

Racking and pressing the pomace
The wine is separated from the pomace. This first wine is called "run wine." The pomace is pressed to extract any remaining juice, which is called "press wine." Press wines have more tannins and color than the run wine.

— 5 —

Fermentation
During maceration, the yeast (those naturally present or added by the winemaker) transform the sugar from the pulp into alcohol. The wine is in the midst of being born. Fermentation lasts about ten days.

4

Run wine   Press wine

Henry participates in the grape harvest

Blending
The winemaker blends the run wine with the press wine.

Aging (either in a tank or a barrel) and malolactic fermentation
The wine is kept for several weeks in barrels or tanks, or up to thirty-six months for wines worth cellaring. During this resting phase, the aromas and the structure of the wine evolves. At the same time, for three to four weeks a second fermentation happens called "malolactic fermentation." The wine becomes less acidic and more stable.

7

SO₂

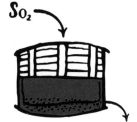

8

Racking and, eventually, sulfiting
The yeast and other deposits fall to the bottom and are removed. A little sulfur can be added to protect the wine from oxygen.

Optional blending
At this point, depending on the region, various vintages or wine from different vineyards that have been harvested separately can be blended.

Refining and filtration
To gather and eliminate any floating particles, a protein-based solution (such as egg white mixed with wine) is used. And to make the wine clearer and more brilliant, you can also filter it. These steps are optional, because they can influence the aromas and the structure of the wine.

10

Bottling
The wine is bottled and closed with a cork or a capsule. Simpler wines can be sold right away, while others age more in the bottle before sale.

11

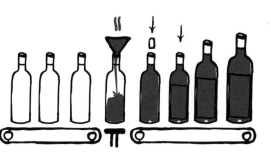

MAKING WHITE WINE

Unlike red wine, there is no maceration and the grapes are pressed as soon as they get to the cellar. Depending on the type of white wine wanted, the aging is done in a tank (for dry and lively wines) or in a barrel (for powerful whites destined for aging).

Pressing
After the stems have been removed, the grapes are pressed right away to separate the juice from the skin. Only the juice is collected.

Settling
The juice is put in a tank. Any floating particles that come from the pressing fall to the bottom of the tank and are removed. This step allows you to make white wines finer.

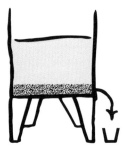

Fermentation
The yeast (naturally present or added by the winemaker) transforms the sugar into alcohol. The wine is on its way to being born! The fermentation lasts about ten days.

— 3 —

First technique

For a lively white wine meant to drink young

— 4 —

Maturing
The juice is transferred to a tank where it will rest for a few weeks to stabilize. This maturation occurs with the yeast slurry in the tank, a technique known as *sur lie*, or aging on the lees.

A

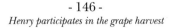

- 146 -
Henry participates in the grape harvest

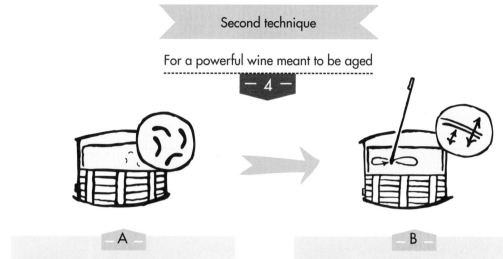

Second technique

For a powerful wine meant to be aged

— 4 —

— A —

Maturing in barrel and malolactic fermentation
The wine is put in a barrel. The second fermentation (malolactic) starts and gives a fatter, rounder feel to the wine.

— B —

Stirring
During maturation, which can last several months, the wine is stirred with a rod to put the lees in suspension and add more smoothness to the wine.

For both white processes

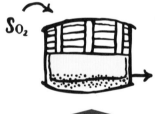

SO_2

— 5 —

Eventually, there is sulfiting, blending, refining, or filtration
To protect the wine from oxygen, you can add a little bit of sulfur. Depending on the region, different vintages or juice from grapes harvested and fermented in separate lots can finally be blended. To gather and eliminate any floating particles, you can use a protein-based solution that binds to these particles. To make the wine clearer and more brilliant, you can also filter it. These steps are optional, because they can influence the aromas and the structure of the wine.

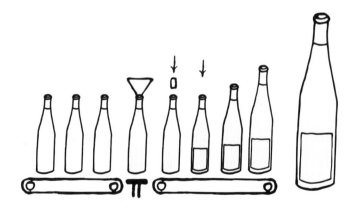

— 6 —

Bottling
The wine is put into bottles and closed with a cork or a capsule. It can age longer in the bottle or be sold right away.

MAKING ROSÉ WINE

The pink color always comes from the skin of red grapes. There are two ways of making rosé: One method is similar to making a red wine and the other is more like making a white wine.

Bleeding rosé

This is the method that is most frequently used. Like a red wine, there is a maceration with the skins and the juice, but for a much shorter time than a red wine. This type of rosé has a sustained color and body.

Direct-pressing rosé

This method is reserved for modern wines and *vin gris* ("gray wine"), which are light-colored, very fruity rosés. This technique presses the grapes right away, like the white-wine process, but the pressing is performed a lot more slowly. These rosés have a light color and are more airy.

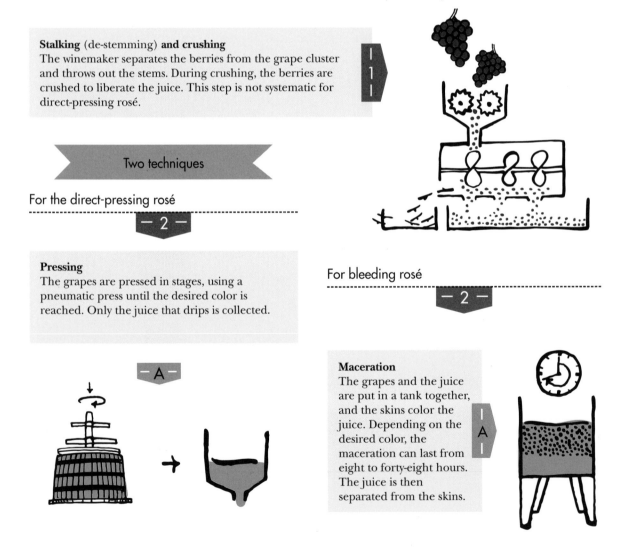

Stalking (de-stemming) **and crushing**
The winemaker separates the berries from the grape cluster and throws out the stems. During crushing, the berries are crushed to liberate the juice. This step is not systematic for direct-pressing rosé.

— 1 —

Two techniques

For the direct-pressing rosé

— 2 —

Pressing
The grapes are pressed in stages, using a pneumatic press until the desired color is reached. Only the juice that drips is collected.

For bleeding rosé

— 2 —

— A —

Maceration
The grapes and the juice are put in a tank together, and the skins color the juice. Depending on the desired color, the maceration can last from eight to forty-eight hours. The juice is then separated from the skins.

— A —

Henry participates in the grape harvest

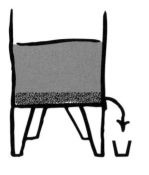

Settling
The juice is transferred into a tank. Any floating particles fall to the bottom of the tank and are removed. This step allows you to make rosés with sharper aromas.

Fermentation
The yeast (naturally present or added by the winemaker) transforms the sugar into alcohol. The wine is on its way to being born! Fermentation lasts about ten days.

— 4 —

Aging
The wine is transferred to a tank where it rests for a few weeks to stabilize. Barrel-aging and malolactic fermentation are rare. Eventually, there will be sulfiting blending, refining, and possibly filtration.

— 5 —

Bottling
The wine is bottled and closed with a cork or a capsule. It is often sold in the spring.

- 149 -
Making wine

MAKING CHAMPAGNE

Champagne can be made with white grapes (Chardonnay) and red grapes (Pinot Noir and Pinot Meunier). For classic Champagnes, three vintages are used. In all cases, the wine ends up white. The technique for making champagne is the same as that for making white wine, with one extra step—the fermentation, which gives birth to its famous bubbles. This is called méthode champenoise. *It is also called* methode traditionelle *(or traditional method), and it is also used to create other sparkling wines.*

Pressing
After the stems have been removed, the red grapes and the white grapes are pressed right away to separate the juice from the skins. Only the juice, which is colorless, is collected. It is generally more acidic and less sweet than the juice used to make non-sparkling wines.

Fermentation
The juice is transferred to a tank or into barrels. The yeast transforms the sugar into alcohol. The wine is about to be born! It will be dryer if it ferments in a tank, fatter if it ferments in barrels.

Blending
The wine is aged in a tank or in barrels, where it can go through a malolactic fermentation. Then the winemaker can blend in the three vintages, and for most non-vintage Champagnes, some older vintages can be added in. The blending with the old wines is adjusted so that the Champagne made every year has the same personality.

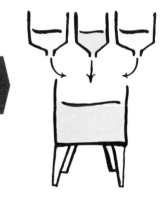

N.B. For rosé Champagnes

Some of the red grapes are made as a red wine. Adding this red wine to the blend (about 10 percent) will color the white wine pink.

Henry participates in the grape harvest

Bottling

The wine is put into bottles and a blend of sugar and yeast is added before the bottle is closed with a temporary capsule.

4

Fermentation

The fresh yeast culture eats the sugar and begins a second fermentation. This produces carbon dioxide that stays trapped inside the bottle. The bubbles are about to be born!

— 5 —

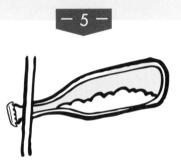

Aging and riddling

The bottles can spend two to five years in a cellar depending on the character of the Champagne, sometimes even longer for great vintages. Initially the bottles are lying down, then they are incrementally spun and tilted up until they are eventually straightened bottleneck down (a process called "riddling"). In the past this was done manually, but it is now done with a machine. The yeast forms a deposit that accumulates against the capsule.

— 6 —

Disgorging

The collar of the bottle is frozen. The capsule is removed, and from the pressure of the carbon dioxide, the yeast deposit is expelled like an ice cube out of the bottle.

— 7 —

Dosing

Before inserting the final cork and the cage that covers it, the winemaker can add a blend of wine and sugar to the Champagne. Depending on the blend used, the Champagne can turn out sweeter or less sweet.

8

Ⓥ Vocabulary

Depending on the style, you talk about Champagne as: Brut Nature (the least sweet), Extra Brut, Brut, Extra Sec, Sec, Demi-Sec, or Doux (the sweetest).

AGING

Between fermentation and bottling, aging in a tank or in a barrel is an essential step.

The goal of aging

To develop the aromas of the wine

To age the wine

To stabilize the color

To mute the tannins (for red wines)

To separate the wine from the particles present (for example, yeast from the fermentation)

Tank-aging

Whether the tank is made of stainless steel, concrete, or resin, these are all neutral materials that won't remove or add any aromas to the wine. This type of aging is used for whites, rosés, or reds that need to stay fruity, lively, and light. Tank-aging is often short, between one to two months for light wines and up to twelve months for more evolved wines, and reds often need to age one year before being made available for sale.

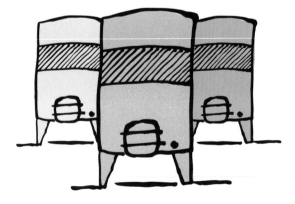

Barrel-aging

Wine interacts a lot with the wood of the barrel, especially if the wine is new. Depending on the choice of wood and the intensity with which it's been heated, the barrel transmits aging aromas to the wine (grilled, toasted, vanilla, brioche, among others). Minuscule amounts of air circulate through the wood and the bung that stoppers the barrel. A small part of the wine actually evaporates through the wood, which is known as the "angel's share." This gas exchange encourages the wine to evolve, smooths out the tannins, and starts the aging process that will continue in the bottle. This aging is used only for powerful wines. To control the influence of the wood, the winemaker generally uses different-aged barrels (from a new barrel to barrels previously used for up to four different wines). The aging can last twelve to thirty-six months.

Henry participates in the grape harvest

Malolactic fermentation

During aging, most reds and some rosés and powerful whites go through a malolactic fermentation: malic acid (similar to the acid from a green apple) transforms into lactic acid (which you find in milk), producing a softer, more velvety, less spicy acidity in the wine. It starts at a certain temperature (about 63°F or 17°C) and doesn't start if it's very cold. It's not activated for whites and reds that must stay light.

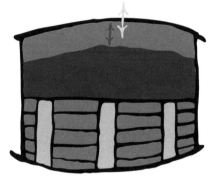

Oxidative aging

Normally, the aging of a wine happens in a barrel that is completely full. To counter evaporation, the winemaker regularly adds wine and tops it up. The wine is never in direct contact with oxygen. However, some wines are intentionally aged in barrels with a big pocket of air left inside. These wines develop very specific aromas of walnuts, curry, dried fruits, or bitter orange due to the oxidative environment.

Sometimes the yeast forms a protective coating on the surface of the liquid. These wines are called *vins de voile* ("veil wines"). Wines that undergo oxidative aging include young wine from Jura, Fino Sherry, Tawny Port, Banyuls, and Madeira.

 Micro-oxygenation (or micro-bubbling)

This process consists of artificially diffusing small quantities of oxygen in the wine (mostly those aged in tanks, rarely those in barrels). This technique replicates the action of aging in a barrel, or it accentuates the effects of aging, which smooths out the tannins and accelerates the maturation of the wine. This practice is somewhat controversial because it can also smooth out the unique character of the wine.

SOFT AND SWEET WINES

Soft and sweet wines are distinguished from each other by their sugar content. A soft wine contains 20 to 45 grams per liter of sugar after fermentation, while a sweet wine has more than 45 grams per liter, up to 200 grams per liter.

The development of entry-level sweet wines is simple: They are the result of chaptalization, a process that adds sugar during the winemaking process. When the fermentation has created an acceptable amount of alcohol, about 12.5 percent, it is stopped by adding sulfur.

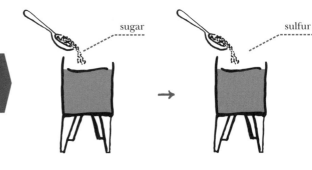

The way of harvesting

For soft or sweet wines of high quality, it's all about the vine. During the harvest, the winegrower picks the grapes that have more sugar than normal. This is achieved in different ways:

Late harvest: The grapes are picked later than for dry wines, and in the best cases, the grape is affected by "noble rot" (*Botrytis*). This fungus concentrates the sugars and gives aromas of roasted fruits. The grapes are now "botrytized."

Straw wine: The grape clusters are collected early but dried on straw or on mats for several months, a method used in Italy, Greece, Spain, and Jura.

Desiccation: The grapes are left to dry at the foot of the vine, helped along by the autumn sun and wind. This method requires a mild climate that is dry and windy, like it is in the South West France or Valais in Switzerland.

The Sélection de Grains Nobles or Beerenauslese: The grape is even sweeter than during a late harvest because it's picked even later and it is affected by "noble rot" (*Botrytis*).

Ice wine: In the colder wine regions, the winemaker waits for winter and picks frozen grapes, as they do in Germany, Austria, and especially in Canada.

During the winemaking process, the grapes are pressed very slowly to extract the little juice that they still contain. The fermentation is slower and is then stopped by the aid of sulfur and lowering the temperature. The winemaker then filters it to separate the yeast from the wine.

Henry participates in the grape harvest

THE FORTIFICATION OF SWEET WINES

A "fortified wine" is a type of wine that has alcohol added to it. These wines are white or red and are generally soft and sometimes dry. In the bottle, the alcohol content is above 15 percent.

alcohol

The winemaking process
At the beginning of fermentation, the winemaker stops the work of the yeast by adding a pure, neutral alcohol that has no taste or aroma, which kills the yeast. The sugar from the grapes is stopped from fermenting into alcohol.

The best-known fortified wine in the world is certainly Port, made in Portugal.

In France, this process is used to produce whites like the Muscats from Beaumes de Venise, Rivesaltes, Frontignan, and Cap Corse.

For reds, you find the soft Rasteau, Banyuls, and Maury, products of the Grenache varietal.

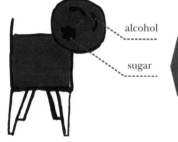

alcohol

sugar

Sherry (Xeres)
Made in Spain in the town of Jerez, it is fortified with alcohol just before it is put into bottles, after the fermentation and aging. All of the sugars present in the grape have been transformed into alcohol during fermentation, which explains why the resulting wine is dry. For some types of Sherry, it is also possible to add sugar before the bottling. It is sometimes put through oxidative aging.

Madeira
Madeira has alcohol added during fermentation, then is heated for several months in big tanks at about 113°F or 45°C. The best are heated again during aging in drums designed to hold heat. This type of aging is particularly oxidative.

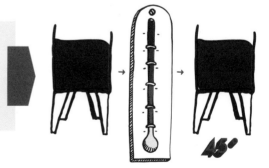

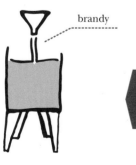

brandy

Liqueur wines
This process is identical to that for making fortified wines, except that the alcohol addition uses an eau de vie, not a neutral alcohol. Among the better-known liqueurs are Pineau des Charentes, which has an addition of Cognac, Floc de Gascogne, which uses Armagnac, and Macvin du Jura with Marc du Jura, a brandy from Franche Comté.

THE DIFFERENT BOTTLES

Piccolo or Split:
187.5 mL

Demi or Half:
275 mL

Clavelin:
620 mL

Standard:
750 mL

Magnum :
2 bottles = 1.5 L

Jeroboam
(or Double Magnum):
4 bottles = 3 L

Imperial:
8 bottles = 6 L

Rehoboam:
6 bottles = 4.5 L

Salmanazar:
12 bottles = 9 L

Balthazar:
16 bottles = 12 L

Nebuchadnezzar:
20 bottles = 15 L

Henry participates in the grape harvest

Bordeaux

Muscat
de Frontignan

Champagne

Sherry Fino

Champagne

Tawny Port

Muscat de
Beaumes de Venise

Madeira

Champagne

Burgundy

Clavelin (Jura)

Alsace

Côtes-du-Rhône

Provence

Banyuls

Muscat
de Rivesaltes

Provence

THE SECRETS OF CORK

The first use of cork goes back to antiquity when it was used to seal amphorae of wine. It then disappeared from use only to reappear in the seventeenth century with the invention of the glass bottle.

Manufacturing

The principal plantations growing cork are found in Portugal, Spain, Morocco, and Algeria. A cork tree lives an average of 125 years and must be twenty-five years old before it can be used to make wine corks. When it reaches maturity it's stripped of its bark approximately every nine years. The bark is dried, cleaned, and cut.

▶ The best wine corks are punched out directly from the bark. They can also be created from pieces of compressed cork. Those are destined for bottles of wine that are drunk quickly.

AIR

▶ The quality of a wine cork depends on the quality of the wood—the fewer cracks along the body (called lenticels) the better seal it will have. If the outside doesn't contain any cracks, it's called a mirror. Corks that possess a mirror on each side are extremely rare and their price can be very high. They are used for exceptional bottles of wine, those that are suitable for aging up to fifty years.

or

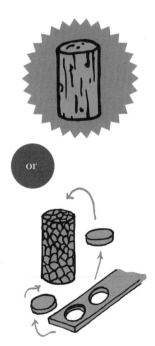

Henry participates in the grape harvest

The advantages

▶ A sound as delicious and unique as the opening of a wine bottle.

▶ **Most important:** It is airtight and keeps oxygen from entering the bottle.

▶ **Consumers prefer it:** They appreciate its natural origin, its history, and see it (sometimes wrongly) as the sign of a quality wine.

▶ A cork's elasticity allows it to fit perfectly in the neck of the bottle and to adapt to subtle variations in temperature to protect the wine from the seasons for several decades.

5 years   15 years   30 years

The disadvantages

▶ The biggest defect of a wine cork is that it can transfer a contaminant to the wine—the infamous taste of being "corked." This comes from a molecule called TCA that sometimes develops in the cork. It takes hardly any to render a bottle undrinkable. Though strong attention is paid to hygiene and careful decontamination of the cork, cork growers have largely reduced the risk of TCA. It's considered to affect only 3 to 4 percent of all bottles with cork closures. This risk is something to take into account when you purchase a bottle of wine.

3 to 4% of bottles

 Laying the bottles down

Be careful, the cork can dry out if it's not moist. That's why it's imperative to lay the bottles on their sides so that the liquid can stay in contact with the cork. Otherwise, the cork loses its elasticity and will no longer keep the oxygen out.

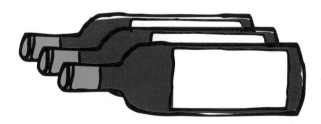

Alternate closures

Synthetic corks

Less expensive to produce than its natural alter-ego, the synthetic cork (often made from silicone) has the same properties as natural cork, at least in the short term.

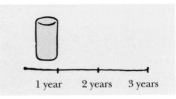

1 year   2 years   3 years

The elasticity of synthetic corks is more limited over time. After about two or three years, it tends to stiffen up and loses its sealing capability. But for most bottles that are drunk soon after release, it does the trick.

The screwcap

The screwcap is the least popular method of sealing a bottle. It's a metallic contraption that's hardly natural, makes no pleasing cork-popping sound when opening a bottle, and renders your favorite corkscrew useless, but they let you open a bottle of wine easily and quickly. This is a real asset for picnics. The Swiss and New Zealanders have happily been using screwcaps for their wines since the 1970s.

The advantages
▸ It is absolutely airtight.
▸ It doesn't degrade, even if there are strong changes in temperature.
▸ It does not cause corked wines.

The disadvantages
However, it is so airtight that some discerning tasters find the wine less evolved or less full than wines sealed with a cork. In fact, comparative tastings show that the aromas of a ten-year-old wine are different between bottles sealed with a cork or with a screwcap. Manufacturers now offer screwcaps with a joint that is more or less porous so as to mimic the effect of natural cork.

The use of screwcap is on the rise. Of the 17 billion bottles sold worldwide, 4 billion have screwcaps. And this number is growing.

Henry participates in the grape harvest

THE ROLE OF SULFUR IN WINE

The advantages

▸ Sulfur is an antioxidant. It protects the juice from oxygen while it is fermenting and limits oxidation that could spoil the wine.
▸ It stops fermentation and helps maintain the residual sugars that are used to develop a sweet wine.
▸ It stabilizes bottled wine, protecting it from oxidation that makes it age prematurely.

The disadvantages

▸ Sulfur has a bad odor (like rotten eggs).
▸ Because sulfur is an antioxidant, it can cause the reduction of the wine and release unpleasant odors when you open the wine (cabbage smell).
▸ It can provoke terrible headaches in consumers (due to its negation of the oxygen).
▸ It stunts the wine and rubs out its character.

For these reasons, most winemakers progressively reduce their doses of sulfur. This is possible as long as the grapes are carefully transported during harvest and don't burst, the cellar is clean, and the wines are well protected from oxygen.

On average, you'll find the lowest to the highest dose of added sulfur:

The quantity of sulfur
Doses of sulfur vary from 3 to 300 milligrams per liter in wine, so you can see the margin is enormous. It also varies in the functions it serves in the wine.

red wine   effervescent wine   rosé wine   white wine   sweet wine

 Wine without sulfur

A few winemakers (as reckless as they are small in number) make some wines without adding sulfur. These wines are not stabilized and are protected in rigorous storage conditions (at a temperature lower than 61°F or 16° C), otherwise the fermentation could begin again or the wine will oxidize rapidly. These unsulfured wines offer surprising flavors and are full of freshness and vitality, but when things go badly they give off odors of overripe apple and horse stable.

One day, Caroline grabbed her backpack, got in her car, and left home. She had a crazy idea: to take a year off and go out and see the world. She did have an idea of what she wanted to do. She wanted to explore other cities and taste some wine. Initially, Caroline plugged in her GPS, but she realized she preferred to get lost on the streets and dirt roads, stopping when she felt like it at wineries, vineyards, and castles. She was guided by the Wine Route signs that peppered the route as she climbed the coasts and descended into valleys. She stopped to look at grapes in the sun, walked on a wide variety of soils, both rocky and claylike, and kicked the stones between the vines.

Henry had warned: "You'll see that the vines can be very different depending on the region and the *terroir*." And this has been true. Some vines line the coasts, some vines are tortured by age, and others show shoots full of promise. And she tasted. Some idiosyncratic white wines from Alsace, some smoother white wines from the Languedoc, green Portuguese wines, silky red wines from Rioja, and strong reds from Tuscany. Caroline took hundreds of photos, but it's the taste of all those nectars that she remembers the most. She knew that the region, the climate, the altitude, the dryness, the history, the work that winemakers put in, and the decisions they made gave each wine a unique personality. The *terroir*, sometimes a very vague term to define, became clear to her; it was an indispensable part of the process.

This chapter is for all the Carolines who like to travel, explore, and learn on the road.

CAROLINE

VISITS THE VINEYARDS

The *terroir* • The wines of France
The wines of Europe • The wines of the world

Terroir *is a difficult concept to grasp. This French word is rarely translated into other languages and doesn't have an equivalent in English. You could say that* terroir *gathers all of the factors that contribute to the individuality of a wine.*

Geographic factors

The climate
Unlike weather, climate encompasses all the atmospheric conditions of a region over time.
You can define the climate of a viticultural region by examining:
▸ the average temperature;
▸ the average rainfall;
▸ the strength of the wind, which dries the grape, refreshes, or reheats (and prevents frost);
▸ the negative aspects like frost, hail, or storms.

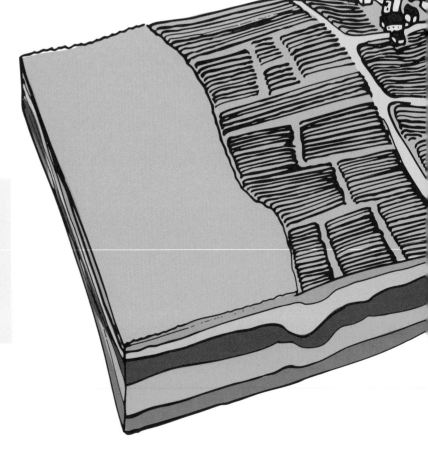

There are climates that are classified as continental, oceanic, mountain, or Mediterranean. To these larger, general areas add the various microclimates, with unique characteristics that modify the overall local climate. Microclimates can be localized to valleys, hillsides, near a body of water, or a forest.

The altitude

A grape cultivated at a higher altitude will not develop the same way as if it had been cultivated near sea level; the deviations in temperature between summer and winter and even between morning and evening will be more important. This factor, like climate, is decisive in the type of grape variety that is grown.

The slope

Topography plays another essential role:
In a vineyard situated on a slope, rainwater flows more easily and doesn't stagnate in contact with the roots. A vineyard planted on a hillside and exposed to the south, southeast, or southwest profits from an ideal sun exposure. However, the soil on a hillside is generally poorer than soil on a plain.
For these reasons, vines planted on a slope (more or less steep) often result in better wines.

The different soils

More than the topsoil, which is generally composed of earth, it's the subsoil that's really important—the bedrock where the roots squeeze through and take hold.

Types of subsoils:

▸ clay, limestone, even clay-limestone
▸ marl left by receding oceans
▸ schist, granite, and gneiss from the mountains

▸ sand and gravel from seas, rivers, and deltas
▸ pebbles, chalky soils, basalt, volcanic rock

In the same viticultural region, there are often different types of soils that succeed and overlap, which mean that a *terroir* is often very complex.

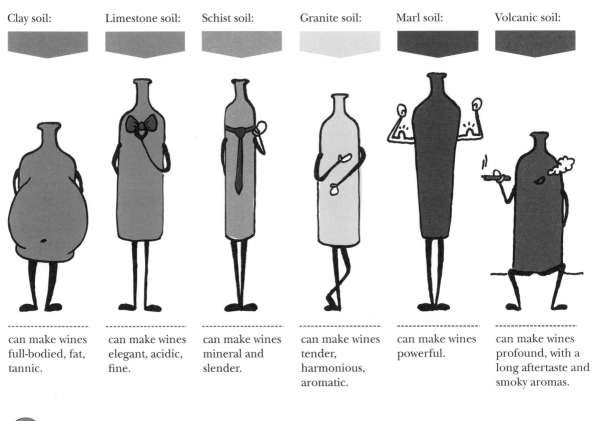

Clay soil:	Limestone soil:	Schist soil:	Granite soil:	Marl soil:	Volcanic soil:
can make wines full-bodied, fat, tannic.	can make wines elegant, acidic, fine.	can make wines mineral and slender.	can make wines tender, harmonious, aromatic.	can make wines powerful.	can make wines profound, with a long aftertaste and smoky aromas.

 The richness of the soil

Good wines are born from soils that are arid and moderate in water and nutrients. This causes the vine to send its roots as deep as possible to search for food, as much as several yards into the ground, for its survival.

The deeper the roots are, the better the wine is. On the other hand, rich, fertile soil will make the vine grow too quickly, and it won't concentrate its juice in the grape.

Caroline vists the vineyards

The work of man

Without man, terroir *is nothing but potential.*

The work of a winegrower consists of developing the *terroir*, of driving a vine toward what's needed for good vinification.

He makes decisions depending on the soil and the climate, the preferred grape varieties, and trellising and pruning techniques. He takes care of the vine and chooses the best time to harvest the grapes.

He strategically selects exactly where to plant. In the eleventh century in Burgundy, monks tasted the earth to decide what to do, but today sophisticated analyses with pH testing lets him evaluate how to care for the soil in a much more scientific way.

At the winery, he opts for the best winemaking process and the best aging conditions to let the *terroir* express itself without smothering or masking the potential with too much technique or carelessness.

He reworks the soil, drains it, maintains it, and nourishes it.

While respecting the *terroir*, man interprets and shapes it. Thus he makes a veritable *vin de terroir* ("wine of the *terroir*") and not simply a varietal wine.

What is a *vin de terroir*?

▸ A wine with highlighted geological and geographical characteristics;
▸ A wine that recalls the history and tradition of the techniques of production in the region (called the "typicality of the region");
▸ A wine that pays no attention to fashion or newfangled methods.

What is a varietal wine?

▸ A wine in which only the aromas of the grape express themselves (called "varietal expression");
▸ A wine without geographic demarcation;
▸ A technological wine, in which the winemaking process doesn't reflect the viticultural region;
▸ A wine made to resemble a fashionable wine, independent of its region of origin.

WINES FROM ALSACE

Whites: around 90%
Reds and rosés: about 10%

HOW TO FIND THEM?

The varietal

These wines are the exception when compared to the rest of the French vineyards. We think of Alsace when we want to drink Muscat or Sylvaner. The choice of varietal is more important than the *terroir*. Each grape varietal has its own personality, from the minerality of Riesling to the spicy character of Gewürztraminer to the smoky notes of Pinot Gris. We also choose according to the occasion: an effervescent wine (a Crémant, generally made with Pinot Gris) or a dry, soft, or sweet wine.

Four varietals, called "noble varieties," can produce these soft wines: Muscat, Pinot Gris, Gewürztraminer, and Riesling. Sweet wines are the late harvests or Sélection de Grains Nobles, depending on the quantity of sugar desired in the berries.

Grand Cru

Once a varietal is chosen, the enlightened amateur will next look for the reference to Grand Cru, reserved for the four noble varietals and designate fifty-one remarkable Alsatian *terroirs* (for example: Osterberg, Rangen, Schlossberg, or Zinnkoepflé). With so many different soil profiles interspersed throughout the area (there are thirteen, from sedimentary volcano to gneissic to sandstone), it is the most geologically complicated region in France. No matter what, you will find beautiful wines at reasonable prices and excellent wineries that will explain everything to you.

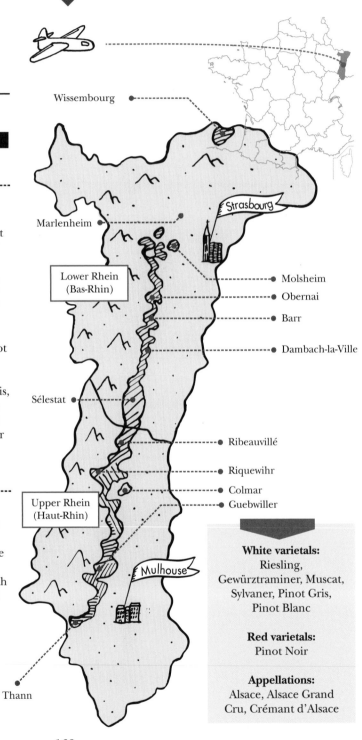

Wissembourg

Strasbourg

Marlenheim

Lower Rhein (Bas-Rhin)

Molsheim

Obernai

Barr

Dambach-la-Ville

Sélestat

Ribeauvillé

Riquewihr

Colmar

Guebwiller

Upper Rhein (Haut-Rhin)

Mulhouse

Thann

White varietals:
Riesling, Gewürztraminer, Muscat, Sylvaner, Pinot Gris, Pinot Blanc

Red varietals:
Pinot Noir

Appellations:
Alsace, Alsace Grand Cru, Crémant d'Alsace

Reds: 98%
Whites and
sparkling wines: 2%

Beaujolais and Beaujolais Nouveau

In terms of popularity, wine from Beaujolais is still too often associated with its little brother, Beaujolais Nouveau. Celebrated around the world on the third Thursday of November, this little primary wine is bottled immediately after it's made. It doesn't have time to develop complex aromas and it's often criticized for its simplicity and its famous "banana taste." But Beaujolais has much more to offer. The home of Gamay, a fruity and lightly tannic grape variety, this region offers wines that are easy to drink, and among the vintage wines, some that are more complex and capable of aging ten years and more.

Which wine to pick?

If you are looking for something that is easy to drink, light, and full of vivacity, a Beaujolais-Villages is a good choice. But you'll make the best discoveries in the vintage wines, and at good prices, too. From Morgon, Chénas, and Moulin-à-Vent, the wines are structured, more tannic, and worth aging. From Chiroubles and Saint-Armour, on the other hand, the Beaujolais is fine and light. From Fleurie, you'll find wines with beautiful aromatic intensity of red fruits and flowers.

White varietals:
Chardonnay

Red varietals:
Gamay

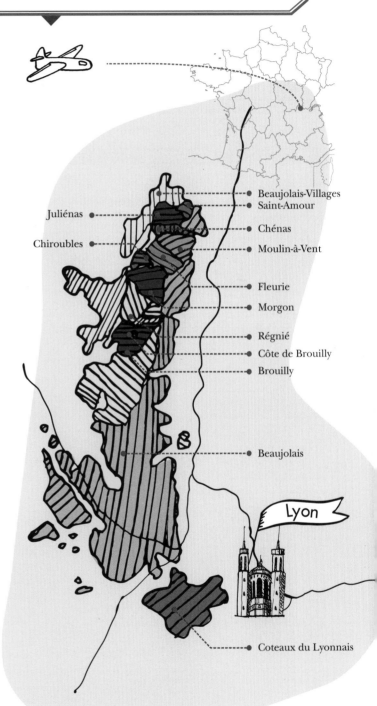

Beaujolais-Villages
Saint-Amour
Juliénas
Chénas
Chiroubles
Moulin-à-Vent
Fleurie
Morgon
Régnié
Côte de Brouilly
Brouilly

Beaujolais

Lyon

Coteaux du Lyonnais

Whites and sparkling wines: about 70%
Reds: about 30%

HOW TO FIND THEM?

There are no châteaux in Burgundy, but there are wineries called Domaines and Clos (if the vines are surrounded by hundred-year-old walls). Apart from Chablis and the Grand Auxerrois, which are situated in a little gap in the Yonne River, Burgundy vineyards extend from north to south, from Dijon to Lyon, on a thin ribbon of land only a few miles wide. There are four distinct regions from north to south: Côte de Nuits, Côte de Beaune, Côte Chalonnaise, and Mâconnais.

White or red?

The wines from the Chablis appellation are always whites. The Côte de Nuits is very well known for its reds (Gevrey-Chambertin, Chambolle-Musigny). The Côte de Beaune is reputable for its whites (Meursault, Chassagne-Montrachet), except for Pommard and Volnay, which produce excellent reds. You'll find whites and reds all over, but also some sparkling wines, like Crémant de Bourgogne. On the other hand, the varietals are very specific: Pinot Noir almost exclusively for the reds, Chardonnay for the whites, with the exception of Aligoté from Bourgogne Aligoté and Sauvignon Blanc from Saint-Bris.

The hierarchy

There are about a hundred appellations in Burgundy, hierarchies between the regional denomination, and Grand Cru status. In more of the appellations, it's possible to add the name of the locality or the parcel of vineyard land, the so-called "climate." There are more than 2,500 of those.

Hierarchy and examples of appellations:

Regional appellation: Burgundy
Subregional appellation: Côte de Nuits

Village appellation: Gevrey-Chambertin, Saint-Véran
Apellation Premier Cru: Gevrey-Chambertin Premier Cru aux Combottes, Gevrey-Chambertin Premier Cru Bel-Air
Appellation Grand Cru: Chablis Grand Cru Vaudesir, Corton Grand Cru "The Foxes" (Côte de Beaune); Les Grands Échezeaux (Côte de Nuits)

How to buy?

Buy what you can afford, of course, because wine from Burgundy is still pretty expensive, except for the sparkling wines, the best of which can easily replace Champagne.

The appellation

Assess the appellation according to the hierarchy. Better to go with an unknown village appellation than a regional or generic appellation, which means that the grapes were harvested a little bit from everywhere. The trick is to choose an unknown village that neighbors a known one. For example, a red from Monthélie rather than Volnay, or a white from Saint-Aubin rather than Meursault. Don't hesitate to try the white wines from Mâconnais. These often offer good quality for the price.

The producer

In addition to the appellations and names of vineyard parcels, you must take into account the name of the producer or the negociant. There are numerous trading houses in Burgundy that purchase the grapes or the wines from the owners and sell them under their own name. They often offer a wide range of appellations, but sometimes the wines from the original owners have more character.

The taste

Pinot Noir is very fine in the north and takes on more and more magnitude as one goes toward the south. Everyone likes the Chardonnay. The Chablis is pure and mineral. The Côte de Beaune is powerful, and the Mâconnais is fat or even smooth.

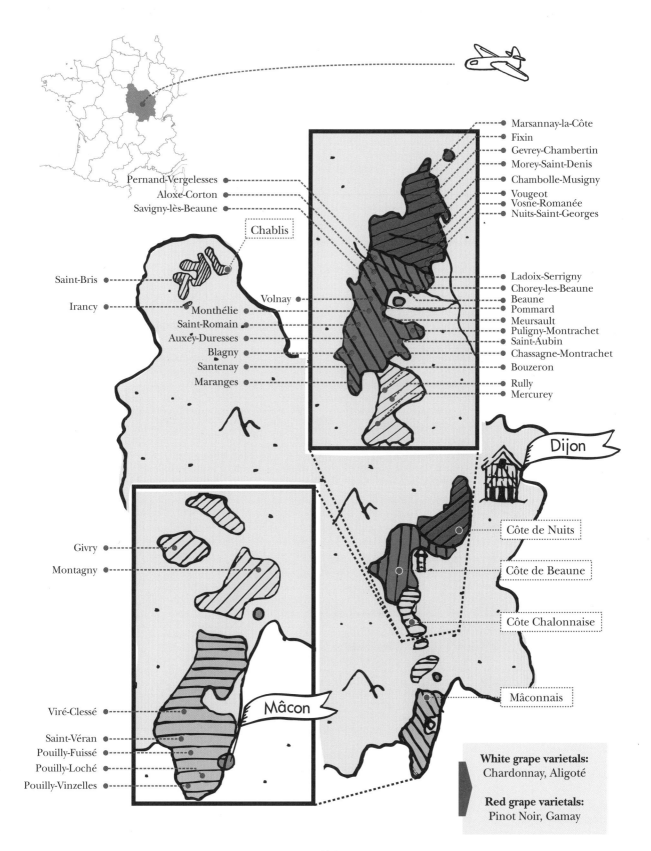

Marsannay-la-Côte
Fixin
Gevrey-Chambertin
Morey-Saint-Denis
Chambolle-Musigny
Vougeot
Vosne-Romanée
Nuits-Saint-Georges

Pernand-Vergelesses
Aloxe-Corton
Savigny-lès-Beaune

Chablis

Saint-Bris
Irancy

Volnay

Ladoix-Serrigny
Chorey-les-Beaune
Beaune
Pommard
Meursault
Puligny-Montrachet
Saint-Aubin
Chassagne-Montrachet
Bouzeron
Rully
Mercurey

Monthélie
Saint-Romain
Auxey-Duresses
Blagny
Santenay
Maranges

Dijon

Côte de Nuits

Côte de Beaune

Côte Chalonnaise

Givry
Montagny

Mâconnais

Mâcon

Viré-Clessé

Saint-Véran
Pouilly-Fuissé
Pouilly-Loché
Pouilly-Vinzelles

White grape varietals:
Chardonnay, Aligoté

Red grape varietals:
Pinot Noir, Gamay

THE WINES FROM BORDEAUX

Reds and rosés: about 90%
Whites: about 10%

Left Bank (Haut-Médoc and Médoc): dominant in Cabernet Sauvignon (with Merlot)

Right Bank (Pomerol, Saint-Émilion): dominant in Merlot (with Cabernet Franc)

HOW TO FIND IT?

Home of the most respected red wines in the world (and the most expensive), you'll also find several good wines at the less well-known or lower-priced châteaux. They are difficult to choose. On the label, you'll see the name of the appellation, the name of the château, and the vintage.

The appellation

The more specific it is, the better it is. Depending on what you drink, a bottle can be labeled Bordeaux or Bordeaux Supérieur. It can also include a more local name like Médoc, and for the most famous wines, communal appellations like Saint-Estèphe, Pauillac, Margaux, Saint-Julien.

The château

For Bordeaux, experts talk about château more than domaine. However, what's called a château is often only a business operation surrounded by vines. Some are very well-known and much valued (the high price goes hand in hand), others are less well-known and less expensive but merit being discovered and followed. Some only exist on paper, invented by a grocery store chain's marketing team, and they aren't very interesting in the glass.

The vintage

Vintage is a very important factor in Bordeaux, because it dictates the year's price curve. A château wine will cost more or less depending upon the weather and the reputation of the vintage. Therefore, a 2010 Bordeaux, already an expensive vintage, will normally cost more than a 2011 or a 2007. In good years, the wine will help small châteaux succeed, and those from the big names will be good for aging.

The classes of Bordeaux wines

The biggest wines from the Médoc, Graves, Saint-Émilion, and Sauternes are classified (often controversially). For example, for the reds from Médoc, there is a classification that was established in 1855 (Les Grands Crus classés en 1855), which was based on the prices of the era. They go from (highest to lowest) First to Fifth Growths (Crus), then move to Crus Bourgeois and Crus Artisans.

The First Growth Grand Cru Classés wines:

First Growths from Médoc:
Château Latour (Pauillac)
Château Lafite Rothschild (Pauillac)
Château Mouton Rothschild (Pauillac)
Château Haut-Brion (Graves)
Château Margaux (Margaux)

Superior First Growth from Sauternes:
Château d'Yquem

First Growths from Saint-Émilion:
Château Ausone
Château Cheval Blanc
Château Pavie (since 2012)
Château Angélus (since 2012)

Some good recent vintages:

| 2010 | 2009 | 2005 |

Visit the Bordeaux wineries:

To discover the wines from Bordeaux, participate in a Médoc marathon or take a more peaceful route, visiting some of the choice châteaux. You can visit the biggest (you may have to pay for tastings), but don't forget to visit the smaller wineries too. You will stumble onto beautiful surprises.

Caroline vists the vineyards

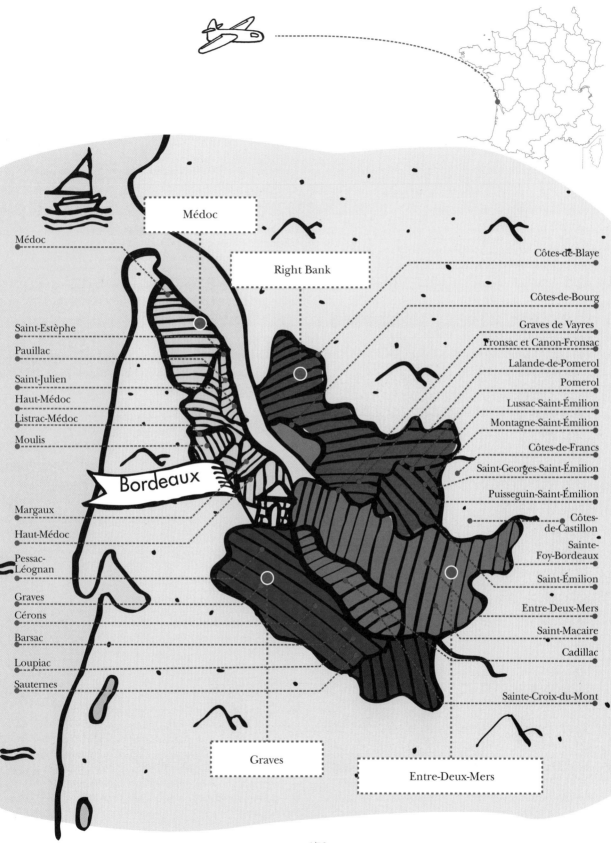

Médoc

Right Bank

Médoc

Côtes-de-Blaye

Côtes-de-Bourg

Saint-Estèphe

Pauillac

Graves de Vayres

Fronsac et Canon-Fronsac

Lalande-de-Pomerol

Saint-Julien

Pomerol

Haut-Médoc

Lussac-Saint-Émilion

Listrac-Médoc

Montagne-Saint-Émilion

Moulis

Côtes-de-Francs

Saint-Georges-Saint-Émilion

Bordeaux

Puisseguin-Saint-Émilion

Margaux

Côtes-de-Castillon

Haut-Médoc

Sainte-Foy-Bordeaux

Pessac-Léognan

Saint-Émilion

Graves

Entre-Deux-Mers

Cérons

Saint-Macaire

Barsac

Cadillac

Loupiac

Sauternes

Sainte-Croix-du-Mont

Graves

Entre-Deux-Mers

THE WINES FROM CHAMPAGNE

The world's best-known celebration wine comes from the most northern vines in France. Three main varietals are used for Champagne: Chardonnay, Pinot Noir, and Pinot Meunier, and they are often blended. A Champagne made solely of Chardonnay is called a "blanc de blancs" (a white Champagne made from white grapes).
A Champagne made from Pinot Noir and Pinot Meunier is a "blanc de noirs" (a white champagne from red grapes). Pink champagne gets its color from maceration or, more often, by the addition of red wine.

HOW TO FIND IT?

There aren't really appellations within the region called Champagne. Especially for the biggest brands, the grapes come from the entire region. Given that, the Côte des Blancs is more Chardonnay oriented, although Pinot Noir readily flourishes on the Reims Mountain and Pinot Meunier in the Val-de-Marne and the Côte des Bar.
There are, nonetheless, levels of quality: Champagne, Champagne Premier Cru (First Growth), and Champagne Grand Cru. The Premiers and Grands Crus are defined by the quality of the grape harvested.

The taste

There are a lot of subtleties but not many obvious differences. Champagnes made from a majority of Chardonnay grapes and other blanc de blancs are often more refined, more acidic, and make perfect aperitifs or an accompaniment to light dishes. The blanc de noirs and the rosés are more powerful and more vinous (with aromas and roundness that make you think of wine), and they can accompany a meal. The soils also influence the taste. The chalky soils around Reims and Épernay give wines much finesse and minerality, while clay soils make wines that are more full-bodied and fat.

Vintage or non-vintage?

Champagne is not generally a vintage wine. Most are made with a blend of wines from the current year and the past, in order to ensure a consistent quality and style each year. Champagne therefore expresses the signature taste of the "house" (the winery) where it's made. At the same time, when the harvest is especially beautiful, the producers will create vintage Champagnes, made entirely with grapes from that year. These wines have a more assertive personality and a good potential for aging for several decades. They are also a lot more expensive.

Dry or sweet?

The base wine added before corking the bottle contains anywhere from 9 grams to more than 50 grams of sugar per liter. Each level gives a radically different profile to the different Champagnes.
You can easily tell the difference between Champagnes depending on what they are: Brut Nature, Extra Brut, Brut, Extra Sec, Sec, Demi-Sec, or Doux.
Extra Brut and Brut Champagnes are appropriate for all parties and aperitifs because of their thirst-quenching properties. Sec, Demi-Sec and Doux Champagnes present a nice alternative to sweet wines for dessert.

Brand or producer?

Champagne is a region where the brand name is queen. This makes the wine easier to buy, as all the big wineries are well-known and sold all over the world. They offer Champagnes consistently. They buy the majority of their grapes from winegrowers.
But certain brands do lack personality, and you sometimes have to turn to the smaller producers to find a good Champagne or one that has better quality for the price.
These are less easy to find, and ideally it's best to visit them in person. If you know a reliable Champagne winemaker your friends will be very jealous, since most people either end up spending a fortune or buying a sub-par bottle at the supermarket.

Caroline vists the vineyards

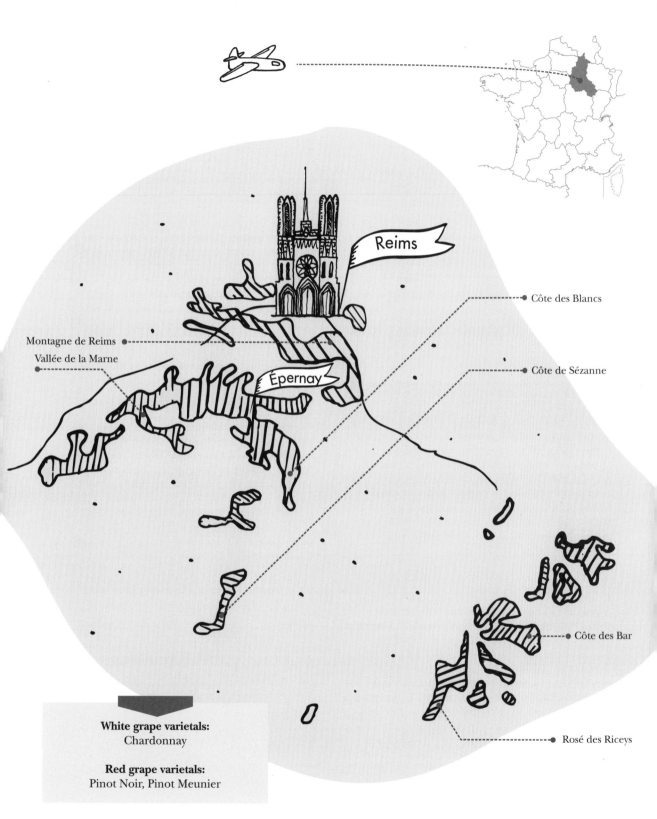

Reims

Côte des Blancs

Montagne de Reims

Vallée de la Marne

Épernay

Côte de Sézanne

Côte des Bar

Rosé des Riceys

White grape varietals:
Chardonnay

Red grape varietals:
Pinot Noir, Pinot Meunier

THE WINES OF LANGUEDOC-ROUSSILLON

Reds and rosés:
about 80%
Whites: about 20%

The Languedoc-Roussillon is the number-one French viticultural region, in terms of volume (40 percent of the total national production) and acreage of vineyards. They extend continuously from Nîmes, where the vineyards touch those of the Côtes du Rhône, all the way to the Spanish border.
Languedoc-Roussillon produces white, red, rosé, dry, and sweet wines.

HOW TO FIND IT?

The volume of wine in this region has been winning over its quality for a long time, but through perseverance, the region now produces wines full of charm and character. At a number of wineries, it is now possible to find very good bottles at more reasonable prices. For example, there are whites from Limoux and reds from Corbières and Pic Saint-Loup, where a lot of naturally sweet wines are enjoying increasing and deserved popularity.

The taste

Don't be surprised if you find some aspects in common with the wines from the southern Rhône Valley. The vintages are practically identical. Only the harsh Carignan, the characteristic varietal of the Languedoc-Roussillon, takes one by surprise. If it's well-worked and from old vines, the result is a wine that's rustic, neutral, and mineral, all at the same time. For whites, although Chardonnay is more and more present, a range of varietals from all over create blends of great richness with aromas of exotic fruits, hazelnuts, and white flowers.

The appellations

Among the appellations, wines from Saint-Chinian, Faugères, and Minervois are generally more delicate and less robust than from Corbières, Languedoc, and Côtes du Roussillon. The wines produced in poor soil and at altitude are more fresh and delicate. The others share an imposing character, marked by aromatic herbs including thyme and bay leaf, and the scrubland that surrounds the vine. In the Languedoc appellation, you will have pleasant surprises among the seventeen local denominations like La Clape or Pic Saint-Loup. But more than appellation, it's the work of the winemaker that makes all the difference. This is a region filled with bargains, provided you do a little digging.

Naturally sweet wines

The region is particularly known for its naturally sweet wines, in red or white.
In white, Muscats (Muscat de Lunel, Muscat de Mireval, Muscat de Frontignan, Muscat de Rivesaltes) deploy powerful aromas and a lovely taste on the palate.
On the red side (Maury, Banyuls), cocoa, coffee, licorice, fig, candied fruits, almonds, and walnuts swim around with smoothness, offering a complexity not unlike the grand Ports.

White grape varieties:
Chardonnay, Clairette, Grenache Blanc, Bourboulenc, Picpoul, Marsanne, Roussane, Macabeu, Mauzac, Muscat

Red grape varieties:
Carignan, Syrah, Grenache, Cinsaut, Mourvèdre, Merlot

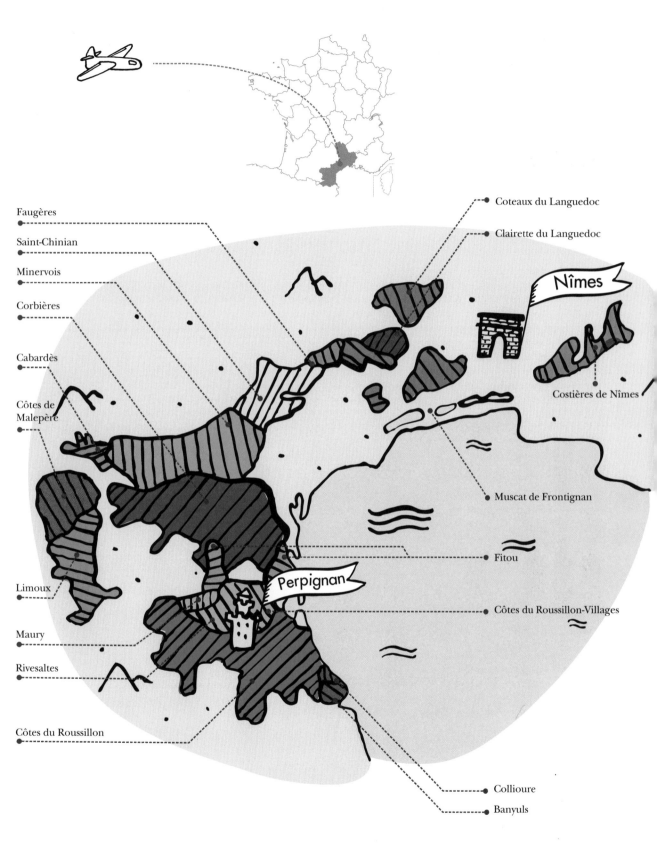

Faugères

Saint-Chinian

Minervois

Corbières

Cabardès

Côtes de
Malepère

Limoux

Maury

Rivesaltes

Côtes du Roussillon

Coteaux du Languedoc

Clairette du Languedoc

Nîmes

Costières de Nîmes

Muscat de Frontignan

Fitou

Perpignan

Côtes du Roussillon-Villages

Collioure

Banyuls

Rosés: about 80%
Reds: about 15%
Whites: about 5%

The dominant rosé

A vacation wine, rosé is the image conveyed by this viticultural region. Provence is characterized by the sea, cicadas, lavender, olives, and rosé. Not surprising, given the amount of production that is dedicated to it, rosé wines are produced year after year to the detriment of reds and whites. Rosé from Provence accounts for nearly half of all French rosés produced. Provence was also the first maker of rosé in the world. Its quality is unassailable, but it is regrettable that it eclipses the crystalline whites and complex reds also worth drinking.

Choose a wine

Even the simplest rosés are fruit bombs, with perfumes of strawberry, raspberry, and candy. There are some rosés that are more complex, with a gastronomic allure perfectly suited to drink with a meal, even when summer is over. They take on aromas of flowers and wild herbs, mint and dill.

White grape varieties:
Rolle (Vermentino), White Grenache, Clairette, Bouboulenc, Ugni Blanc

Red grape varieties:
Carignan, Syrah, Grenache, Cinsaut, Mourvèdre, Cabernet Sauvignon

Rosés: about 45%
Reds: about 40%
Whites: about 15%

Delicate and absolutely worthy of interest, white wines from Corsica are delicious, aromatic blends with the freshness of wild herbs and the finesse of flowers. The reds from the Patrimonio appellation are no exception. The popularity of Muscat du Cap Corse, a vin doux naturel *("naturally sweet wine"), has grown rapidly.*

White grape varieties:
Vermentino, Muscat

Red grape varieties:
Nielluccio, Sciacarello, Grenache

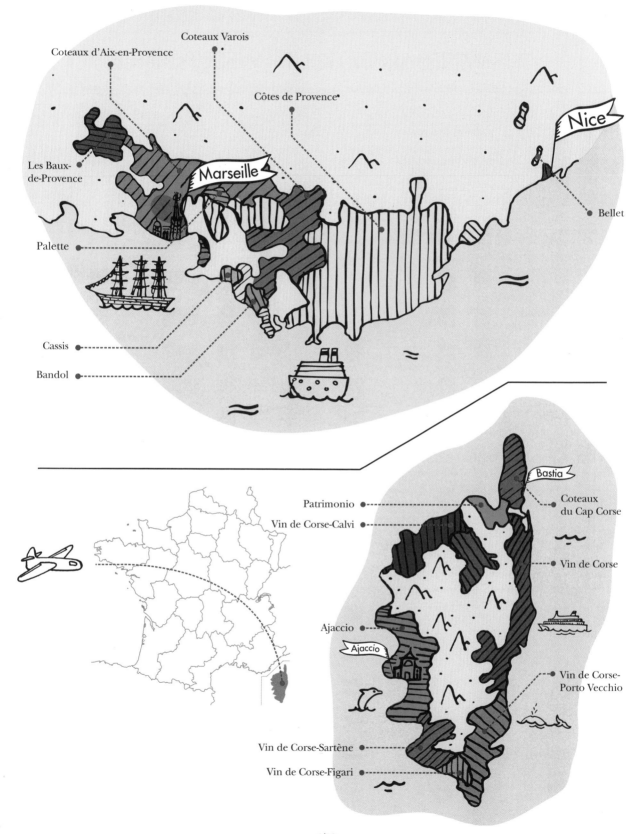

Coteaux Varois

Coteaux d'Aix-en-Provence

Côtes de Provence

Nice

Les Baux-
de-Provence

Marseille

Palette

Bellet

Cassis

Bandol

Patrimonio

Bastia

Coteaux
du Cap Corse

Vin de Corse-Calvi

Vin de Corse

Ajaccio

Ajaccio

Vin de Corse-
Porto Vecchio

Vin de Corse-Sartène

Vin de Corse-Figari

THE WINES FROM SOUTH WEST FRANCE

Reds and rosés:
about 80%
Whites: about 20%

HOW TO FIND IT?

The vineyards of South West France are very scattered, in clusters of little viticultural zones, from Bordeaux to the Basque country. Although the wines have in common a friendliness, a rugged and endearing character, the grape varietals that they're made from are quite varied and reflect the diversity of the region.

Good deals

Although the quality of the wines from the region directly affect their price, there are some good deals to be had. Sweet whites are particularly attractive and they are a lot less expensive here than in Bordeaux—the Monbazillac, after a soft period, is recovering a bit of acidity and the Jurançon continues its rise. The Pacherenc du Vic-Bilh, ignored despite its complexity and delicacy, is truly a good deal.
The dry whites generally don't cost very much. The supple reds are rather good deals. The Madirans, outside of some star wineries that have explosive prices, are still affordable given their longevity.

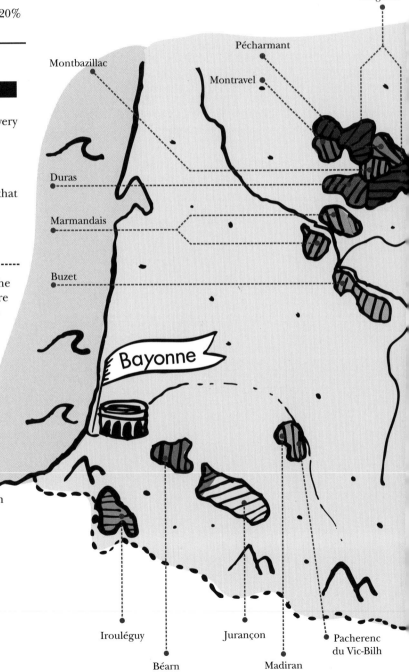

Montbazillac

Bergerac

Pécharmant

Montravel

Duras

Marmandais

Buzet

Bayonne

Irouléguy

Béarn

Jurançon

Madiran

Pacherenc du Vic-Bilh

Caroline vists the vineyards

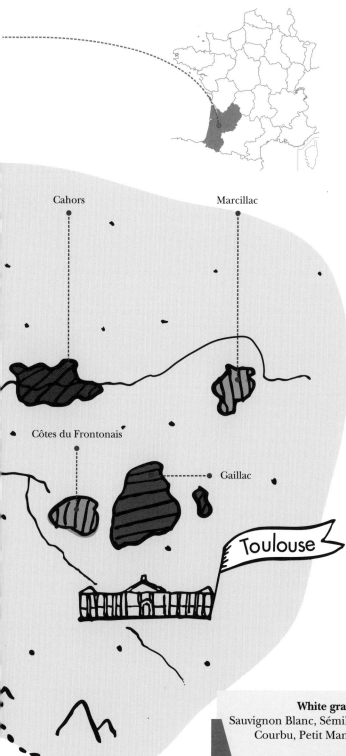

Varietals

Bergerac and Marmandais, near the capital of Gironde, use Bordeaux grape varietals including Cabernet Sauvignon and Merlot. At Cahors, Malbec is king. Fronton uses an honored local grape varietal called Négrette, a lot like Madiran with its intense Tannat grape.

The countryside also grows a wide variety of white grapes, from the classic Bordeaux duo of Sauvignon Blanc and Sémillon to the baroque couple Petit Manseng and Gros Manseng, further south.

Taste

The mosaic of *terroirs* is very much reflected in the glass. Near Bordeaux, the wines naturally resemble Bordeaux wines, but maybe with a little more *bonhomie*. The farther inland you go, the more the wine takes on muscle, structure, spices on the nose, and mouthfeel. Cahors unwinds a host of chocolatey aromas, from cocoa to praline. Irouléguy leans more toward wildflowers and woodland scents. Négrette from Fronton has a perfume that is very much like violets.

Aging

While the people there appreciate drinking these wines while they're young, it has taken years for Madiran and Cahors to refine their wines with extremely solid and vigorous tannins. This makes them good wines for aging, to bring out in ten to twenty years.

White grape varieties:
Sauvignon Blanc, Sémillon, Muscadelle, Mauzac, Courbu, Petit Manseng, Gros Manseng

Red grape varieties:
Cabernet Sauvignon, Cabernet Franc, Merlot, Malbec, Tannat, Négrette, Fer Servadou

THE WINES FROM THE LOIRE VALLEY

Whites:
about 55%
Reds and rosés:
about 45%

HOW TO FIND IT?

The Loire Valley is the most widespread viticultural area in France. Part of it meets the Atlantic Ocean near Nantes then goes up the Loire to Orléans and Bourges.
This region offers all types of wine: white, rosé, red, soft, sweet, and sparkling. A lot of young vineyards are planted in the region, and winemakers are achieving true prowess, offering little gems at all prices and in all styles.
There are four distinct big zones: the Nantes region, Anjou, Touraine, and the Central Loire. Each has a very different personality.

The big regions

Size matters. Appellations are numerous but not hierarchical.
The differences between the wines are, however, enormous. Each region has its favorite varietals.

The Nantes region

Muscadet reigns in this area (the Burgundy varietal Melon de Bourgogne). This wine, never known for its great quality, is experiencing a rebirth. Muscadet grapes turn into dry and acidic wines of great quality, which allows them to age several years, and are a good choice for a low-priced aperitif. In the hills of Ancenis, you'll find a lively and light red from Gamay.

Anjou, Saumur, and Touraine

In these regions, the wines have more fullness and structure. The wine uses a base of Chenin Blanc, which gives it great aromatic richness, in dry and in sweet wines.

The dry wines are, to the happiness of our wallets, unjustly unknown and sometimes grandiose. The soft and sweet versions of these wines are perfect for dessert and can be kept for several decades. Their aromas are very complex and evoke white flowers, honey, and quince. The Chenin Blanc also produces elegant sparkling wines.
In red, the Cabernet Francs can be kept for between two and ten years. They present a lot of freshness and suppleness, with aromas of raspberry and strawberry. Easy to drink, they are the joy of Parisian bistros. Simpler and lighter still is Gamay. On the other hand, the rosés from Anjou don't hold a lot of gustatory interest.

Central Loire

Sauvignon Blanc reigns as master. Thanks to this region, and to Sancerre in particular, this wine is known everywhere for its very expressive aromas, of tender grass, lemon, and grapefruit. Its prices however are also higher, and you'd do better to look to neighboring appellations, such as Menetou-Salon or Reuilly, to find a more affordable version. Red wine from the Central Loire is, like a Burgundy, made with Pinot Noir. Supple and fruity, it can even accompany fish.

White grape varieties:
Melon de Bourgogne, Chenin Blanc, Sauvignon Blanc, Chardonnay

Red grape varieties:
Cabernet Franc, Gamay, Pinot Noir

Caroline vists the vineyards

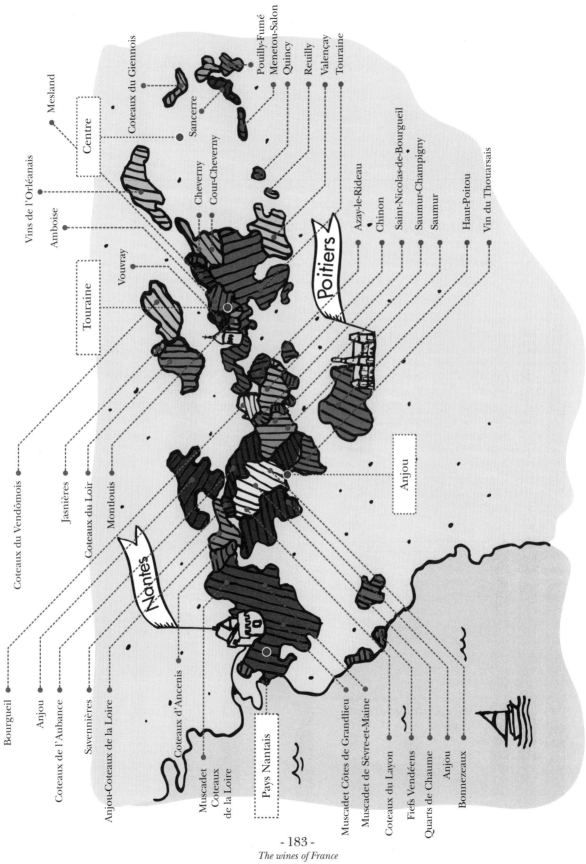

Mesland

Vins de l'Orléanais

Centre

Amboise

Coteaux du Giennois

Sancerre

Pouilly-Fumé
Menetou-Salon
Quincy
Reuilly
Valençay
Touraine

Cheverny
Cour-Cheverny

Touraine

Vouvray

Azay-le-Rideau
Chinon
Saint-Nicolas-de-Bourgueil
Saumur-Champigny
Saumur

Haut-Poitou
Vin du Thouarsais

Poitiers

Coteaux du Vendômois

Jasnières

Coteaux du Loir

Montlouis

Anjou

Bourgueil

Anjou

Coteaux de l'Aubance

Savennières

Anjou-Coteaux de la Loire

Nantes

Coteaux d'Ancenis

Pays Nantais

Muscadet
Coteaux
de la Loire

Muscadet Côtes de Grandlieu

Muscadet de Sèvre-et-Maine

Coteaux du Layon

Fiefs Vendéens

Quarts de Chaume

Anjou

Bonnezeaux

WINES FROM THE RHÔNE VALLEY

Reds and rosés:
about 90%
Whites:
about 10%

The regions and the grape varieties

Vineyards from the Côtes du Rhône consist of two principal regions: Northern Rhône up to Valence, and Southern Rhône. In the north, the reds are exclusively produced with Syrah and the whites are mainly made from Viognier, but you will also find some made with Marsanne and Roussanne. In the south, the number of varietals is a lot higher: at Châteauneuf-du-Pape, for example, thirteen grape varietals are authorized to be used for making red wine blends. In addition to the white, red, and rosé wines, the Rhône offers some naturally sweet wines, with a base of Muscat for the whites (Muscat de Beaumes-de-Venise) and Grenache for the reds (Rasteau). Finally, there are sparkling wines made with Muscat and Clairette from the Clairette de Die region.

The taste

Syrah from the north end of the Côtes du Rhône produces powerful and tannic wines that are racy, with aromas of pepper and cassis (black currant). In their youth, the tannins can render them austere, but they loosen up after several years to become sublime. In the south, the wine is also powerful, sometimes even more so, but it is also rounder, thanks to the addition of Grenache. In both camps, there are wines that are extremely famous, Côte-Rôtie and Hermitage on one side, and Châteauneuf-du-Pape on the other. When it comes to whites, those from the north are exceptional: the Condrieu and the Château-Grillet are among the most aromatic in the world, and Viognier explodes in flowers, cream, and apricot. The quality of the white wines from the south is more varied. They can express charming aromas of beeswax, chamomile, and *fines herbes*. But if the sun is too intense, they can become watery. This is equally true for the reds and the rosés from Tavel, which can be tasty when they are not too overwhelming. It's common to see alcohol percentages on these wines as high as 15 percent! The alcohol and the tannins are often enveloped by the fat of the wine, which makes it very easy to drink—and get a little too tipsy!

White grape varieties:
Viognier, Marsanne, Roussane, Clairette, Bourboulenc, Picpoul, Grenache Blanc, Ugni Blanc

Red grape varieties:
Syrah, Grenache, Mourvèdre, Carignan, Cinsaut, Counoise, Vaccarèse

Caroline vists the vineyards

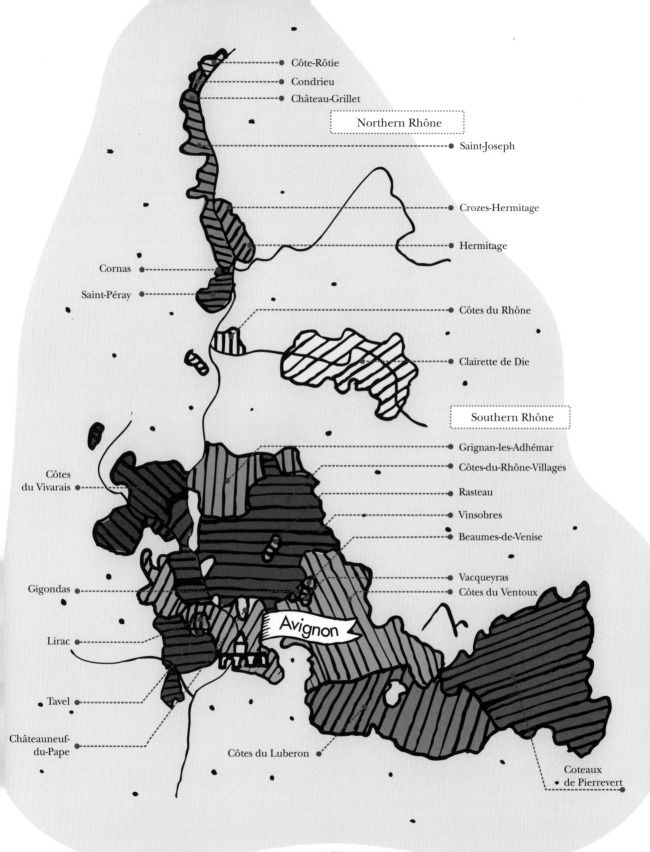

Côte-Rôtie
Condrieu
Château-Grillet

Northern Rhône

Saint-Joseph

Crozes-Hermitage

Hermitage

Cornas
Saint-Péray

Côtes du Rhône

Clairette de Die

Southern Rhône

Grignan-les-Adhémar
Côtes-du-Rhône-Villages
Côtes
du Vivarais
Rasteau

Vinsobres

Beaumes-de-Venise

Gigondas
Vacqueyras
Côtes du Ventoux

Avignon

Lirac

Tavel

Châteauneuf-
du-Pape
Côtes du Luberon

Coteaux
de Pierrevert

WINES FROM OTHER REGIONS OF FRANCE

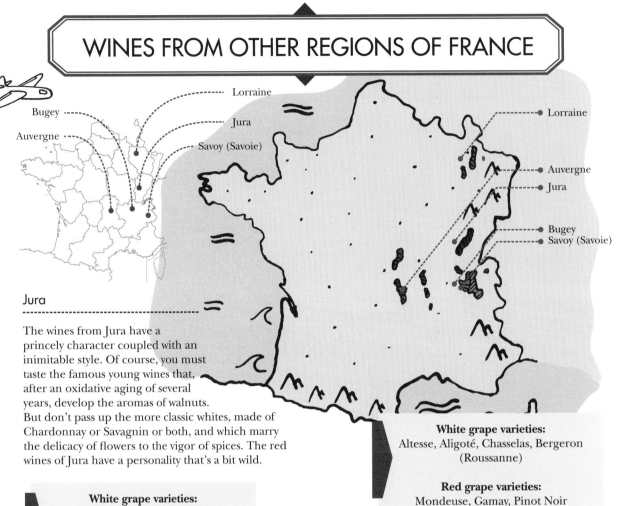

Jura

The wines from Jura have a princely character coupled with an inimitable style. Of course, you must taste the famous young wines that, after an oxidative aging of several years, develop the aromas of walnuts.
But don't pass up the more classic whites, made of Chardonnay or Savagnin or both, and which marry the delicacy of flowers to the vigor of spices. The red wines of Jura have a personality that's a bit wild.

White grape varieties:
Chardonnay, Savagnin

Red grape varieties:
Poulsard, Trousseau, Pinot Noir

Bugey

At the crossroads of cultures between Jura, the Savoy, and Burgundy, the wines of Bugey can be sparkling, white, red, or rosé. Exemplary, reds are made from Mondeuse, Pinot Noir, Gamay, and Poulsard du Jura.

Lorraine

Known for its "gray rosé" wines from Toul (in fact, the rosés are the color of onion skin), the region also produces whites close in style to those of Alsace-Moselle.

White grape varieties:
Altesse, Aligoté, Chasselas, Bergeron (Roussanne)

Red grape varieties:
Mondeuse, Gamay, Pinot Noir

Auvergne

The vines of Auvergne are interesting for their production of Gamay and Pinot Noir. They make a fruity and very light red wine at Saint-Pourçain-sur-Sioule and the Côtes d'Auvergne.
It is sometimes more structured, depending on the color in the skins and the producer's deft hand. The Roanne coast produces reds and rosés that are also fruity.

Savoy (Savoie)

The Savoy produces very acidic whites, which often accompany Savoy fondues, but the wines based on Bergeron (the local name for Roussanne) are smoother and great to serve with fish dishes. The reds have a wild berry, pepper, and hummus character, and you can age them a few years before drinking them.

WINES FROM GERMANY

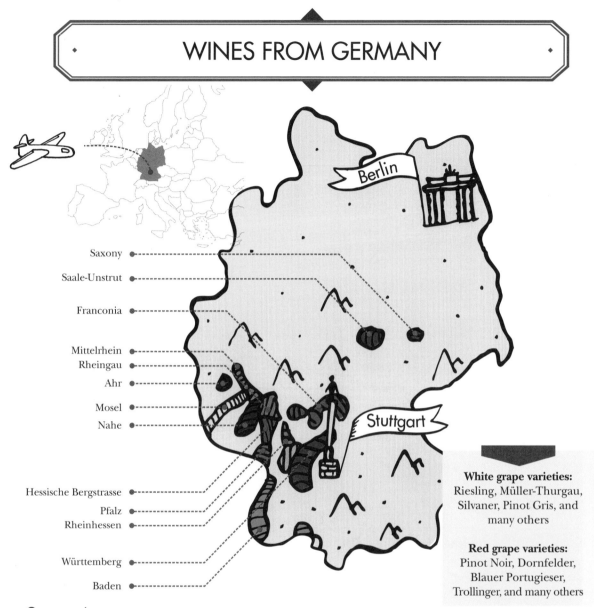

Saxony
Saale-Unstrut
Franconia
Mittelrhein
Rheingau
Ahr
Mosel
Nahe
Hessische Bergstrasse
Pfalz
Rheinhessen
Württemberg
Baden

Berlin

Stuttgart

White grape varieties:
Riesling, Müller-Thurgau,
Silvaner, Pinot Gris, and
many others

Red grape varieties:
Pinot Noir, Dornfelder,
Blauer Portugieser,
Trollinger, and many others

German wines

Vineyards in Germany encompass thirteen regions, all situated in the southern reaches of the country where the climate is milder. These wines are less well-known to the general public, but the big German white wines are among the most elegant in the world and can hold up for several decades. They have a great acidity with a little sugar to keep them balanced. Unfortunately, there are some less pleasing wines too, so leave the less aromatic varietals alone and opt for the Riesling, a carefully cultivated grape in high demand. Its character varies depending upon the *terroir*. The best

grow along the banks of the Mosel River, in the Rheingau, the Hessische Bergstrasse or the Pfalz. Germany also produces red wines that are bright and fruity.

Sugar content

German wines are often sweet or semi-sweet and the label identifies each type. From driest to sweetest: Kabinett, Spätlese, Auslese, Beerenauslese, Trockenbeerenauslese, and Eiswein (Ice wine).

The regions

Switzerland is at the crossroads of three great viticultural countries, France, Italy, and Germany, so it's no surprise that it produces wines similar to those of its neighbors. Three-quarters of the vineyards are situated in French-speaking Switzerland (Romandy), and nearly all the rest is in the north of German-speaking Switzerland. The Italian canton of Ticino, at the extreme south of the country, specializes in Merlot. Valais is a fascinating region to discover, because it abounds in grape varieties that no longer exist anywhere else.

The grape varietals

Switzerland is the only country that knows how to get the best out of Chasselas, a less aromatic variety (called Fendant in the Valais). Here it becomes a sharp white wine, often beading in its youth, with aromas of green apple and fern. When made by the best producers, it exudes purity. Chasselas cultivation takes up nearly 75 percent of all the vineyards. The reds, based on Gamay, are jammy or wild on the nose, but light on the palate.

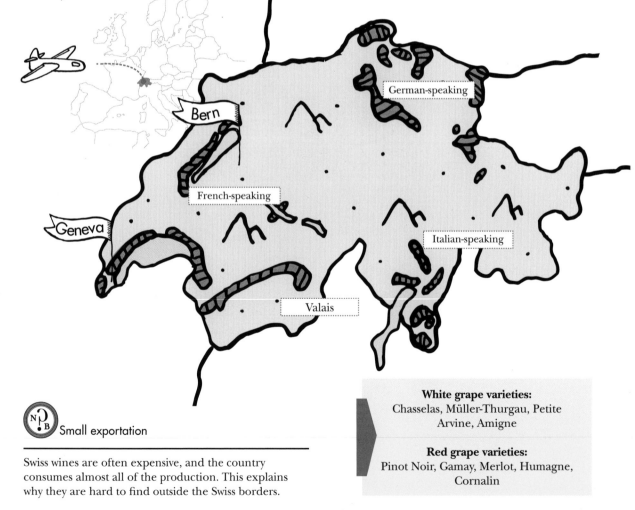

German-speaking

Bern

French-speaking

Geneva

Italian-speaking

Valais

Small exportation

Swiss wines are often expensive, and the country consumes almost all of the production. This explains why they are hard to find outside the Swiss borders.

White grape varieties:
Chasselas, Müller-Thurgau, Petite Arvine, Amigne

Red grape varieties:
Pinot Noir, Gamay, Merlot, Humagne, Cornalin

Caroline vists the vineyards

WINES FROM PORTUGAL

Portugal is first, and above all, known for producing the best sweet wine in the world, capable of aging and improving over decades: Port.
The country also invented Madeira, which is drier than Port, with smoky aromas. These two fortified wines, sold all over the world, make you nearly forget that Portugal also knows how to produce good red and white wines.

The other wines

Vinho Verde ("green wine") is a very young white wine. It's aggressive, with a freshness that makes it appealing in summer, and it's ridiculously inexpensive. The red wines from the Douro Valley, where they make Port, are rich in fruits and spices. You must taste these wines, developed from Touriga Nacional grapes–the grape of Port–with their sunny aromas of resin, blackberry, and pine. In the South, the Alentejo produces wines that are more supple and fruity that improve over time.

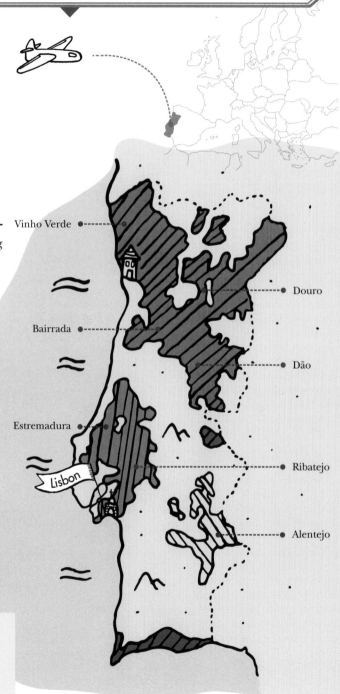

White grape varieties:
Loureiro, Treixadura, Arinto, Malvasia

Red grape varieties:
Touriga Nacional, Tinta Pinheira (Rufete), Tinta Roriz, Tempranillo, Souzãho (Vinhão)

WINES FROM ITALY

The Italian vineyard, as rich, complex, and passionate as the French vineyard, never ceases to amaze wine lovers. If the Italian production sold in the 1980s with an image of little charming and inexpensive wines, it has since regained its titles of noblesse. There are now all kinds of wine: some very good, some excellent sparklings and formidable reds, from more fruity to more powerful, wines with finesse, exuberance, seduction. There's something for every taste.

A multiplicity of *terroirs*

Such diversity of style is defined by the infinite variations of climate. Along the mountain to the edge of the sea, the hillside vineyards benefit from the influence of both types of climates. And the limestone soil in the north and volcanic soil in the south give the wines a range of character.
Italian wines profit also from the impressive number of native wine grape varieties that cover the region. There are more than 1,000 varietals in the country, of which 400 are officially recognized! You'll understand then that with such numbers of *terroirs*, Italy has no reason to envy France. Then add the complexity of appellations, and the variations become incomprehensible, even to the Italians. It gets to the point that the name of a producer takes precedence over the appellation.

The big regions

Wine is produced almost everywhere in the country. Italy and France argue all the time about which country is the premiere producer in the world. At the very least, Italy leads in exports.

The North West

Lombardy (Val d'Aosta, and specifically Piedmont) is a region of beefy red wines. Barolo and Barbaresco, which come from tannic Nebbiolo grapes, are global giants. They have strong tannins and powerful aromatics (leather, tobacco, tar, prune, rose). The tannins are persistent, unless you choose vintages aged at least fifteen years. They are otherwise very expensive. The Barbera varietal, less costly but more widespread, is less tannic and more acidic.
The wines produced in Dolcetto are very fruity and bittersweet in the mouth.

The North East

This region, composed of Veneto, Friuli, and Trentino, produces airy, elegant, nearly sparkling whites, which are ideal for aperitifs or for accompanying light dishes. Prosecco, which is very well known, is as lively and fresh as a Champagne. When it comes to reds, the celebrated Valpolicellas are very light.

The Center

Tuscany is the country's premier viticultural region. The top grape in Tuscany is Sangiovese, which gives birth to the famous Chiantis, and their quality never ceases to get better. It's a favorite companion for tomato-based dishes. But true wine lovers prefer the Brunello di Montalcino, which is fruity but more structured, and the Vino Nobile di Montepulciano. There are also wines called Super Tuscans, which use a base of Bordeaux grapes (Merlot and Cabernet) mixed with Italian grape varieties, but they are extremely expensive.

The South

This is a region of discoveries and good deals. In fact, the wines there are rarely expensive and the grape varieties grown here make wines with rare personality, from the peppery Aglianico to Primitivo, with its scents of almond, to the Negroamaro and Nero d'Avola, which both produce wines of great quality. As for the whites, there are equally fascinating wines, dry and sweet, not to mention Marsala.

Caroline vists the vineyards

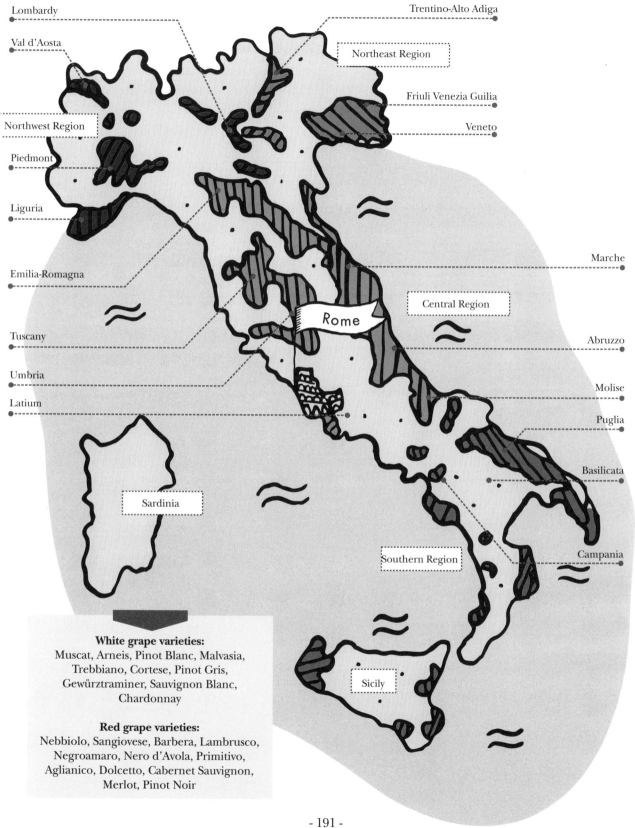

Lombardy

Val d'Aosta

Northwest Region

Piedmont

Liguria

Emilia-Romagna

Tuscany

Umbria

Latium

Trentino-Alto Adiga

Northeast Region

Friuli Venezia Guilia

Veneto

Marche

Central Region

Rome

Abruzzo

Molise

Puglia

Basilicata

Campania

Sardinia

Southern Region

Sicily

White grape varieties:
Muscat, Arneis, Pinot Blanc, Malvasia,
Trebbiano, Cortese, Pinot Gris,
Gewürztraminer, Sauvignon Blanc,
Chardonnay

Red grape varieties:
Nebbiolo, Sangiovese, Barbera, Lambrusco,
Negroamaro, Nero d'Avola, Primitivo,
Aglianico, Dolcetto, Cabernet Sauvignon,
Merlot, Pinot Noir

WINES FROM SPAIN

Spain is the third-largest producer of wine in the world, as well as the third-largest exporter. One reason it's so successful is that the country produces all styles of wine, from easy-to-drink to more structured, from very simple to highly prestigious. Midrange Spanish wines are often full-bodied with a lot of fruit. These wines are full of camaraderie and smiles, and are very friendly. To drink them is to immerse oneself in the same frame of mind.

The Northeast

Penedès

This region produces full-bodied, powerful whites and intense reds, but it's really known for its specialty: Cava. This sparkling wine, produced like Champagne, is getting better and better and remains a good deal. It is consumed in the same manner as its French cousin—for festive occasions, as an aperitif, and for lighter moments.

Priorat

Its production is adored by intense wine lovers. It is almost exclusively devoted to concentrated, red wines that are very ripe, with great intensity. They keep a long time in the cellar. Their renown is enormous, as are their prices.

Navarra

The wine style of Navarra has been close to those of Rioja for a long time: fruity and velvety. But the region has diversified and now you'll find numerous Spanish and international varietals as well as wines with diverse characteristics, from crisp whites to oaky barrel-aged reds. There's a range of round, enjoyable, easy-to-drink wines.

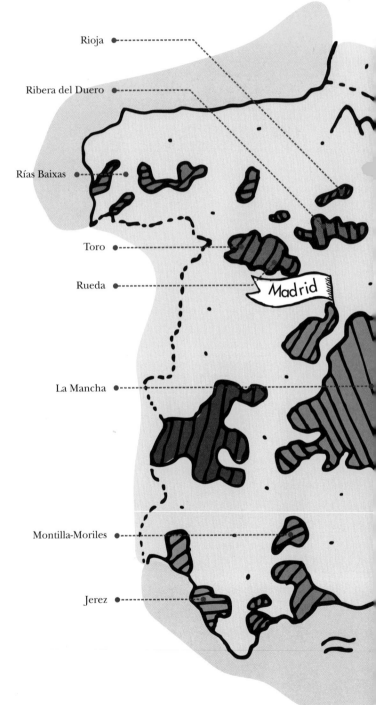

Rioja

Ribera del Duero

Rías Baixas

Toro

Rueda

Madrid

La Mancha

Montilla-Moriles

Jerez

Caroline vists the vineyards

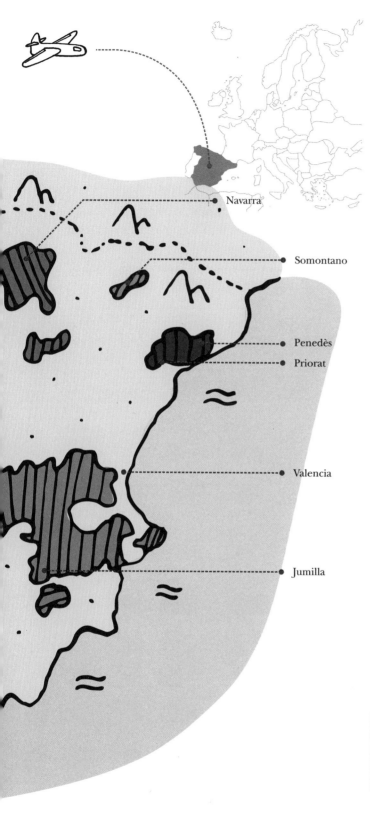

North and Northwest

Rioja

The traditional red wines of the region are well known, and they are all about roundness, with silky texture and vanilla and fruity notes. But Rioja also develops wines that can be lighter or denser, depending on the winery making it. Whites are often powerful with aromas of pralines.

Ribera del Duero

These wines are among the most sought after in the country for their structure, their blackness, and their depth, but, alas, they are terribly expensive.

Toro

Although less complex and more robust than the Ribera del Duero wines, they are an interesting alternative at a lower price.

Rueda

Here you'll find excellent whites, fresh and astringent, with aromas of tender grass, developed from the Verdejo grape.

Central and South

La Mancha

These wines are honest, simple, fruity, and accessible in all colors, like the wines from Valdepeñas. Manchuela wines are more complex and more expensive.

Jerez

The homeland of fantastic Sherry. In contrast to its sweet counterpart, the most bewitching is dry Sherry.

> **White grape varieties:**
> Verdejo, Albariño, Sauvignon Blanc, Muscat, Parellada, Macabeo, Chardonnay, Malvasia
>
> **Red grape varieties:**
> Grenache, Tempranillo, Carignan, Mourvèdre, Cabernet Sauvignon

WINES FROM GREECE

The vineyards in Greece have had a checkered past. Its wines have been among the most studied from antiquity to the Middle Ages. But then the vines collapsed from the fifteenth century until the nineteenth century, after the war of independence. Over the last several decades, the country has planted its 300 native varietals with an aim to build up its reputation for producing fine wines. Today you'll find whites with great mineral purity from its volcanic soils, sweet Muscats from the island of Samos, dense red wines that age well from the heights of the Peloponnese, and very beautiful reds and rosés from Macedonia. Unfortunately, the economic crisis in Greece has had a big impact on the industry and it has forced a drop in consumption of wine. Let's hope it doesn't suffer too much.

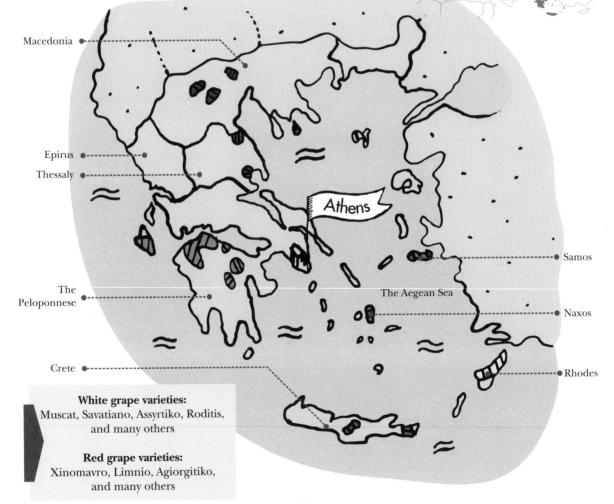

Macedonia

Epirus

Thessaly

Athens

The Peloponnese

The Aegean Sea

Samos

Naxos

Crete

Rhodes

White grape varieties:
Muscat, Savatiano, Assyrtiko, Roditis, and many others

Red grape varieties:
Xinomavro, Limnio, Agiorgitiko, and many others

Caroline vists the vineyards

Bulgaria, Slovenia, Serbia, Romania—these old vineyards may surprise us in the next few years. Wine is an old tradition in the Balkan states, but the communist period hurt the vineyards. Happily, over the past fifteen years or so, new winemakers have rebuilt the wineries and have turned their eyes to the forgotten varietals.

In **Serbia**, for example, a former prime minister recently became a winemaker! With the help of some young winemakers, he will hopefully give a boost to this vineyard, which was prosperous in the nineteenth century, but fell into disrepair. It still has a good reputation and has good potential to succeed.

Macedonia makes good red wines, **Moldavia** profits from the aid of the European Union, which has helped them modernize their production facilities. **Slovakia** produces whites that are becoming increasingly well known in international tasting rooms. Revered around the world, Tokaji from **Hungary** (also known as Tokay) is a sweet wine that can be aged for a hundred years. It has lovely aromas of honey and a surprisingly long mouthfeel. The country produces very nice dry whites and sweet wines.

Farther away, in the eastern Mediterranean, the little island of **Cyprus** carefully nurtures its vineyards, and its wines enjoy an excellent reputation that far exceeds its borders. The country is predominantly known for its sweet wine from dried grapes, the Commandaria, but also knows how to make hearty red wines.

Some popular wines:
Hungarian Tokaji,
Commandaria

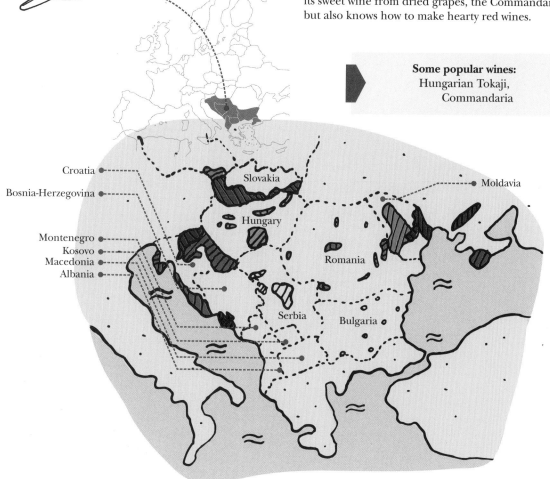

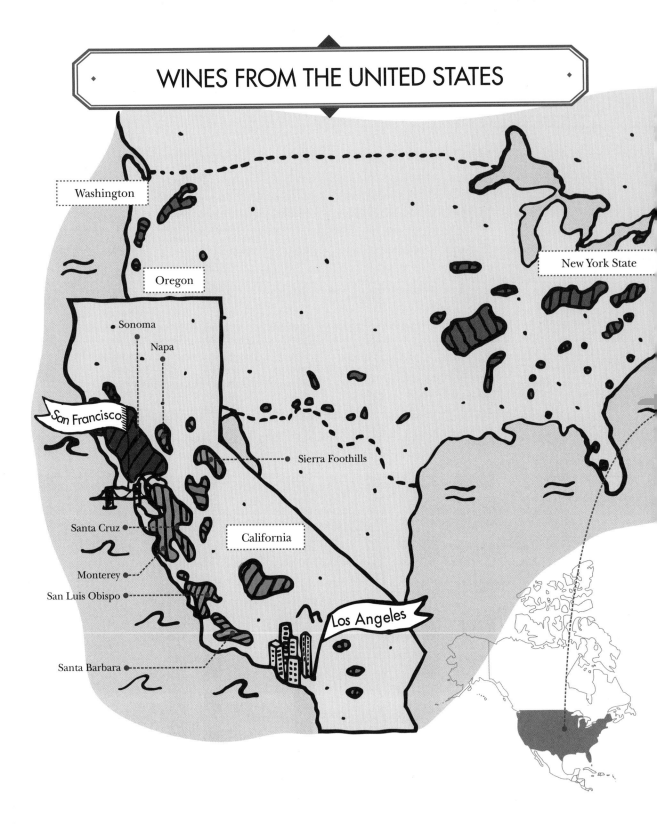

WINES FROM THE UNITED STATES

Washington

Oregon

New York State

Sonoma

Napa

San Francisco

Sierra Foothills

Santa Cruz

California

Monterey

San Luis Obispo

Los Angeles

Santa Barbara

Caroline vists the vineyards

The United States is the birthplace of the New World wines. Their style is different from that of Old World, European wines. There is more sweetness present in the red wines, the whites are oakier and creamier, and there's more forward fruitiness in both reds and whites.

These wines are referred to as "modern," a term increasingly common in some French vineyards, and evidence of the influence that American wines now have on the wine world. Critics accuse them of displaying a character that is too seductive. This is sometimes true, but they have the advantage of being easy to drink. The United States also produces some small wines that are practically works of art. Today, the greatest wines from California and Oregon compare in price to major Bordeaux and Burgundy wines.

Understanding New World wines is a lot easier than understanding those from Europe. There are fewer appellations, and they are more spread out. And the rules governing them are much less complicated. The wines are traditionally labeled with the main grape variety, and there are only about a dozen.

The United States is the fourth largest producer of wine in the world, behind France, Italy, and Spain. Today, almost every state makes wine, but California alone accounts for almost 90 percent of the entire American production!

White grape varieties:
Chardonnay, Sauvignon Blanc, Riesling

Red grape varieties:
Merlot, Cabernet Sauvignon, Syrah, Grenache, Zinfandel, Pinot Noir, Barbera

California

Bright sunshine and little rainfall gives rise to wonderfully ripe grapes. Aromatic richness and fullness in the mouth are the signature of California wines. California brings together ideal soil and climate, the best wine university in the country, and above all, people who love wine! Admittedly, Italian and Spanish immigrants brought centuries of winemaking traditions in their luggage when they arrived there. The best producing regions are located along the northern coast of California, where the fresh breezes of the Pacific Ocean slow the maturity of the grapes. There are two main regions—to the north and to the south of the San Francisco Bay. The north coast is a paradise for wine lovers and includes the most famous appellations, including the Napa Valley and the Russian River in Sonoma. The Central Coast stretches from San Francisco to Santa Barbara and has some appellations to watch including Paso Robles and Monterey. The Central Valley produces decent table wine, but its climate is too hot to make super high-quality wines.

The North Coast

Located north of San Francisco, this is the most prestigious area within the United States for its vineyards. There are four major zones: Mendocino, Sonoma, Lake County, and Napa Valley.
Sonoma was long considered the little sister of Napa, and though it had excellent wines, they sold for much less. But a new generation of winemakers have been quick to align their prices with those of their prestigious neighbors while, fortunately, continuing to raise the quality of their wines.
Sonoma has a varied environment. Near water, as in the Russian River Valley and Carneros, fog from the sea is common, and it's here that we find varieties that thrive in cool climates: Chardonnay, Sauvignon Blanc, and Pinot Noir. There are good sparkling wines, too, in particular from Carneros. Away from the coast, including Alexander Valley and Dry Creek Valley, the weather is warmer and more conducive to producing powerful reds from Cabernet Sauvignon or Zinfandel. A little farther north, in Mendocino, the landscape is similar to Sonoma, and you will appreciate this region's Zinfandels and sparkling wines.

The Napa Valley is the most famous of all, and although it has densely planted vines and some 400 wine producers, it is actually smaller than Sonoma. Bordered by a chain of mountains, temperatures in the Napa Valley are more constant—that is, hot. This is ideal for creating typical Bordeaux blends of Merlot and Cabernet Sauvignon (also called Meritage). One finds the duo both in plain designations like Rutherford and on the steeper terrain of Howell Mountain and Stags Leap. Although less known, Lake County offers features similar to the northern Napa Valley.

Finally, in the northeast of the state, near Sacramento, the Sierra Foothills provide the ideal conditions for Syrahs and Zinfandels that are sturdy and plump as can be.

Red wines from California

Cabernet Sauvignon, or King Cab, is powerful and fruity: a reflection of the California sun. In the Napa Valley and Paso Robles, you'll find some that are internationally renowned. Napa has also specialized in Bordeaux-style wines. And any doubt about the quality of these great Napa reds compared to those of Bordeaux was dispelled in 1976, during the famous Paris competition where a Winiarski Cabernet beat out every Premier Cru French wine there.

Zinfandel was thought to be a variety of American origin until recently. It makes wines that are structured and tasty, and it likes warm climates, which draws out color and alcohol, and gives the wine flavors of stewed fruit. The oldest vineyards are located in Lodi and Dry Creek.

Merlot is often underestimated, and you'll find excellent ones in Napa. This is a velvety red wine that's very aromatic, with supple tannins and not too oaky.

Pinot Noir is both seductive and very structured. It thrives on the breezy coasts of Sonoma, Santa Barbara, and Monterey.

The Central Coast

This region extends south from the San Francisco Bay area to Santa Barbara. Its valleys are often quite cool, thanks to the wind that blows in from the Pacific. There are some excellent Chardonnays, Pinot Noirs, and Syrahs from as far north as Santa Cruz and Monterey to San Luis Obispo and on to the southern reaches of Santa Barbara.

The Santa Cruz Mountain vineyards have been around longer than those in Napa. Surrounded by forests, grapes are difficult to grow but can create inexpensive reds with good aging potential.

Monterey Bay, at its best, is sunny and produces equally sunny Chardonnays.

Santa Barbara offers a multitude of microclimates with temperatures that jump from one plot to the next. Newer winegrowing areas like the Santa Maria Valley, Santa Ynez Valley, and Santa Rita Hills are covered with small vineyards offering a wide variety of grapes, from very Burgundian Pinot Noir to the very Rhône-like Syrah. The area around Paso Robles is growing very quickly and has a very promising future. It is revered for its dense and powerful reds, Cabernet Sauvignon and Zinfandel.

White wines from California

Chardonnay is the number-one grape in California, and it produces rich, buttery wines that are fruity and sometimes taste toasty if kept in barrels.

Sauvignon Blanc (sometimes called Fumé Blanc) is bright and sharp but generally less acidic and vegetal than in Europe. It is not uncommon to find aromas of pineapple.

White grapes grow throughout California, but it's in the coastal regions where Chardonnay, Viognier, Riesling, or Sauvignon Blanc are able to keep their beautiful acidity. Chardonnay reigns in Sonoma, but the Russian River Valley is also very welcoming to Pinot Gris. Mendocino, with its cooler climate, is very suitable for Riesling and Gewürztraminer. Superb Sauvignon Blancs can be found in Napa Valley. That said, between Mendocino and Santa Barbara, you can grow almost any variety.

Other American States

Today all states in the U.S. produce wine, but not all can grow quality grapes. So they buy the grapes or the must (the freshly pressed juice) from winemakers in neighboring states and ferment in their own facilities. Despite this, 98 percent of American production is in the hands of just four states: California, New York, Washington, and Oregon. If California is the biggest American producer by far, New York and Washington are next, producing approximately 4 percent each. Although they have an excellent reputation, Oregon produces only 0.9 percent of the total wine production in the United States. Very close behind Oregon are Texas, Virginia, Pennsylvania, New Jersey, and Ohio. Note: AVAs (American Viticultural Areas) are equivalent to AOCs in France. They refer to defined geographical areas where viticulture plays an important role. In contrast, and unlike French or Italian regulations, they do not specify any mandatory requirements nor set limits on grape yields, which leaves a lot of freedom to the tenants.

Washington and Oregon are geographically close, yet their styles of wine are quite different. Oregon is known for its tiny boutique production of Pinot Noir, while Washington offers large amounts of Merlot, Cabernet Sauvignon, Chardonnay, and Riesling at affordable prices.

Oregon

The main wine-producing region of Oregon is the Willamette Valley south of Portland. From the mountains of the Cascade Range in the east to the Pacific Ocean in the west, the valley is perfect for Pinot Noir, which demands a relatively cool climate. In fact, it's there that you will find showcased treasures of delicacy, and these wines are among the highest rated in the world. As you might guess, prices tend to be pretty steep.

The wines

Pinot Noir is one of the most beautiful expressions of the grape outside of Burgundy, with elegant aromas of strawberry, cherry, and underbrush, couched in a silky and balanced mouthfeel.

Pinot Gris here is heavier than the ones produced in Italy, but it's lighter than its French equivalent. Pinot Gris from Oregon is often balanced, dry, and unoaked. It has flavors of pear, apple, and sometimes melon.

Washington

East of the Cascades lies Columbia Valley. This large region dotted with vineyards is an arid plateau where the sun beats down and gives rise to dark and powerful wines. But the night is as cold as the day is hot, which prevents the grapes from burning and ensures wines have good acidity. These temperature differences are accompanied by essential irrigation and careful attention to detail, the efforts of a group determined to produce the richest and most flavorful wines in the country. This area is very promising!

The wines

Syrah is intense in all respects: in its color, in its spicy aromas, and in its structure on the palate. The wines from this grape are richer here than from the French Rhône and more powerful than from Australia.

Merlot exploits the uncommon power in the Columbia Valley, far from the light and fruity standards to which it is too often confined.

Riesling's character is close to the German version: floral and slightly sweet.

There are also Chardonnay, Cabernet Sauvignon, and Cabernet Franc, which are all expressed with opulence.

The Midwest

Colorado, New Mexico, Texas, and Missouri also make wine! Because of the climate, they are rarely wines worth aging because they lack the needed acidity. But thanks to the inclusion of international varietals, there are some nice young drinkable wines to be had. The vineyards are no longer regarded as an extravagance that will go out of fashion. And Texas has announced its commitment by launching an ad campaign with this slogan a few years ago: "Wine, the next big thing from Texas!"

Vines also grow in Ohio and Michigan, where the sun is more discreet. As in the Canadian province of Ontario, they grow varieties that are used to the cold including Riesling, Cabernet Franc, and Pinot Noir. They create crisp and refreshing wines.

The East Coast

The state of New York is no slouch when it comes to wine! Their volume of production follows close on the heels of the state of Washington. There are about 150 wine producers, versus the thousand producers of grape juice. Indeed, the grapes barely have a chance to ripen and winemakers often have to add sugar. Rieslings and Chardonnays from the state are winning awards.

WINES FROM CHILE

The quality-versus-price relationship in Chilean wines can rarely be equaled. Even the entry-level wines offer immediate pleasure. They are sun-kissed and spiced without heaviness. It's possible that Chile is the winemaking star of tomorrow—the country possesses wonderful climatic conditions. The sun beats down strong and it's hot, but the air is cooled and dried during the day by the glacial wind from the ocean and at night by the fresh air that comes down from the Andes. The country is also crossed with rivers from the mountains that flow toward the Pacific Ocean, irrigating the vines as they pass.

The grape varieties

The grapes cultivated are the international standards: Cabernet Sauvignon, Merlot, and Chardonnay, with the notable exception of Carménère. This grape variety, which almost disappeared, has had a comeback—and surprisingly now creates Grand Cru levels of wines.

The regions

The wines of Chile grow in the Central Valley, south of Santiago, but there are also several sub-regions in the surrounding area that create a mosaic of styles.

White grape varieties:
Chardonnay, Sauvignon Blanc, Sémillon, Torontel

Red grape varieties:
Merlot, Cabernet Sauvignon, Pinot Noir, Malbec, Syrah, Carménère

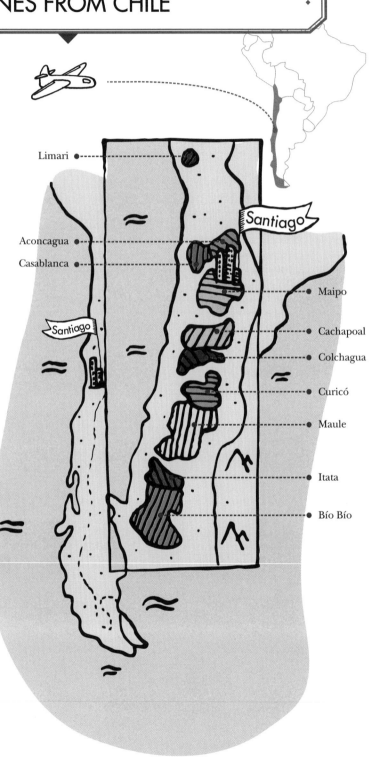

Limari
Aconcagua
Casablanca
Santiago
Maipo
Cachapoal
Colchagua
Curicó
Maule
Itata
Bío Bío
Santiago

Caroline vists the vineyards

WINES FROM ARGENTINA

Unlike in Chile, the vines of Argentina are on the other side of the Andes Cordillera and are not cooled by ocean breezes. But the mountain valleys offer a welcoming *terroir*, with the vivacity of the altitude and the perfect amount of sunshine. The wines are generally richer and more structured than those from Chile.

The grape varieties

Malbec is the most interesting varietal from Argentina, and the most reputable too, because of the powerful and mature wines it produces. But Bonarda, Merlot, Cabernet, and Syrah, all of which need sun, grow well there too. Those wines are less stimulating, though. Among the whites, Argentina is noted for some very perfumed Torrontés.

The regions

The main area of production is Mendoza, in the center of the country. You'll also find a great production in Patagonia, notably in the Río Negro region.

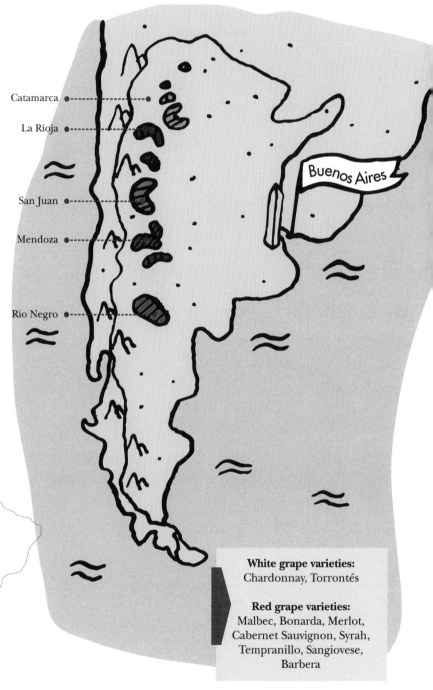

Catamarca

La Rioja

Buenos Aires

San Juan

Mendoza

Rio Negro

White grape varieties:
Chardonnay, Torrontés

Red grape varieties:
Malbec, Bonarda, Merlot,
Cabernet Sauvignon, Syrah,
Tempranillo, Sangiovese,
Barbera

THE WINES OF AUSTRALIA

Australian wine has almost everything, including modern technology and the work of men. They have performed miracles to overcome the challenges of the climate—Australia is one of the driest countries in the world—to produce great wines. On this continent, there is little talk of *terroir* but lots of discussion about the many techniques involved in cultivation and winemaking. Hard work and innovations that have paid off: Australia knows how to create world-renowned wines with a distinct style. The success of Australia's vineyards is one of the most significant events in the modern history of wine.

The climate and the wine

The vines thrive in the most temperate area of the island, the southeastern and southwestern points. But even when the grapes come from the coolest regions, Australian wines are always very mature or ripe. Rather than trying to hide this feature, producers have made their mark with their deep and opulent Shiraz. Good prices (between $15 and $25 a bottle) except for a few superstars whose prices soar to over $500. The country is worried though, as there has been a drought in recent years and water reserves are depleted and polluted. Two-thirds of production is irrigated and the vines are dangerously threatened.

Exploitation

Australian wine is in the hands of commercial giants. The four largest make up 80 percent of exports. Their blends, made from southern plots, dominate the market and leave no room for the character of *terroir* (that's the case with the inevitable, yet friendly Yellowtail). But the global market is beginning to tire of this industrial and standardized production that's been happening for the past ten years. In response, new pioneers are doing the opposite: refusing to use irrigation and synthetic products, handpicking, deploying biodynamic conversion, and using corks (instead of screwcaps). They are also moving toward Mediterranean grape varieties that are better adapted to drought conditions, including Barbera, Sangiovese, Tannat, and Dolcetto.

Varietals

Australia is the fourth largest wine exporter in the world and its area of vines has tripled in twenty years. The country grows mainly two varieties: Syrah (called Shiraz here) for red wines and Chardonnay for white wines. Far behind, there are many international varieties like Cabernet Sauvignon, Sémillon, and Riesling. The South Australia region has hardly been affected by phylloxera, and still-young vines are planted often without rootstock.

The Regions

The historic heart of the vineyard remains the southeastern tip of Australia, in the state of Victoria, but new areas have been brilliantly developed in the far west of the country, Margaret River, very favorable to white varieties and red Bordeaux, or the island of Tasmania with its distinguished Pinot Noirs. New areas of future growth appear north of Sydney to Orange, or in the Yarra Valley just outside Melbourne. The best vineyards are located 190 miles from the coast, the smallest situated mostly in the interior, in warm, irrigated areas.

Western Australia

In this vast region, the vineyard land is confined to the extreme southwestern tip, near Perth, and brings together brilliant independent winemakers. The most notable area is the Margaret River, with a mild climate, a place of stunning Chardonnays and Shiraz as well as fine, mature Cabernet Sauvignons.

South Australia

Nicknamed "The Wine State," its capital, Adelaide, is surrounded by vineyards. Among the star regions,

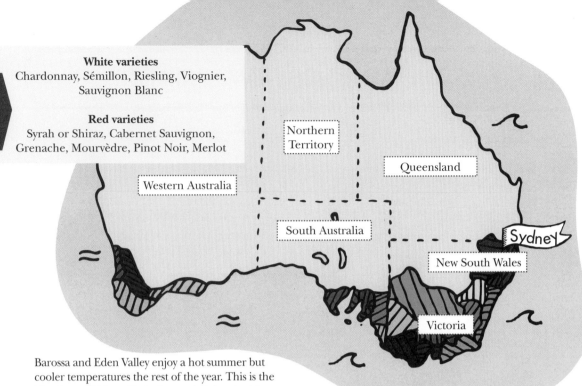

Northern Territory

Queensland

Western Australia

South Australia

Sydney

New South Wales

Victoria

Barossa and Eden Valley enjoy a hot summer but cooler temperatures the rest of the year. This is the kingdom of Shiraz. First of a wooded, heady style, producers now add Viognier to soften its power and reduce the wood. There is also a blend of a lot of wines nicknamed "GSM," for Grenache-Shiraz-Mourvèdre. Eden Valley is also known for its Riesling made in a Germanic style, with floral notes.

Margaret River

Just next door, in the Clare Valley, where the nights are very cold, the area welcomes Cabernet Sauvignon and Shiraz, and also creates splendid dry Riesling.
At McLaren Vale, in coastal areas, land has little need for irrigation and takes advantage of the cool ocean breezes that give acidity conducive to great wines. Its Shiraz, Cabernet Sauvignon, GSM, and Sauvignon Blanc are all very refined. The Adelaide Hills, temperate and well protected from winds, offers Sauvignon Blanc, with fresh aromas of citrus, and more and more Chardonnay. It also grows beautiful Pinot Noir at higher altitudes. Coonawarra grows Cabernet Sauvignon and Merlot with exotic aromas and also specializes in Chardonnay-based sparkling wines.

Victoria

Colder than South Australia, Victoria has beautiful land in areas close to the ocean and at higher altitudes. The Rutherglen area has long specialized

in Port-style fortified wines, the famous "stickies" with a base of Muscat and Muscadelle. But other producers are attracting attention. Bendigo and Heathcote produce powerful Shiraz; Henty makes exciting Riesling suitable for aging; and Mornington Peninsula, south of Melbourne, specializes in Pinot Noir and Chardonnays with a crystalline structure. Finally, the Yarra Valley, the main area, produces profound Pinot Noirs and sparkling wines inspired by Champagne.

New South Wales

Birthplace of Australian viticulture, this region is losing ground because its summers are hot and falls quite humid. However, the Hunter Valley, with a subtropical climate, creates rich and intense Sémillon-based sweet wines.

The island of Tasmania

In the coldest of cold-climate countries, Tasmania is in the midst of a complete vineyard expansion. The varieties that thrive here, notably Pinot Noir, Chardonnay, and Riesling, enjoy these brisk conditions and like it a lot. Sparkling wines from Tasmania are winning awards.

THE WINES OF NEW ZEALAND

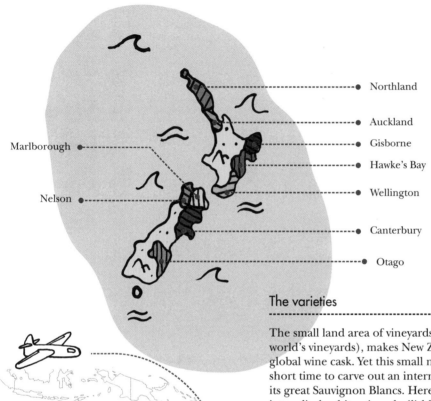

- Northland
- Auckland
- Gisborne
- Hawke's Bay
- Wellington
- Canterbury
- Otago

Marlborough

Nelson

The varieties

The small land area of vineyards (less than 0.5 percent of the world's vineyards), makes New Zealand wine a drop in the global wine cask. Yet this small nation has succeeded in a very short time to carve out an international reputation, thanks to its great Sauvignon Blancs. Here, the grape is transformed into a lively white wine, devilishly aromatic and with a palate ranging from lime to pineapple by way of mango and passion fruit. It is particularly successful in the regions of Hawke's Bay and Marlborough (the first wine region of the country). Its greatest export success is certainly from Cloudy Bay, made in stainless steel tanks and paving the way for this new style of wine. These powerful Sauvignon Blancs have pioneered their next specialty, Chardonnay, which now has twice as many vineyards as Sauvignon Blanc planted in the Marlborough area. Also found are good Rieslings and Gewürztraminers. Generally, white wine makes up two thirds of the production of New Zealand.

When it comes to red wines, the other pearl of the country is Pinot Noir. This grape prefers cool climates and thrives in the vineyards of the South Island and Wellington. It creates fine wines, close in style to Burgundy. New Zealand has managed a matchless, yet unlikely union, which combines the style of New World wines to the European climate where there is high acidity and elegance. Their method of viticulture, with mainly

Caroline vists the vineyards

mechanical harvesting and irrigation produces very high yields, and even though bottles are mostly sealed with screw caps, their prices are very competitive with traditionally made French wines. This island has seen exponential growth—from less than a thousand acres in 1960 to nearly 62,000 acres that are now being cultivated.

The regions

New Zealand consists of two large islands. The North Island is warm, almost subtropical in the more northern regions. The South Island has a more temperate oceanic climate, sunny and windy, with temperatures that do not exceed 77°F (25°C). There is little difference in temperature between seasons but a big difference between day and night. Rainfall and humidity are important, except in the region of Marlborough where the mountains trap the clouds.

The North Island

Wellington or Martinborough (or Wairapa) in the extreme south of the island. The climate is relatively cold, with strong climatic variations and frost in the spring. The soil is poor. This is the kingdom of Pinot Noir, but it does not have the usual personality of the New World wines. Instead, you will find a Burgundy-style wine. There are also some Bordeaux varietals, some Gewürztraminer, Riesling, and Chardonnay. Hawke's Bay, on the southeastern part of the island, enjoys a moderate climate protected from the wind by the mountains and has a fairly low rainfall. Soils are varied and their water retention capacity uneven, resulting in a sustained irrigation. Here they grow Merlot, Syrah, Pinot Noir, and opulent Chardonnays. Gisborne, on the East Coast, is warmer and wetter than nearby Hawke's Bay. There they make remarkable Gewürztraminer, a little Sémillon, and Chenin Blanc. Auckland, in the north, has a subtropical climate and menacing heavy rains. Rot is common, but the wines have been made for the past a century by Yugoslav immigrants who, through heroic efforts, produce beautiful Chardonnays.

White grape varieties
Sauvignon Blanc, Chardonnay, Riesling, Gewürztraminer, Sémillon, Chenin Blanc, Viognier

Red grape varieties
Pinot Noir, Merlot, Syrah

The South Island

Marlborough, on the northern tip of the island, is the first wine region in the country. It combines bright sun, cold nights, and mainly dry weather. The growers harvest as late as possible to be sure the grape is ripe, without fear of harm from the characteristic acidity of wines of the region. The Sauvignon Blancs are paradise. The best are made by blending several parcels with varied soils and microclimates. They're often aged in vats, rarely in wooden casks. Surprisingly, Sauvignon Blanc made here often goes through malolactic fermentation. There are also many bright, unoaked Chardonnays (without barrel-aging) and Viogniers with excellent aromas of apricot. Canterbury, in the cool plains surrounding Christchurch gives birth to honest Rieslings and Chardonnays. This area, though promising, is still underdeveloped. Pinot Noir could also be a possibility.
Otago is the most southern wine region on the planet! The climate is very continental, with dry, sunny summers and frequent freezing in winter. You can taste fabulous Pinot Noirs from here with fruity and spicy aromas that are rich in alcohol. They are among the most sought after by wine lovers.

WINES OF SOUTH AFRICA

The history of South African wine

South Africa has produced wine for a very long time. In fact, the sweet wines from Klein Constantia were Napoleon's favorite during his exile. But the vineyards you see today are very different. Its renaissance dates back to the end of Apartheid in 1991 and the recovery of business relations with other countries.

The grape varieties

Nowadays, South Africa produces very diverse styles of wines, though the quality is just as variable. You'll find classic wines, whites like Chardonnay and reds like Cabernet Sauvignon. Syrah and Merlot are also cultivated. But the most typical red wine in South Africa is made from a local grape, the very original Pinotage, which is equally fruity and wild. Surprisingly, a white varietal, Chenin Blanc, is found here. You won't find the grape much outside of the Loire Valley, but here they produce elegant wines, either dry or sweet, that don't skimp on glamour.

The regions

Some young winemakers are investing in vineyards and are trying to highlight the notion of *terroir*, particularly winemakers in the Swartland region. The best wines come from the regions neighboring the Cape, which benefits from its maritime freshness. Paarl and Stellenbosch are the most developed regions.

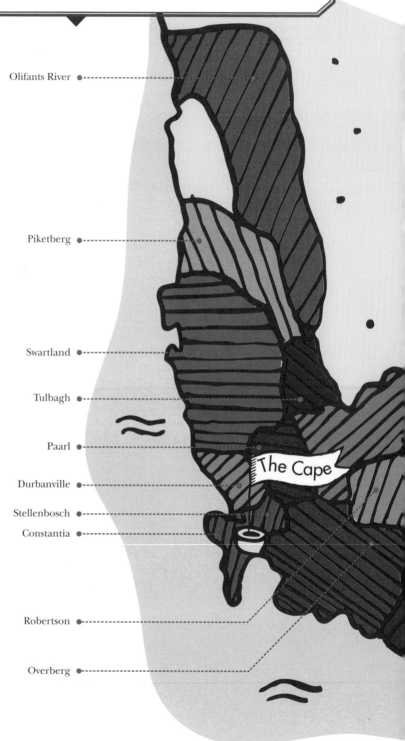

Olifants River

Piketberg

Swartland

Tulbagh

Paarl

The Cape

Durbanville

Stellenbosch

Constantia

Robertson

Overberg

Caroline vists the vineyards

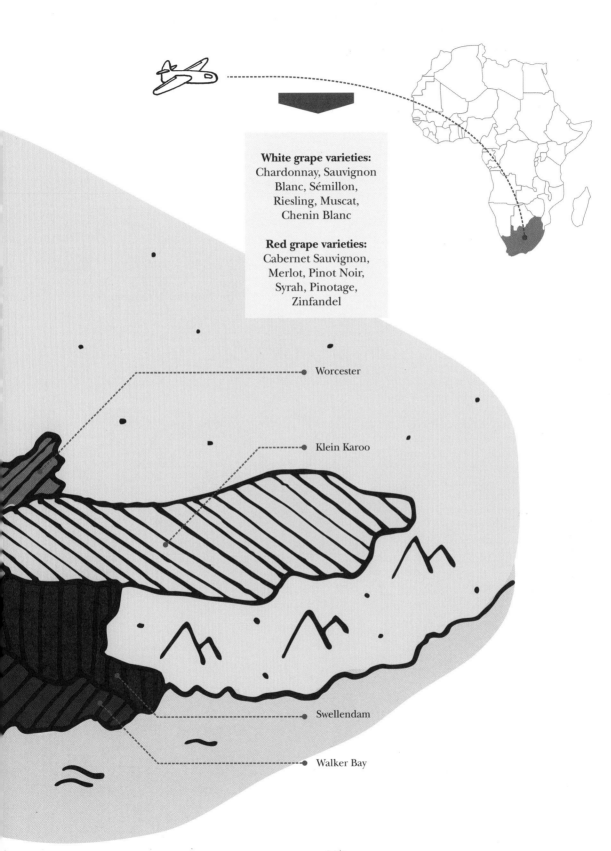

White grape varieties:
Chardonnay, Sauvignon Blanc, Sémillon, Riesling, Muscat, Chenin Blanc

Red grape varieties:
Cabernet Sauvignon, Merlot, Pinot Noir, Syrah, Pinotage, Zinfandel

Worcester

Klein Karoo

Swellendam

Walker Bay

OTHER WINES OF THE WORLD

Winemaking regions exist across the planet, mostly consolidated in certain countries, with appearances in others, and they have been conquering new territories. The map of the world of wine will be without a doubt very different in thirty years. The amelioration of winemaking and winegrowing techniques allows new vineyards to exist in places where it was inconceivable just a few years ago. In response to this emergence, traditional winemaking countries are giving their vines another look and engaging in the race with a surprising dynamic quality.

Is it global warming, more attentive workers, or the use of technology? **England** manages to get better and better at making their grapes ripen and producing some honest wine. The most promising results to this day rest with sparkling wines from the coast with their chalky terriors.

In the **Near East**, **Lebanon** produces wines whose fame never stops climbing. The tradition of wine in this country dates to the Phoenicians, 3,000 years ago. Romans then constructed a temple dedicated to Bacchus in the plains of the Bekaa, where today the vineyards are concentrated. The castles of Ksara, Kefraya and the grand Musar create superb spicy and chocolatey red wines, and intense and perfumed whites. Faced with these big classics, a fourth of the vineyards have been around for the past twenty years and are demonstrating great vitality. Some, like the Wardy domaine, offer very good wines.

We often forget that they also produce wines in the neighboring countries of **Israel**, **Syria**, and even **Afghanistan**. Let's hope that the conflicts in those countries don't end that. Even in Egypt, you can find some remarkable wines, like those from the Jardin du Nil property.

In **Maghreb**, the wine growing tradition is firmly anchored. There you'll taste rosés and spicy reds, some of which, most notably from Morocco, deserve to be at good gourmet restaurants.

Caroline vists the vineyards

In **China**, the production and consumption of wine has grown exponentially. Today, 80 percent of the wine drunk by the Chinese is made in-country. And producers are also exporting abroad. The vineyards are planted on gigantic pieces of land in northern China, particularly in the northeast, at latitudes close to those of the Mediterranean basin. The French are investing heavily in these new vineyards. Big corporations like Pernod Ricard, LVMH, and Lafite-Rothschild are part of the adventure.

Japanese wine production is very limited but of good quality.

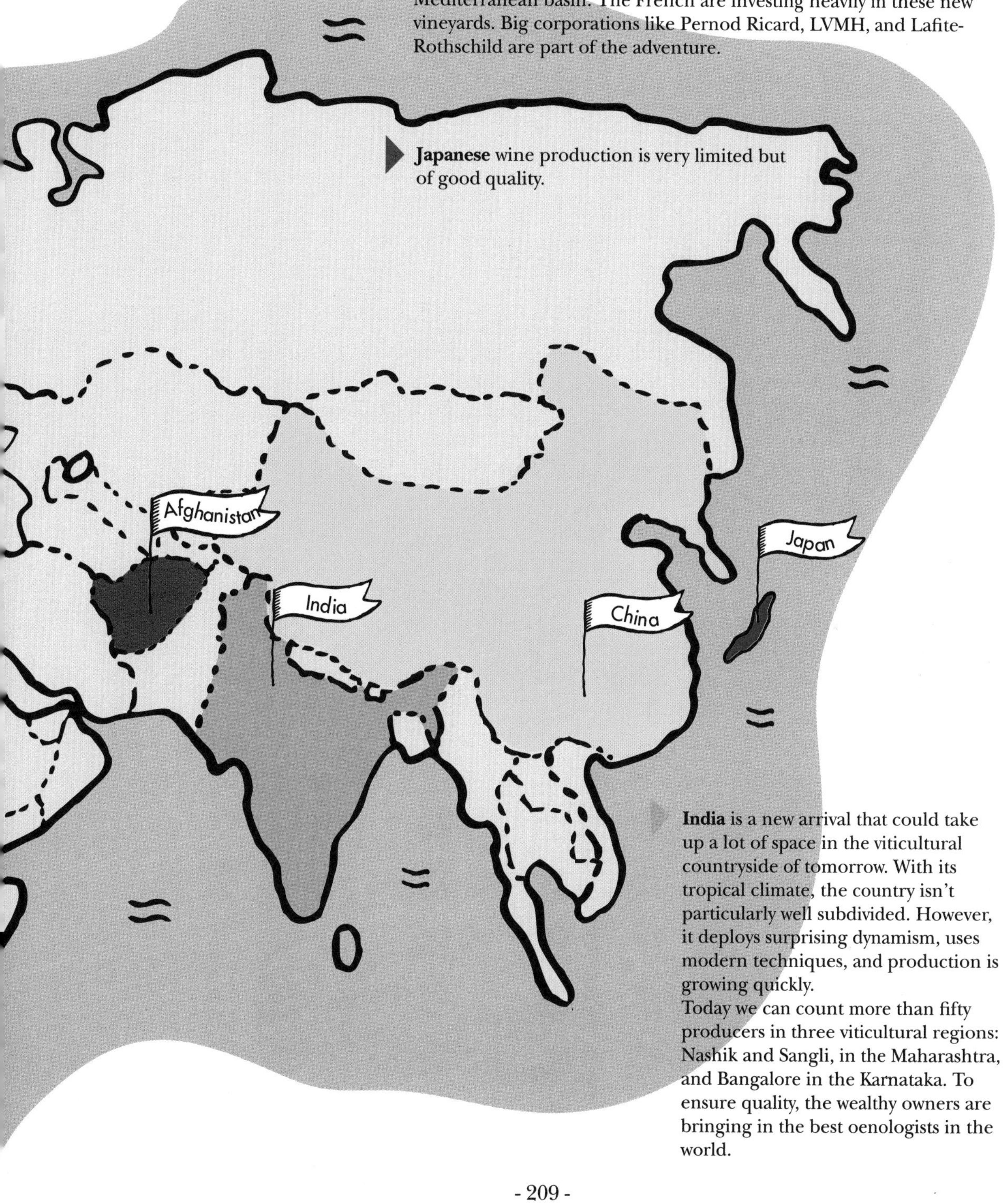

Afghanistan

India

China

Japan

India is a new arrival that could take up a lot of space in the viticultural countryside of tomorrow. With its tropical climate, the country isn't particularly well subdivided. However, it deploys surprising dynamism, uses modern techniques, and production is growing quickly.

Today we can count more than fifty producers in three viticultural regions: Nashik and Sangli, in the Maharashtra, and Bangalore in the Karnataka. To ensure quality, the wealthy owners are bringing in the best oenologists in the world.

Elizabeth remembers the day she first became interested in wine. It was at a simple family meal. She'd just taken a bite of food and then tried a sip of her dad's wine. Then she had another bite of food . . . and that's when it happened. The flavors of the food were enhanced. Elizabeth had just discovered the power of wine and food pairing.

Ever since that day, Elizabeth has made it her mission to find just the right wine to drink with dinner or serve with a meal. Sometimes she even opens two or three bottles with a meal to compare how it would taste alongside what she's serving. At a recent dinner party she served oysters with a Sauternes. She'd read somewhere that this was a good pairing. Some of her guests admitted that they were underwhelmed by the combination, while while others loved it. What she learned from this experience was that wine pairing rules are not universal; they depend very much on taste and cultures!

This chapter is for all of the Elizabeths, who like to play and discover new tastes.

ELIZABETH

BECOMES AN APPRENTICE SOMMELIER

The basics of food and wine pairing
Which wine goes with my meal?
Food assassins
Which dish goes with my wine?

· THE BASICS OF FOOD AND WINE PAIRINGS ·

Rule of thumb for wine pairings

A pairing of food and wine is like a marriage: If it's successful, each party flourishes in the presence of the other, seeming better together than had they been alone. If it fails, both parties, at best, ignore each other; at worst, they argue and lose interest in each other. To judge this marriage, the idea is to taste the wine separately, in the kitchen if possible. Then try it again with the dish and see how well the food goes with the wine. Note that a marriage of tastes is just that—a matter of taste. You may like something that your neighbor appreciates less than you do.

You will find in the following pages some principles and suggestions to help you find classic combinations of food and wine. Feel free to follow the rules, or you can try something else!

According to color

One of the easiest tricks when trying to pair food and wine is to match their colors.

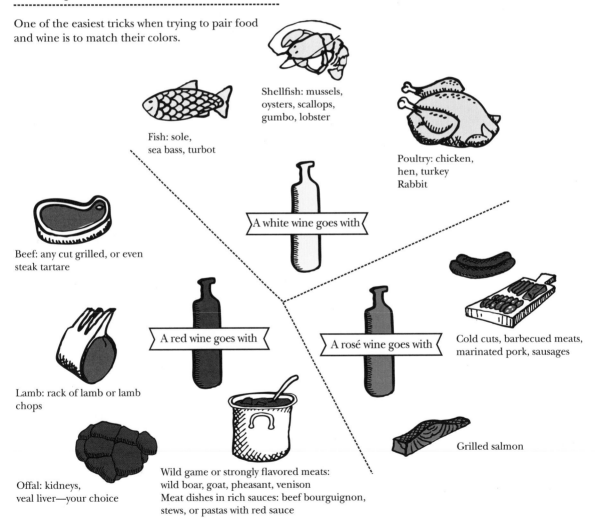

Fish: sole,
sea bass, turbot

Shellfish: mussels,
oysters, scallops,
gumbo, lobster

Poultry: chicken,
hen, turkey
Rabbit

Beef: any cut grilled, or even
steak tartare

A white wine goes with

Cold cuts, barbecued meats,
marinated pork, sausages

A red wine goes with

A rosé wine goes with

Lamb: rack of lamb or lamb
chops

Grilled salmon

Offal: kidneys,
veal liver—your choice

Wild game or strongly flavored meats:
wild boar, goat, pheasant, venison
Meat dishes in rich sauces: beef bourguignon,
stews, or pastas with red sauce

Elizabeth becomes an apprentice sommelier

Matching *terroirs*

When serving a special food from a particular region, especially if it is a main dish, you should always try to select a wine that comes from the same geographic area: a sauerkraut with a Riesling or a Pinot Blanc from Alsace; Prosciutto di Parma with Pinot Grigio from Italy; a Raclette (or cheese fondue) with a white from Jura; Pacific Northwest salmon with an Oregon Pinot Noir; barbecued pork with a California Zinfandel; a Spanish Mencia with paella; lamb from a certain region with a wine from the same region; a sweet Tokaji from Hungary with foie gras.

Matches that contrast

The objective of this style of pairing is not so much to accompany the plate than to surpass it, unveiling new aromas and new sensations. A new taste sensation can then emerge between the flavors of the dish and the wine. The most pleasing combinations surprisingly come from matches with wines that one rarely drinks: bubblies, sweet wines, and fortified wines.

Here are some short cuts

With brut Champagne (or a good Cava from Spain), try some runny Camembert. The effervescence of the wine gives a boost to the rich fat in the cheese. Try the pairing with cider too.

Matches that merge

Choose tastes that are related between the wines and foods: fat with fat, dry with dry, salty with salty. Tastes that resemble each other tend to go together: a salty Muscadet or a Chablis with iodine notes with oysters; a Sauternes or Ice wine that has aromas of pineapple with pineapple flambé; a powerful wine with a highly flavorful dish; a light wine with a plate of delicate foods. If you cook with a (good) wine, save some to serve at the table or choose a wine for the meal from the same region, or made from the same grape variety.

A Grüner Veltliner from Austria with a chicken curry. The curry aromas are present in the wine, but they accompanied by a bouquet of lime, ginger, and spicy pepper notes.

A soft, slightly sweet wine with a Thai meal (or Peking duck). How about combining sweet and salty tastes like you find in Asian foods? An added plus with a spicy dish: A sweet wine extinguishes the fire to soften the spiciness.

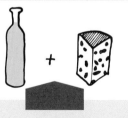

A licorice wine with a Fourme d'Ambert (or a Sauternes with a Roquefort). The softness of the wine brings out the sharpness of the cheese and accentuates its roundness.

The basics of food and wine pairing

· PAIRINGS FOR BEEF, PORK, LAMB AND VEAL ·

When selecting wine to drink with meat, it's important to seek a balance. The wine should not be overwhelmed by a strong-tasting meat, but it also must not crush a meat that has subtler flavors. Try to balance a fatty meat with a wine that has strong tannins or vivacity that can cut the fat and revitalize the dish.

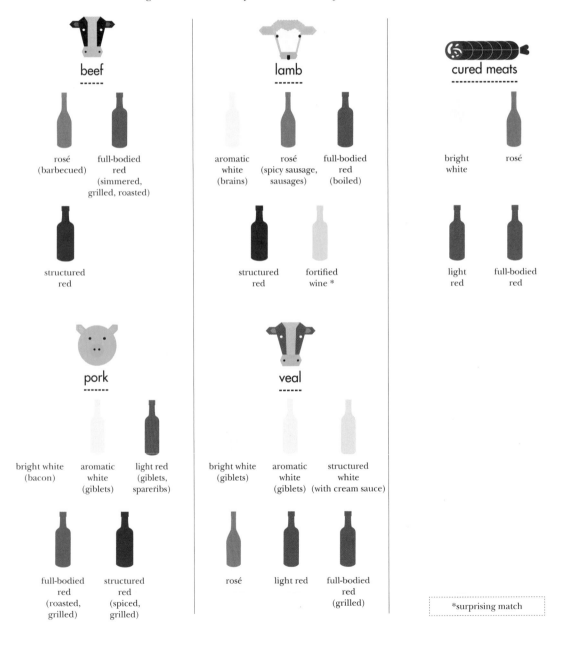

beef
- rosé (barbecued)
- full-bodied red (simmered, grilled, roasted)
- structured red

lamb
- aromatic white (brains)
- rosé (spicy sausage, sausages)
- full-bodied red (boiled)
- structured red
- fortified wine *

cured meats
- bright white
- rosé
- light red
- full-bodied red

pork
- bright white (bacon)
- aromatic white (giblets)
- light red (giblets, spareribs)
- full-bodied red (roasted, grilled)
- structured red (spiced, grilled)

veal
- bright white (giblets)
- aromatic white (giblets)
- structured white (with cream sauce)
- rosé
- light red
- full-bodied red (grilled)

*surprising match

Elizabeth becomes an apprentice sommelier

PAIRINGS FOR POULTRY AND GAME

With poultry, avoid a powerful red wine, which will completely dominate it. With game, aim for elegance, but don't forget that certain strongly flavored meats demand a wine that knows how to assert itself.

chicken, turkey

structured white (roasted, with cream sauce) — rosé — light red (roasted)

* sparkling (with cream sauce) — * soft, sweet

duck

full-bodied red (breast) — structured red (roasted, foie gras*)

soft, sweet (foie gras) — fortified wine (flambé)

rabbit

aromatic white — structured white

light red — * sparkling (with cream sauce)

eggs

bright white (quiche) — aromatic white (omelets)

round red (poached) — * soft, sweet

game birds

light red — full-bodied red

*structured white

wild game

full-bodied red (rabbit) — structured red (in stew, with a sauce)

*surprising match

With fish, avoid strong tannins that will unleash a metallic taste and favor the lighter, more aromatic wines.

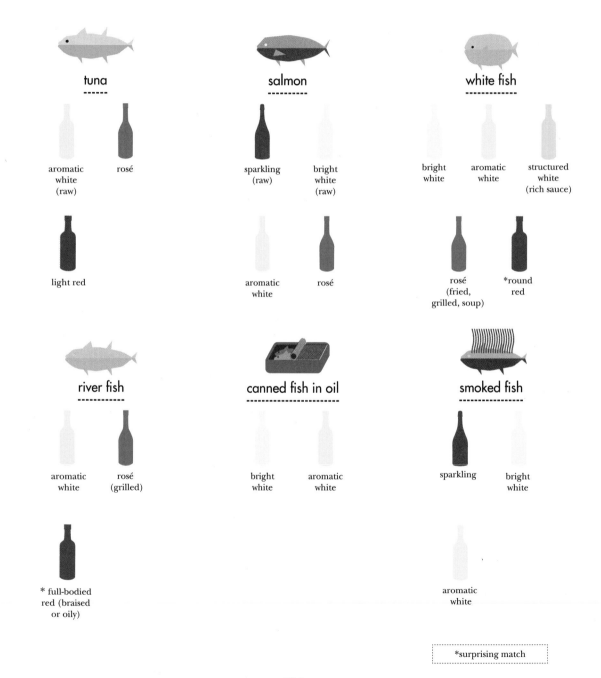

tuna

aromatic white (raw)

rosé

light red

salmon

sparkling (raw)

bright white (raw)

aromatic white

rosé

white fish

bright white

aromatic white

structured white (rich sauce)

rosé (fried, grilled, soup)

*round red

river fish

aromatic white

rosé (grilled)

* full-bodied red (braised or oily)

canned fish in oil

bright white

aromatic white

smoked fish

sparkling

bright white

aromatic white

*surprising match

Elizabeth becomes an apprentice sommelier

Without exception, these dishes belong with white wines, either with or without bubbles. These wines will best accompany the iodine and salty notes of the shellfish and highlight the delicacy of their flesh.

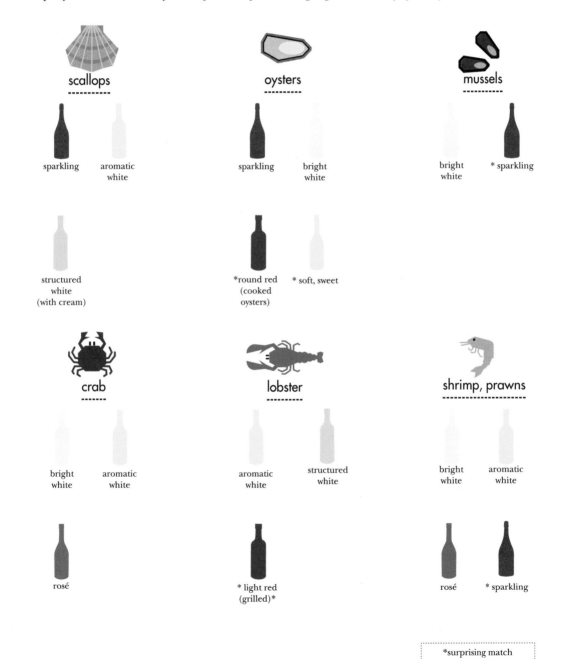

scallops

sparkling aromatic white

structured white (with cream)

oysters

sparkling bright white

*round red (cooked oysters) * soft, sweet

mussels

bright white * sparkling

crab

bright white aromatic white

rosé

lobster

aromatic white structured white

* light red (grilled)*

shrimp, prawns

bright white aromatic white

rosé * sparkling

*surprising match

PAIRINGS FOR VEGETARIAN DISHES

Vegetarian dishes can be a headache for sommeliers because vegetables are not as robust in texture or flavor as meat or fish. Yet magnificent pairings are possible with fine or aromatic wines. Fungi love old wines that evoke very similar flavors.

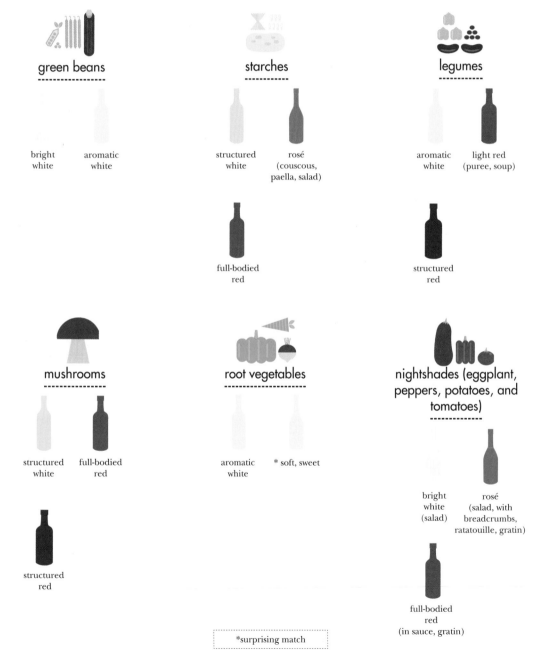

green beans

bright
white

aromatic
white

starches

structured
white

rosé
(couscous,
paella, salad)

full-bodied
red

legumes

aromatic
white

light red
(puree, soup)

structured
red

mushrooms

structured
white

full-bodied
red

structured
red

root vegetables

aromatic
white

* soft, sweet

nightshades (eggplant, peppers, potatoes, and tomatoes)

bright
white
(salad)

rosé
(salad, with
breadcrumbs,
ratatouille, gratin)

full-bodied
red
(in sauce, gratin)

*surprising match

Elizabeth becomes an apprentice sommelier

PAIRINGS FOR HERBS AND SPICES

Herbs with a subtle taste require a wine that will emphasize their freshness. The most powerful herbs require a wine with character. As for spices, they are an opportunity to match an unusual wine. Note that nothing works like a sweet wine to soothe the fire from a chile pepper.

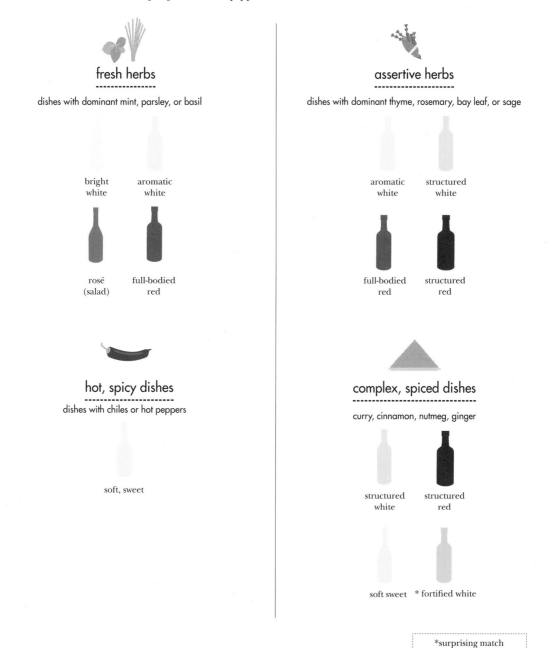

fresh herbs

dishes with dominant mint, parsley, or basil

bright
white

aromatic
white

rosé
(salad)

full-bodied
red

assertive herbs

dishes with dominant thyme, rosemary, bay leaf, or sage

aromatic
white

structured
white

full-bodied
red

structured
red

hot, spicy dishes

dishes with chiles or hot peppers

soft, sweet

complex, spiced dishes

curry, cinnamon, nutmeg, ginger

structured
white

structured
red

soft sweet

* fortified white

*surprising match

PAIRINGS FOR CHEESE AND DESSERT

You can try to resist white wines, but they make the best pairing with cheese of all types because they avoid overwhelming the taste buds. Desserts offer the opportunity to taste sweet and fortified wines that match the aromas of yellow fruit or berries.

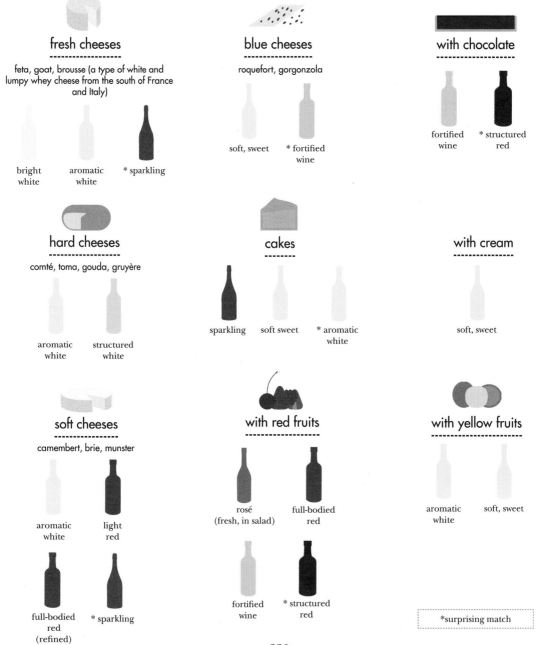

fresh cheeses
feta, goat, brousse (a type of white and lumpy whey cheese from the south of France and Italy)

bright white   aromatic white   * sparkling

blue cheeses
roquefort, gorgonzola

soft, sweet   * fortified wine

with chocolate

fortified wine   * structured red

hard cheeses
comté, toma, gouda, gruyère

aromatic white   structured white

cakes

sparkling   soft sweet   * aromatic white

with cream

soft, sweet

soft cheeses
camembert, brie, munster

aromatic white   light red

full-bodied red (refined)   * sparkling

with red fruits

rosé (fresh, in salad)   full-bodied red

fortified wine   * structured red

with yellow fruits

aromatic white   soft, sweet

*surprising match

Elizabeth becomes an apprentice sommelier

Some foods don't appreciate the presence of wine. Not only do they not enhance the wine but, even worse, they seem hell-bent on destroying its wonderful qualities.

Vinaigrette turns wine into the living dead, a zombie.

The vegetable platter makes you look the other way.

Garlic is a strangler of wine.

Artichokes, endives, leeks, and spinach are serial killers.

The grapefruit is a kamikaze.

You also risk being disappointed if you try:

▸ A tannic red wine with fish or crustaceans. Light, supple red wines (Loire, Burgundy, Beaujolais) can go well with seafood, but fish gives a metallic taste to the tannins.

▸ Dry white with a sweet dessert. The wine stiffens in the face of the sugar and assaults the dessert.

WITH SPARKLING WINE

Sparkling wines go well with many dishes. They have very different profiles, from the powerful vintage Champagne to light and fruity sparkling wines such as Cava and even sparkling reds like Lambrusco. All share a fine effervescence that gives pep to both simple and sophisticated dishes. Avoid drinking it with a dish that is too strong in flavor, which can overwhelm it.

fish
salmon (raw)

smoked fish

seafood
oysters

scallops

desserts
cakes (if the wine is not too dry)

varietals
Chardonnay, Pinot Noir, Pinot Meunier, Pinot Auxerrois, Riesling, Chenin Blanc, Lambrusco, Grasparossa, Glera (Prosecco), Macebeo, Muscat, Mauzac, and many blends

appellations
Champagne, Crémant du Jura, Crémant d'Alsace, Crémant de Bordeaux, Crémant de Bourgogne, Crémant Limoux, Crémant de Loire, Clairette de Die, Blanquette de Limoux, Cava, Gaillac, Spumante, Prosecco

*surprising matches
chicken and turkey (with cream sauce)

rabbit (with cream sauce)

mussels

shrimp and prawns

strong herbs

fresh cheeses

hard cheeses

Elizabeth becomes an apprentice sommelier

WITH A BRIGHT WHITE

As invigorating as a cold blast of air, a good, lively white wine awakens the taste buds and appetite. It is never heavy, tiring, or overbearing. Its acidity may surprise you, but it's the guarantee of freshness and purity. Its salty mineral notes and citrus zest augment the simplest of dishes.

meats

pork (bacon)

veal (giblets)

cured meats

eggs (quiche)

fish

salmon (raw)

white fish

canned fish in oil

smoked fish

herbs & spices

fresh herbs

seafood

oysters

mussels

crab

shrimp and prawns

vegetables

green beans

nightshades (eggplant, peppers, potatoes, and tomatoes)

cheeses

fresh cheeses

varietals

Sauvignon Blanc, Melon de Bourgogne, Chenin Blanc, Pinot Blanc, Pinot Auxerrois, Silvaner, Chasselas, Aligoté, Assyrtiko, Grüner Veltliner

appellations

Sancerre, Pouilly-Fumé, Muscadet, Anjou, Saumur, Alsace, Savoy, Burgundy Aligoté, Santorini, Marlborough, Monterey, Burgenland

Which dish goes with my wine?

WITH AN AROMATIC WHITE

Aromatic whites offer explosions of flowers, fruits, and rare perfumes, which can be very different depending on the variety. Their specificity allows real gastronomic experiences, which are sometimes daring but magnificent when they are successful. Some of them become structured with time.

meats
----

pork (giblets)

veal (giblets)

mutton, lamb (brains)

rabbit

fish
-----

salmon

tuna (raw)

white fish

river fish

canned fish in oil

smoked fish

herbs and spices
----

fresh herbs

seasonings

varietals

Chardonnay (oaked),
Gewürztraminer, Muscat,
Riesling, Vermentino, Viognier,
Savagnin, Gros and Petit
Manseng, Albariño, Torrontés

appellations

Alsace, Condrieu, Corsica,
Palette, Bellet, Jura, Jurançon,
Gaillac, Coteaux du Languedoc,
Limoux, Burgundy (unoaked),
Rías Baixas, Rioja

seafood
----

scallops

crab

lobster

shrimp and prawns

vegetables
----

green beans

beans (legumes)

root vegetables and squash

cheeses and desserts
----

fresh cheeses

hard cheeses

soft cheeses

desserts with yellow fruits

Elizabeth becomes an apprentice sommelier

WITH A STRUCTURED WHITE

Often made in oak barrels, structured whites are fat and full in the mouth. They may give off aromas of butter mixed with flowers or fruit. At the table, they add class and presence thanks to their rich texture.

meats
- - - - - - - -

chicken, turkey (roasted, with cream sauce)

veal (with cream sauce)

rabbit

fish
- - - - -

white fish (rich sauce)

seafood
- - - - - - - - -

scallops (with cream sauce)

lobster

varietals
- - - - - - - - -

Chardonnay (oaked), Sémillon, Marsanne, Roussanne, Grenache Blanc

appellations
- - - - - - - - - - - - - - -

Côte de Beaune, Chablis Grand Cru, Meursault, Chassagne, Puligny Montrachet, Mâconnais, Pouilly-Fuissé, Graves, Côtes du Rhône, Hermitage, Châteauneuf-du-Pape, Coteaux du Languedoc, California Chardonnay

vegetables
- - - - - - - - - - -

starches

mushrooms

herbs & spices
- - - - - - - - - - - - - - - - -

seasonings

spices

cheeses
- - - - - - - - -

hard cheeses

*surprising match
- - - - - - - - - - - - - - - -

game birds

Which dish goes with my wine?

WITH A ROSÉ

Rosés have very diverse personalities depending on their origin and the style in which they are made. Whether pale, light, or more structured, all rosés have very expressive fruit and discreet tannins. They are easy to match with food from both land and sea, because they combine the acidity of white and the aromas of red.

meats

beef (sausages, spicy sausages)

veal (offal)

sheep, lamb (spicy sausage)

chicken, turkey

cured meats

fish

salmon

tuna

white fish (fried, grilled, soup)

river fish (grilled)

seafood

crab

shrimp and prawns

vegetables

starchy foods (couscous, paella, salad)

nightshades (salad, gratin)

herbs & spices

fresh herbs (salad)

desserts

with red fruits

varietals

Pinot Noir, Cabernet Franc, Cabernet Sauvignon, Merlot, Grenache, Syrah, Cinsaut, Mourvèdre, Pineau d'Aunis, and almost all other red varieties!

appellations

Côtes de Provence, Tavel, Corsica, Bordeaux Rosé, Anjou, Bandol, Coteaux du Vendôme, Bourgogne Rosé, Côtes-de-Toul, Boulaouane Gris, Sonoma Coast, Greve (in Chianti)

Elizabeth becomes an apprentice sommelier

WITH A LIGHT RED

Its aromas move toward small red fruits, and its fluid texture quenches thirst and can revive a dish. They often come from cool or temperate climates. Note: the term "light" is not always synonymous with simplicity! Delicate Pinot Noirs from the Côte de Nuits in Burgundy are as fine as they are complex and elegant.

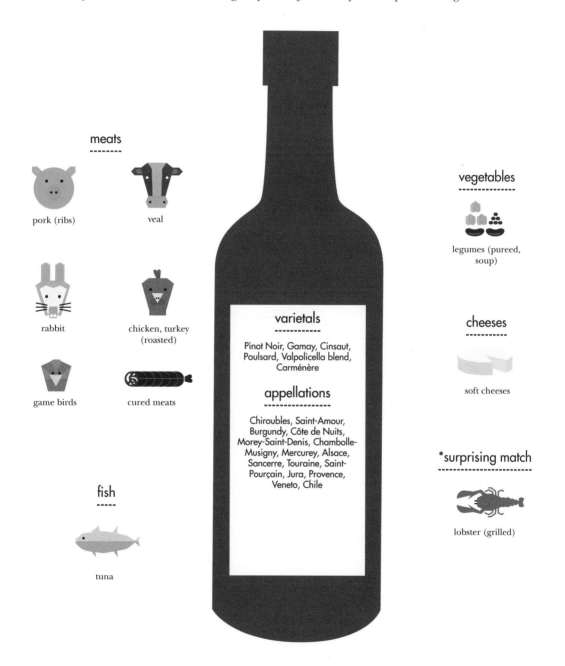

meats

pork (ribs)

veal

rabbit

chicken, turkey (roasted)

game birds

cured meats

fish

tuna

vegetables

legumes (pureed, soup)

cheeses

soft cheeses

*surprising match

lobster (grilled)

varietals

Pinot Noir, Gamay, Cinsaut, Poulsard, Valpolicella blend, Carménère

appellations

Chiroubles, Saint-Amour, Burgundy, Côte de Nuits, Morey-Saint-Denis, Chambolle-Musigny, Mercurey, Alsace, Sancerre, Touraine, Saint-Pourçain, Jura, Provence, Veneto, Chile

Which dish goes with my wine?

WITH A FULL-BODIED RED

Sometimes called "greedy" or "fleshy," a full-bodied red isn't known for its strength or its structure, but rather for its roundness. It's often fruity, and sometimes spicy, with a velvety, soft texture. Sometimes it can be a little greasy. It brings softness and richness to food and coats the meal like a sauce.

meats
-----

pork
(roasted, grilled)

beef
(simmered, grilled)

sheep, lamb
(boiled)

veal
(grilled)

duck
(breast)

game
(rabbit)

game birds

cured meats

vegetables
-----

starches

mushrooms

nightshades
(in sauce, gratin)

varietals

Grenache, Merlot, Cabernet Franc, Carignan, Sangiovese, Touriga Nacional, Petite Sirah, Zinfandel, and many blends

appellations

Côtes-du-Rhône-Villages, Lirac, Gigondas, Vacqueyras, Châteauneuf-du-Pape, Costières de Nîmes, Saint-Joseph, Coteaux du Languedoc, Saint-Émilion, Pomerol, Côtes de Blaye, Côtes de Bourg, Bordeaux Supérieur, Côte de Beaune, Côte de Provence, Corsica, Anjou, Chinon, Bourgueil, Saumur-Champigny, Tuscany, Sicily, Rioja, Napa Valley, Portugal, Chile

herbs & spices
-----

fresh herbs

seasonings

cheese
-----

soft cheeses

desserts
-----

with red fruits

surprising matches
-----

white fish

river fish

oysters

Elizabeth becomes an apprentice sommelier

WITH A STRUCTURED RED

With muscular structure, strong tannins, and a lasting power on the palate, the structured red has dark color and aromas of black fruits and spices. It pairs well with full-flavored dishes characterized by a rich sauce or a little fat, which give the tannins something to grab. It is often aged before drinking.

meats

pork
(spiced, grilled)

beef

sheep, lamb

duck
(roasted)

game
(in stew, with
sauce)

vegetables

legumes

mushrooms

varietals

Tannat, Cabernet Sauvignon,
Mourvèdre, Malbec, Syrah (Shiraz),
Tempranillo, Nebbiolo, Nero
d'Avola, Montepulciano

appellations

Haut-Médoc, Pauillac, Saint-
Estèphe, Saint-Julien, Margaux,
Graves, Corbières, Fitou, Minervois,
Saint-Chinian, Faugères, Côtes du
Roussillon, Bandol, Madiran,
Irouléguy, Fronton, Buzet, Cahors,
Côte-Rôtie, Hermitage, Crozes
Hermitage, Cornas, Pommard,
Echezeaux, Chambertin, Priorat,
Ribera del Duero, Barolo,
Barbaresco, Napa Valley,
Argentina, Australia

herbs & spices

seasonings

spices

surprising matches

duck
(foie gras)

dessert with
red fruits

chocolate desserts

Which dish goes with my wine?

WITH A SOFT OR SWEET WINE

They are often reserved for foie gras (liver pâté) and desserts, but sweet wines can be paired with poultry, seafood, spicy dishes, sweet or savory recipes, and cheese. A soft wine will marry more easily with a main course, and a sweet wine will bring character to shellfish, cheese, or dessert.

meats

duck
(foie gras)

herbs & spices

chiles

spices

cheeses

blue cheeses

varietals

Chenin Blanc, Sémillon, Petit and Gros Manseng, Riesling, Gewürztraminer, Pinot Gris, Muscat, Furmint, Malvasia

appellations

Alsace late harvest, Alsace Sélection de Grains Nobles, Barsac, Sauternes, Loupiac, Monbazillac, Jurançon, Pacherenc du Vic-Bihl, Bonnezeaux, Quarts-de-Chaume, Vouvray, Coteaux du Layon, Montlouis, straw wine (Jura, South West France, Italy, Greece, Spain, Switzerland), Tokaji from Hungary, Auslese and Beerenauslese (Germany), Ice wines (Austria, Canada)

desserts

with white and yellow fruits

cakes

with whipped cream

surprising matches

chicken, turkey

eggs

oysters, mussels, octopus

root vegetables and squash

Elizabeth becomes an apprentice sommelier

Just as sweet as a soft sweet wine, but loaded with more alcohol, vin doux naturel, *meaning "natural sweet wine" (as well as* vin de liqueur*), is more robust, especially when it is red. It goes easily with chocolate desserts but also with powerful meats. This type of wine, as well as traditional fortified wines from the rest of Europe, demand accompaniments that are strong and can adorn the meal with deep complexity.*

desserts

with red fruits

with chocolate

surprising matches

sheep, lamb
(in sauce)

duck
(flambé)

game

spices

blue cheeses

varietals

Muscat, Grenache, Malvasia, Maccabeu, Touriga Nacional, Francesa, Tinta Roriz, Sercial, Verdelho, Bual, among others

appellations

Muscat de Beaumes-de-Venise, Muscat de Rivesaltes, Muscat de Frontignan, Muscat-du-Cap-Corse, Banyuls, Maury, Rasteau, Port, Sherry, Madeira, Málaga, Marsala, Vins de Liqueurs (including Pineau des Charentes, Macvin du Jura, Floc de Gascogne)

Paul is the type of bon vivant who loves to invite people over to his place. Invariably, he'll announce as soon as you've entered the door: "I bought a new bottle of wine! Tell me what's going on!"

Paul has excellent taste in wine and knows exactly which wine goes with every occasion and every type of food. However, it wasn't always this way. His buddies remember a time when Paul would bring out the worst wines. He'd just grab the closest bottle from the supermarket shelf or take a gamble based on the look of the label. Then one day he walked into a wine store and asked for a recommendation. He discovered that he'd found a very good shop; one where the wine sellers gave useful advice and really understood his likes and dislikes. Paul was hooked. Soon he was attending wine-tasting events and buying wines by the case to drink at home.

As Paul gained a better understanding of wine and greater confidence in his own knowledge and tastes, he decided to create a personal wine cellar, so he would always have good wines within reach. He bought directly from wineries, starting with the ones he had found at wine-tasting events.

Over the years he amassed a beautiful collection that is widely varied and includes wines suited for aging and others ready to drink right away. He is quite proud of it, but he wonders how he could ever drink it all. That is why he has his friends to help him!

This chapter is for all of the people like Paul who want to be sure they have the right wine at the right time for every occasion.

BUYS WINE

At a restaurant • How to decode a wine label
How to buy a bottle • How to build a wine cellar

The wine list

Choosing a good wine at a restaurant can often be the most vexing part of the meal. There are weak wine lists where nothing looks good and there are lists as thick as dictionaries that you don't dare to open. How do you find the right wine at the right price?

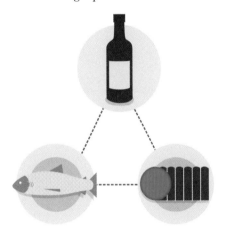

Rule one: Have confidence in your choice. After all, if the wine is bad, it's not your fault but that of the restaurateur.

Rule two: Choose a wine that will adapt to everyone's meal: no tannic red if someone is getting fish, no lively white wine if there is red meat. If the orders are varied, take a light red or a powerful white that will go with just about anything.

Rule three: If all prices are equal, choose the most modest appellation. At $45, a country wine (vin de pays) will certainly be better than a Médoc. At the same time, it's better to choose the most expensive wine of a small appellation or a region that is less expensive than a prestigious appellation or region.

 Inventive menus

For wine newbies, a classic wine list, even if it's very descriptive, can be very confusing. That's why restaurants are getting inventive with their lists to make your work easier. Here are three examples of how three different restaurants approach their wine lists:

▶ **Tasting comments**
Each wine is summarized by a descriptive phrase that evokes the feel of the wine: "A wine like a bald man who has as much money as allure." "A sweet Cinderella, voluptuous and naive." "Funny and inspiring."

▶ **Wine list on a tablet (or iPad)**
By clicking on a specific wine, a page displays a wealth of information: maybe a map of the vineyard, the grape varieties, or information about the winery. This can be playful and very thorough.

▶ **Classified by style**
The diner can choose a style of wine—square and powerful, round and velvety, light and fruity—then they can decide the region and the appellation. This is simple and illuminating.

WINE · LIST

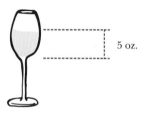

5 oz.

WINE BY THE GLASS

(5 oz.)

WHITE
Loire, Sancerre, "Floris" Domaine V. Pinard $10

RED
Vin de Pays du Cantal IGP Gamay—Gilles Monier 2011 $9

BOTTLES

BURGUNDY AND BEAUJOLAIS
1

Marsannay "Le Clos"—R. Bouvier 2010 $60
Burgundy Nerthus Domaine Roblet-Monnot 2011 $50
Chablis 1er Cru les Vaillons—J. Drouhin 2011 (5) $48

2   **3**   **4**   **5**

THE RHÔNE VALLEY
Saint-Joseph "Silice"—P.&J. Coursodon 2012 $60

THE LOIRE VALLEY
Vouvray "Le Portail"—D&C, Champalou 2010 $48
Quincy Domaine Trotereau 2012 $40

ITALY
Tuscany "Insoglio" del Cinghiale—Campo di Sasso 2011 $42

Wine by the glass

A restaurant menu usually offers at least one wine by the glass. These are generally simple wines, but don't dismiss them. If only the region is listed, though, be careful. Are there a lot of wines by the glass on the menu? Ask how the open bottles are stored. After a few days, if the wine isn't kept in special machines or with a cork that keeps the wine airtight, the quality of the wine will deteriorate.

The following should always be included:

1 The region

2 The appellation

3 The name of the winery, producer, or négociant

4 The vintage

5 The price!

The menu could also include:
- the name of the parcel (examples: Premier Cru de Vaillons)
- the name of the cuvée (or blend) (example: Cuvée Silice, Cuvée du Portail)
- the country, if it's an international wine list

Is the list not telling you enough?

Ask the server or the sommelier to clarify for you. It's their job to know the wines they serve. If they don't know how to answer, that means that perhaps the restaurant doesn't pay a lot of attention to their wine list. That doesn't bode well for the choices they have made.

Pricing

Wines by the glass

Ounce for ounce, it is often more expensive than a whole bottle. Although a glass is only a sixth of the bottle, a glass is frequently sold at a fourth of the price of the whole bottle. If the same wine is offered by the glass and by the bottle, calculate to know if the glass is priced honestly.

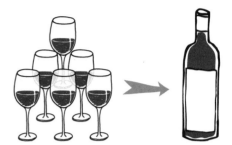

The bottle at a restaurant

The margin that restaurants take on wine is deemed to be very high. On average, a restaurant triples the wholesale price of its bottles. Knowing that they buy them less expensively than a consumer does, it's reasonable to think that they cost between two and two and a half times more than you would have paid at the winery. For example, a wine sold for $15 at the winery can be found on a restaurant menu for $35.

More troublesome (and more horrifying) is that it is not rare to find restaurants that might price their wine at five to six times their cost, banking on the ignorance of their customers!

Our advice
There are several smartphone applications that can help you find the average price of a bottle of wine (as long as it's not too confidential). This should help you judge whether the cost of the wine you want at a restaurant is worth it.

Bring your own bottle

If you have a well-stocked wine cellar, bring your own bottle, which will be subject to a corkage fee. Even if the fee is high, this could be a good deal if you bring a very good bottle.

THE ROLE OF THE SOMMELIER

In a fine dining restaurant, there will likely be a sommelier. He and he alone (or she) will take your wine order. His job is to advise what the best match is between the food you order and a wine. Often, he is the one who has selected and purchased the bottles. His goal is to offer wine service at as high a quality as your meal.

A good sommelier:

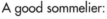

▸ Knows the wine perfectly but never pushes it on the client.
▸ Knows the wine list and ensures it is current (with good vintages). If a wine is out of stock, he will let you know and suggest a close alternative.
▸ Is a fine psychologist and understands how to read between the lines of what you want and what you are likely to like.
▸ Tries to tactfully guess your taste.

▸ Offers suggestions if you don't know what to pick. He will not choose the most expensive, but only the best wine for your table's meal choices—and for your tastes, of course.
▸ Helps you decide between two or three wines if you can't. Even better, he offers you a skillful synthesis of your likes.
▸ Never judges your choice. He might make a suggestion for you, but he should never make you feel like your decision was a bad one.
▸ Will ask you to sample it first, if you choose a wine by the glass, to make sure you like it.

At the time of service

The sommelier will uncork the bottle in front of you. If it's already open, you could think it's a defective bottle sent back by a previous client. Be vigilant during tasting!

The sommelier asks who wants to taste the wine. The person who ordered it is usually the one who tastes it.
You taste and, if you approve, the sommelier fills the glasses of everyone else at the table, and finishes filling yours last.

Why do you taste a wine?

To see if there is a defect, such as cork taint, oxidation, reduction, or incorrect temperature.

 If the wine is corked or oxidized, send it back. The sommelier must bring an identical bottle, and make sure it's unopened. And he should not contradict you and smell the cork himself! On the other hand, you can't blame him if the wine is corked, it's not his fault.

 If the wine is too cold, tell him. There is nothing to do but wrap your hands around the glass to warm up the wine. But don't forget that the cold masks aromas. You could be surprised when its character appears.

 If the wine is reduced or closed (it has no aromas), ask the sommelier to decant it. A sommelier who knows his wines well will do this instinctively or at least prompt you.

 If the wine doesn't have a defect but you don't like it, you can't send it back. You can, however, talk about it with the sommelier to find out why he put this wine on the menu.

 If the wine is too warm, ask for an ice bucket.

HOW TO DECODE A WINE LABEL

The different elements

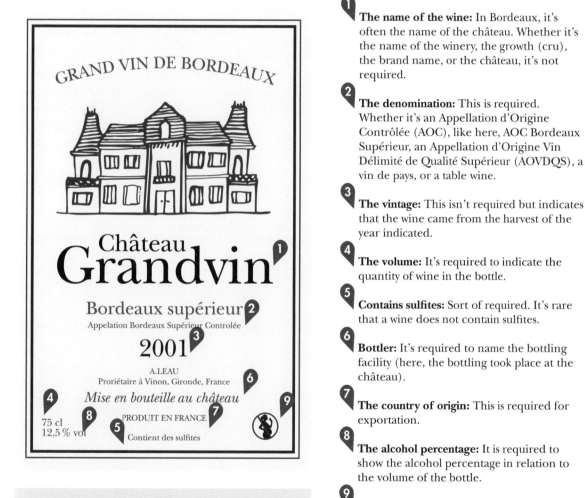

1 **The name of the wine:** In Bordeaux, it's often the name of the château. Whether it's the name of the winery, the growth (cru), the brand name, or the château, it's not required.

2 **The denomination:** This is required. Whether it's an Appellation d'Origine Contrôlée (AOC), like here, AOC Bordeaux Supérieur, an Appellation d'Origine Vin Délimité de Qualité Supérieur (AOVDQS), a vin de pays, or a table wine.

3 **The vintage:** This isn't required but indicates that the wine came from the harvest of the year indicated.

4 **The volume:** It's required to indicate the quantity of wine in the bottle.

5 **Contains sulfites:** Sort of required. It's rare that a wine does not contain sulfites.

6 **Bottler:** It's required to name the bottling facility (here, the bottling took place at the château).

7 **The country of origin:** This is required for exportation.

8 **The alcohol percentage:** It is required to show the alcohol percentage in relation to the volume of the bottle.

9 **This is required on French labels.** In the Unites States you would see the Surgeon General's warning, recommending that pregnant women not drink alcohol.

The example shown here conforms to French wine label requirements. Different countries will have different requirements. And it should be mentioned that there are two other pieces of information often found on the label: the number of the lot to assure traceability on fine wines and information on recycling the bottle.

Another example: Burgundy wine label

1 **Appellation:** In the case of a Burgundy Premier Cru or Grand Cru, the region of Burgundy is sometimes not mentioned but the appellation must be indicated below, along with, in the case of a Premier Cru, the name of the parcel of land (here: Les Chaffots). It's the opposite of Bordeaux, which prioritizes wines by Domaines. Burgundy classifies wines according to *terroir*. That's why you must distinguish at the same time the *terroir* and the producer.

2 **Name of the vineyard:** It could be a producer (or harvester, same thing) or a négociant, as in this example.

Optional terms

1 Exact or stylized representation of the château, winery, or brand name.

2 The mode of manufacture, the type of aging, or other traditional reference. Example: "aged in oak," "old vines."

3 The name of the varietals used.

4 A medal or distinction.

5 Type of wine: Brut, Dry, Semi-Dry, Sweet. This reference is only required for sparkling wines.

The back Label

In the goal of refining the label presentation, some producers decide to put a label on the back of the bottle. This back label can provide more detailed information:

1 **Presentation of the vineyard:** its history, its traditions, its ideas about wine.

2 **Advice:** the optimal serving temperature, food-pairing suggestions, whether it's necessary to carafe the wine.

3 **A logo or supplementary certification:** for example, a seal certifying that it is organic, from Ecocert, Demeter, or Biodyvin.

In the middle of all of these references, you should look for signs that are guarantees of a good quality wine that is carefully produced:

A cru class: Grand Cru in Alsace, 1st thorugh 5th Grand Cru Classé and Cru Bourgeois in Bordeaux, Premier Cru and Grand Cru in Burgundy. Nevertheless, there are excellent wines that aren't classified.

Mise en bouteille à la propriété: This means the wine was bottled at the winery or the château. Sure, there are mediocre wines that are bottled at the property and good wines that have been bottled outside of the winery. But in general, a wine bottled at the producer is a good sign. In any case, avoid the mention "*mise en bouteille dans la region de production*" (bottled in the region of production), which means that it bottled outside the specific appellation and nearly always suggests a wine without identity that is quite average, and maybe even bad.

An acceptable alcohol percentage: A grape that is not quite ripe has a weak alcoholic potential and a green taste. So choose red or white wines with a minimum of 12 percent alcohol. For sweetened wines, try to choose a bottle with 13.5 percent or more alcohol.

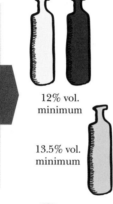

12% vol. minimum

13.5% vol. minimum

An original back label: The standard descriptions and the classic wine pairings are often written by a team of marketers, the text is becoming more and more annoying, and they all are all starting to sound alike. A poem, a message, or a surprising story about the winery means the opposite. It signifies the producer wants to surprise you and express their personality. Chances are that they will express it equally well in the glass.

The pure tin capsule : Pure tin capsules are another tool to brand the wine and are associated with wines of the greatest quality. You'll know it's pure tin when it fits the neck of the bottle snugly and cuts off the bottle cleanly without leaving any sharp edges. Pure tin is also natural and recyclable (versus plastic), a characteristic associated with high quality. New World wines generally use the capsule to brand their winery; French wineries also use the capsule to denote the association between the grapes and the winery: R signifies the wine was bottled by the same person who owns the grapes, N means the grapes are not owned by the bottler but they probably have some say in the farming, and E means the grapes were likely purchased in bulk and marketed by the bottler.

THE MARKETING GAME

Sometimes you'll fine references or phrases that can make the label seem very pretty but don't actually mean anything. Marketing folks wisely highlight certain aspects of the wine on the label, but sometimes they add words just for looks because they think it will entice the customer.

Grand Vin de Bordeaux

This reference means nothing! It's simply there to decorate the bottles with AOC and pretend to play on the regional fame. This term is no guarantee of the quality.

Grande Cuvée, Tête de Cuvée, Cuvée Prestige

Like the reference above, these don't mean anything either. Don't be fooled. This type of denomination simply means, in general, that the bottle is a more prestigious Cuvée than the basic blend.

Aged in oak barrels

This is an indication of the style of the wine, not of the quality. It's optional. Some wines that are aged in barrels never mention that fact. Plus, you don't know how long they've been aged in oak barrels. And you don't know if the wine has enough character to support aging in oak. So be careful when you see this reference prominently placed on a label.

Old vines

Old vines are not truly old unless they are forty years old or more, and their age influences the taste of the wine. Nevertheless, some producers don't hesitate to put this on the label of a vine that's between twenty and thirty years old. There is no legal definition of how old is old.

The shape of the label

Bold producers aren't afraid to make labels in any shape—teardrop, round, cut or split into several parts. These wines are aimed at novices more than the wine lovers who fall for the imitation parchment. These last seem to get more and more tacky to the eyes of consumers. It's all about the package design and has little to do with the quality of the wine. If you like the label design, why not?

The design

New World wines are unrivaled in ingenuity for decorating their labels with designs or photos to give a youthful edge to their wines. Some French wines also use a different illustration every vintage. Among them, the most well known, and pioneer of the genre, is Mouton-Rothschild, which commissions a contemporary artist every year to design their label. Picasso, Keith Haring, or more recently Jeff Koons were ready to play.

Girly wine label

Women drink and buy wine, and more women than men shop at grocery stores. Not surprising, then, that they constitute a prime target for marketing specialists. Where pink labels of varying degrees of good taste flourish on the shelves, there have been some good sales. However, surveys show that women aren't as easily influenced as once thought, and they are reluctant to buy visually feminine wine if they plan to serve it at a table with both men and women. There are some great successes, however.

The Château
The use of the word *Château* on a bottle corresponds to a very particular law. In order to put it on the label, the wine must come from an Appellation d'Origine Contrôlée (AOC), be produced on a property that includes both the vines and a cellar. So, a cooperative winery or an independent winemaker can claim the name.

Bottled in cooperative
A cooperative wine can sometimes tack on the phrase *mise en bouteille à la propriété* (bottled at the property). It shouldn't be a surprise if the winemakers are part owners of the cooperative. It's their own property.

A logo bigger than the name
An Organic, ECOCERT, or Demeter logo is often a sign that the producer, anxious to heal the land of his vineyards, has put much care into vinifying the wine. Even so, these logos, very prized by consumers, are also the target of marketing. If one of these logos is big, maybe too big, it's possible it's a wine where the vine was treated organically but the wine was made in an industrial cellar.

A misspelled name
Château Lafite exists, Château Laffite too. But they're not the same wines! The first is one of the best wines from Bordeaux, a Premier Grand Cru Classe that commands astronomical prices. The second is the name of a wine that is a lot more modest from Saint-Estèphe as well as another in the Madiran.

Vin de pays (highest rank in the French table-wine category)
They are rare, but fabulous Vin de pays wines exist, some more reputable than most AOC wines. Often it's a position taken by the producer, for which he has voluntarily decided to leave the appellation off to create a wine that he wants without conforming to the AOC requirements. Some winemakers, already well known among wine lovers, choose to use a varietal that isn't authorized by the appellation or to ignore the proportion of a varietal required by the appellation, which means their wine must be labeled under the more generic Vin de France (wine of France) appellation. Nevertheless, the price remains high, and you won't find it at the supermarket.

HOW TO BUY A BOTTLE

At the corner store

Some observations

In a little corner grocery store, the wines are stored upright, at room temperature. These storage conditions are not really ideal. The wine gets overheated and the corks can dry out. If possible, find a bottle with a screwcap, which protects the wine better if mishandled.

What to choose?

If you are going to drink it right away, ignore the big appellations, which are expensive and demand a few years of aging. The tannins will be too much in the reds, and the wood influence from aging will be too prominent in the whites.

Opt for fruity wines to drink young

For red: Loire (Chinon, Saumur-Champigny, Bourgueil), Côtes du Rhône (supple tannins, warm wines), Beaujolais (not Beaujolais Nouveau but a Brouilly, a Saint-Amour, or a Chiroubles). Barbera from Italy, Malbec from Argentina, Zinfandel from California, and wines from Spain or Chile are good alternatives. They are supple and easy to drink and often reasonably priced.
For white: Forget dry wines with marked acidity. Go for round and fruity whites like you find in Mâconnais, in Provence, or in the Languedoc. Soave from Italy and Pinot Gris from Oregon are also good choices.
Sparkling: Choose a Champagne from a known winery, so the quality is reliable. If not, better to take an expensive Crémant, Italian Prosecco, or Spanish Cava than a bargain Champagne.

If you can, shop at wine stores where the quality is more reliable among the less expensive wines. For example: a Burgundy from Jadot or Bouchard, a Languedoc from Gérard Bertrand, a Côtes du Rhône from Chapoutier or Guigal, a Dolcetto from Vietti, a Malbec from Montes Alpha.

AT THE SUPERMARKET

You'll find lots to drink on the wine shelves at the supermarket. In other words, there's a little bit of everything: lots of choices in a wide range of prices.

The advantage of buying at the supermarket
More than the number of wines offered (two thirds of which are not worth it), the prices are what attract us. Big supermarket chains negotiate very tight cost margins in order to sell them for less than other places charge.

Disadvantage
Most of the time, there is no one who can help you.

Neck tags

These additional notes hanging from the neck of the bottle tell you that the wine has been chosen (or approved, or recommended) by a guide: Wine Spectator, Hachette, Gault and Millau. This doesn't mean that the wine is great, but it does guarantee an acceptable quality that you can trust.

RED WINES   ROSÉ WINES   WH

Medals

These are appearing more and more on bottles. But beware, not all wine tasting competitions are created equal. A bronze medal from an unknown contest does not guarantee a good wine. It's the fame of the show and its competition that give validity to a medal. The most well-known medals are awarded by the Salon des vins Vignerons Independent, the Salon International de l'Agriculture, the Concours General Agricole, and the Concours Mondial de Bruxelles, and you can trust them. Keep in mind that an awarded wine is not the best in its category for all its existence, but only that it was appreciated among others, at a certain moment, by certain judges. Plus, you have to pay to participate in tasting contests.

Paul buys wine

Brand name wines

Wines from big names are easier to find. They are the sure bets to choose and will have a consistent quality. Note that there many stores that have private-label bottles: Two-buck Chuck was created by Trader Joe's, and Costco created its own brand called Kirkland.

They don't have a lot of personality, but oenologically speaking, they are well made and don't present defects.

Winemaker wines

The big stores are sometimes exclusive resellers of specific winemakers, but more often they prefer to sell big producers who can stock several stores over the course of the year. These are often wines with consistent though not super-refined personality. To find wines from a sharp winemaker with atypical character or produced in small batches is a difficult feat.

 Scan the labels

Bring your smartphone with an app that can identify numerous wines and likely give you an informed opinion (Delectable Cor.kz, Drync, Vivino, Plonk, and many others). Look for QR codes, which are found more and more frequently on labels, if you want to know more about the winery.

These are the best places to learn about wines that you might want to buy. You can taste them beforehand! The goal of the tasting rooms, where winemakers come to pour you their wine, is for you to discover and buy their wine. Even at a little producer, you'll find a table and glasses ready for tasting.

The price

A wine bought directly from the producer is always less expensive. There are no intermediaries between you and him, so no markups added to the price.

The range

A winery never produces just one blend. It always offers a range of entry-level wines and others that are more complex. It can also vinify different parcels separately and sell several wines by *terroir*, appellation, varietal blend, or type of aging. Buying a wine onsite gives you the chance to taste the entire range. Of course, you aren't obligated to like the most expensive wine. On the contrary, you might actually prefer the simplest. A good winemaker must care for his small wine with the same attention he gives to his big wines. Nothing should prohibit you from buying the simplest and coming back the next year to try a wine with a little more complexity. It's a good way of progressing.

Paul buys wine

The discussion

At wine festivals, a winemaker is often overwhelmed by visitors and doesn't have time to talk. But if you come to see him at his place, there's a good chance he'll be happy to spend some more time with you.

Visiting the winemaker

Only he can tell you the average age of his vines, the composition and orientation of the soil, the rain that was missing or that was too present this year, or about his work in the cellar. You can therefore learn why this wine is more gluttonous, why this other is more elegant. Be careful not to waste his time or hospitality. Staying two hours to chat with the winemaker to only buy a half bottle is not polite. If you can't take several bottles, tell him right away. Same thing if you visit a big winery without being able to afford to buy anything. Many wineries now charge for tastings and will offer a discount if you actually buy a bottle.

Horizontal or vertical

To taste horizontally means to taste several blends from the same vintage and same winery. It's a frequent exercise if you visit a winery. It's also a good way of exploring the consistency of wines from one producer.

To do a vertical tasting is less common, which means tasting the same wine over several vintages. Winemakers who have a little stock sometimes sell several vintages at the same time, and it's an excellent way to understand the effect of weather on wine and to observe its evolution.

 Basic rules when visiting vineyards and wine cellars

Preview your venue. Négociants and wine cooperatives are open without an appointment, but winemakers can't always see you if you show up unexpectedly. During the harvest, for example, is not a good time for visits, especially at very small wineries.

A good wine store manager is always passionate—and often chatty. He is one of the most precious contacts for wine lovers. He will guide you from one bottle to another, he encourages tasting wines that you haven't thought about buying, and he can open the door to beautiful surprises and great discoveries.

Chain wine stores

A wine seller who works for a chain chooses from a large catalog of wines. He will choose to stock certain bottles over others depending on each store's clientele. Even if the selection is more classic at an independent wine store, you will always find something to satisfy a craving, and the wine store manager will be able to guide you.

Independent wine stores

This wine seller often meets the winemakers directly to taste their wines. He invites them to his store sometimes, chooses one or several wines, and negotiates prices. Depending on what he likes and his personality, he can point you toward wines, essentials, local wine varietals that have fallen out of favor, less well-known appellations, wines from charming countries, and organic wines. A good wine store manager will offer you some great classics but also some surprising wines.

A good wine store manager

▸ Doesn't direct you to the most expensive wine if you give him a price point. He should offer you average, high, and low.
▸ Doesn't just read off the label if you ask him for information about a bottle. He should be able to tell you the name of the producer, or even better, give you some information about the vineyard.

▸ Can bring out his current favorite. He drinks the wines that he sells and he has his own preferences.
▸ Has available for sale some good Beaujolais, a good Muscadet, a good Riesling, and some good wines from other parts of the world. A wine store manager can't turn his nose up at wines that don't have a great reputation because all appellations have good wines.

AT A WINE FESTIVAL

Do you have the soul of an explorer? You can throw yourself into the wine festivals. In France, these have been around for about thirty years. Festivals of wine represent for the exhibitors more than half the year's sales in the wine sector. The next time you are in France you should try to attend one.

How they work

This phenomenon, which you won't find anywhere else in the world, happens twice a year, in spring and fall, and it lasts about two weeks.

The September fair is a lot more interesting. The new vintage has just been bottled and, for big stores, it's the ideal moment to empty their shelves to make room for the new harvest. One thing is certain—you can always find good deals at wine fairs. The competition is so fierce among retailers during this period that margins are kept to a minimum.

Fancy a stroll?

You can also buy a range of wines, taste them, and return them to buy a bigger quantity of the wine that's won your heart.

Be prepared

Be sure to consult online and print wine publications so that you'll be armed with the latest news and information before you go.

Good deals

The best deals are often on the first day, or even the day before. To take advantage, you have to be invited to the opening parties. It's not very hard to get an invitation, though. All you need to do is meet someone involved. Be quick. The shopping carts fill, and the shelves empty all too quickly.

How to buy a bottle

ON THE INTERNET

Online sales are exploding. Since 2007, sales of wine on the Internet show an increase of 33 percent per year on average. As a result, some sites have closed and some are just starting up. How do you know which ones to rely on?

Look for clues

The wine description
The first thing to look for when judging online wine sites is how detailed their information is. If you find a website where the wine is described precisely according to its character and its aromas, and if it is also accompanied by a technical sheet—listing AOC, the grape variety (or varieties), and the alcohol percent—these are all very good signs. If, however, the site doesn't offer any details about the wine, it might be better to look elsewhere.

Practical information
Storage conditions, although essential, are often neglected. If nothing is mentioned about this on the website, avoid buying older vintages. Other concerns include the price, the time, and the quality of shipping service. All this must be clearly indicated, not just written in small type under the terms of sale.

False promotions
A classic marketing technique is to show the price crossed out or a "sale" logo written really big. Is it really a good deal? Don't hesitate to compare costs by using specialized websites like WineDecider, Snooth, or Wine-Searcher.

The wines offered
Make sure that the wines offered for sale are actually available! There are countless sites that have displayed the sale of wine futures they had not yet acquired and they were ultimately unable to purchase—to the dismay of customers on the other side of the screen that had already placed an order.

Some classic sites, among others

Reliable consensus: Vinatis, Nicolas, Vin-Malin, Millesima, K&L Wines, Wine.com
Private sales: 1Jour1Vin, Ventealapropriete, Vinfolio
Auctions: IDealwine, WineBid, CellarBid
Subscription: Trois Fois Vin, Amicalement vin, Le Petit Ballon, Club W, Lot18
Wine store sites: Savour Club, Lavinia, Legrand Filles et Fils, La Contre-Etiquette, Sherry-Lehmann, Astor Wines

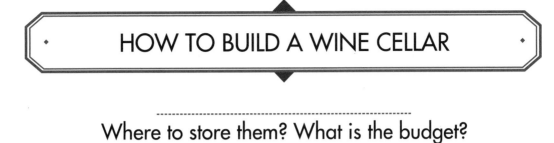

HOW TO BUILD A WINE CELLAR

Where to store them? What is the budget?

You only need one bottle to start a wine cellar. Next, it all depends on the space you have available and your budget. The ideal, of course, is to own a bunch of wines that can adapt to all situations.

4 to 8 bottles

Buy some bottles of white wine and some bottles of red wine for everyday drinking—to have on hand for aperitifs or impromptu dinners. Look for wines that are fruity and drinkable: reds from the Loire, Languedoc, Tuscany, Chile, and Argentina; for whites a Chablis, a Vermentino, or a white from Provence. Also buy a sparkling, Champagne, or Cava, to open when there is something to celebrate.
Budget: between $10 and $20 per bottle.

8 to 12 bottles

Expand your stash with a sweet wine for dessert or a Sunday afternoon with friends around a cake. Plan a sweet wine for the end of parties or for lovers of sugary aperitifs (Port, Muscat de Rivesaltes), and one or two rosés for summer. Finally, get a good-quality red wine (and eventually a white wine), from a respected appellation. It can be a Pomerol or a South African Bordeaux blend in red and a Meursault or Sonoma Coast Chardonnay in white, for example. These are the wines that you can keep several years and can uncork for a beautiful occasion: a birthday, a declaration of love, a happy reunion.
Budget: between $10 and $40 per bottle.

 Don't bankrupt yourself!

Whatever your bank balance, never buy wine that is beyond your means, under the pretext of going "a little crazy." Because this little crazy will make you build up unrealistic expectations. And the day you finally uncork that bottle, those expectations will be so high that you will risk being strongly disappointed. Plus, very expensive wines generally call for longer aging, and if you don't have the optimal storage conditions for wine, you will have wasted all that money you spent.

12 to 30 bottles

It's time to diversify your collection. Choose wines from different regions, even different countries, to vary your pleasures. The important thing is that they have varied aromatic and taste profiles: Wines that are lively and light, fine and complex, intense and spicy, silky and powerful. Then, you will always have the perfect bottle for any situation. Don't forget some eccentric wines, made from a rare varietal or from an undiscovered appellation. And it's even better if they have a nice story to tell.
Budget: between $10 and $45 per bottle.

More than 30 bottles

Buy your favorite bottles in mixed cases, choosing three each of the same or six each. You will then have the pleasure of seeing a wine evolve with time, of observing how the wine shows at six months, one year, and two years or more after purchase.

Begin to interest yourself in vintage
At this stage, you will without a doubt have some special winemakers who you visit regularly. Buy their wine from one year to the next and notice the influence of vintage.

Distinguish the wines worth aging
Separate the wines for drinking right away from the wines to age. The former will be a revolving door of bottles that you will renew as often as necessary. You will keep the latter several years (sometimes more than a decade) before beginning to drink them. Nevertheless, you will continue to buy them regularly. You will have them always within arm's reach—some young wines, some mature wines, and some aged wines.
Budget: no limit.

Paul buys wine

CONDITIONS FOR AGING WINE

According to the conditions of how you store your wine, the bottles will evolve more or less quickly. A bottle exposed to a temperature of 64°F, will evolve and age more quickly than one at 54°F. However, as with human beings, a wine ages best if it ages slowly.

For optimum storage, a wine cellar must respect certain criteria:

Temperature

The ideal temperature for aging wine over decades, is from 52° to 57°F. But the majority of bottles keep very well for several years if held between 43° and 64°F. The aging is slowed by the cold and accelerated by heat. The slow and natural rhythm of the seasons in a wine cellar allows a wine to age harmoniously. Most of all, avoid abrupt variations in temperature, which will ruin the wine. Avoid storing the wine near a radiator, an oven, or some other source of heat. This will degrade the wine very quickly.

Bottles stacked horizontally

Wine bottles must always be stored lying down, especially if closed with a natural cork. This will keep the liquid in contact with the cork and allow it to stay hydrated and well sealed.

Humidity

This is very important. If the air is too dry, the cork will dry out and become porous to the air. The best conditions include fresh humid air, with about 75 to 90 percent humidity. The only risk is too much humidity (quite rare), because the cork will mold and the labels will become unglued.

Light

This is harmful to the wine. It will deteriorate the color as well as the aromas. Always keep wine away from bright light. A cabinet under the stairs or even draped with a cloth can do the job.

Calm

Just like us when we sleep, wine needs calm surroundings. Bumps and vibrations break up the molecules and disturb the aromas. Avoid storing wine above a subway tunnel or on a washing machine.

Bad odors

Bad smells can infiltrate the wine through the cork. Don't store wine near garlic cloves, a bleach-soaked mop, or motor oil. Even a moist cardboard box, if it's around a bottle for a long time, can influence the bouquet.

The big question is: Should this wine be aged? Aging a wine starts with knowing when to drink it.

Wines to drink young

Most wines that are less expensive. Sparkling, whites, rosés, or light and less tannic reds can be consumed right when you buy them. These are the majority of wines that you will probably buy. They are very strong in their youthful spirit, fruit-forward, and they won't gain anything by aging.

Which wines?
There are some exceptions, but in general, wines made from Pinot Blanc, Viognier, Sauvignon Blanc, and Gamay, for example, are best to drink in their youth.
This being the case, you can still try to save them for several years if the wine is powerful enough. You could be surprised.

Wines to drink old

These are often the wines that are more prestigious and more expensive. They are very powerful when they are young and need time to open up, become refined, and develop a complex and harmonious bouquet.

Which wines?
You'll find among others among the reds big Bordeaux wines and great Burgundies, Hermitages, Châteauneuf-du-Papes, Madirans, Spanish Priorats and Ribera del Dueros, Italian Barolos and Barbarescos, Ports, big wines from Argentina, California, and Australia. Among whites you'll find certain dry and sweet Chenin Blancs from the Loire Valley and from South Africa, big Burgundies, German sweet and dry Rieslings, syrupy Sauternes, Tokajis from Hungary and Italian Moscatos.

How do you know if you should age a wine?

Educate yourself: Ask the winemaker or the wine store manager who sold you the wine, read the back label of the bottle, and look on the Internet.

How does the wine age in the bottle?

Oxygen makes wine age. There's always a little bubble of air in the bottle. This little bubble is just enough to allow the wine to mature, reach its peak, and then decline. If the bottle is lying down, the bubble of air is in contact with more of the wine and makes it evolve better. This is another good reason to lay your bottles down.

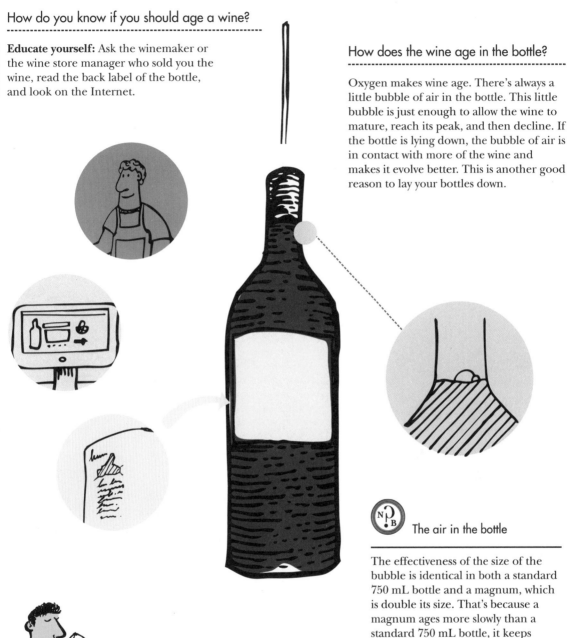

NB The air in the bottle

The effectiveness of the size of the bubble is identical in both a standard 750 mL bottle and a magnum, which is double its size. That's because a magnum ages more slowly than a standard 750 mL bottle, it keeps better, and (bonus!) costs less in proportion to the amount of wine.

Taste it: If you have at least two bottles of the same wine, open one.
Does the wine seem closed, compact, dense, barely aromatic?
From all evidence, it is not ready to be awakened so early. You must wait.
It is very powerful, with acidity and very strong tannins?
It can wait several more years.

Building a wine cellar

In a small apartment

Use a cabinet or a bureau drawer. If you have a non-working fireplace, put your bottles in it. It will generally stay cooler there than in the rest of the house. The important thing in all of these solutions is to make sure the wine is lying down, away from bright light, and far from a source of heat. If you own a wine rack, make sure it won't be hit by the sun's rays.

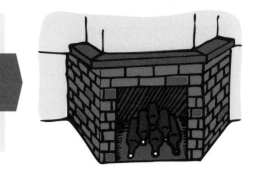

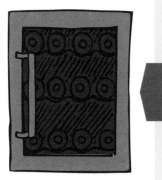

In a bigger apartment or a house

You have a little money and a lot of bottles but no wine cellar? Invest in an electric cellar. These wine refrigerators do a good job, keeping constant temperature and humidity while protecting bottles from light. They range in size from quite small to very big. Depending on the model, they can hold between 12 and 300 bottles. There are three types: wine coolers that store wines for several months; aging cellars, which are more expensive, but they will keep the temperature constant at 54°F; and the really high-end types, the dual-zone cellars, which combine different temperatures according to the compartments. Winemakers advise using electric cellars to vary the temperature 3 to 5°F, according to the time of year, to reproduce the natural cycle of the seasons.

In a house

You have a lot of money and ambition but no wine cellar? Have one built! With some work, it's possible to create a special room just for your bottles—with good isolation, no windows, sealed, air conditioned, and humidified. And lastly, a solid door and a strong lock. Some companies specialize in excavation and insert cylindrical cellars with integrated storage. You can access it by a ladder or, even more luxurious, a spiral staircase through the center. You can stock between 500 and 5,000 bottles there.

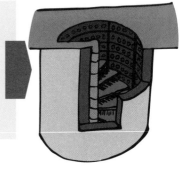

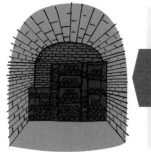

You have a cellar?

You are lucky or have foresight. If you have an underground cellar—with thick walls, in old stone and clay soil—that's ideal. Is the cellar modern, concrete, and warm enough? See if you can isolate it and even install a humidifier. To avoid wasting too much energy, you can stock 150 bottles in 30 cubic feet. If you arrange the room well, stacking the wines from the ground to the ceiling and leaving a little passageway, it's possible to stock some 1,200 bottles in a space that is 15 feet square.

Paul buys wine

How do you stack the bottles?

Shelves: They can be plastic or metal. They are bought as a unit and hold from six to twelve bottles and stack on top of each other. These are perfectly modifiable and adaptable to spaces. Avoid tall stacks, which can become unsteady.

Fixed bins: Attached to the walls, bins are strong and offer good protection for the bottles. You can construct them yourself to fit, or find specialized shelves.

Original cases: Sure, as long as they are in pristine wood or in an environment that's not too humid. Be careful: If the humidity is high, the carton or even the wood of the case can mold and transmit mildew through the cork of the wine.

How do you arrange the wines?

By region
This is a classic way to arrange the wine that will allow you to easily find the right style for the meal.

By vintage
It's a good way to separate bottles that should be drunk within two years from those that can age longer.

By priority
Store bottles that will be drunk quickly at a level that is easiest to reach. Bottles that can age for a few years can be stored close to the floor or very high near the ceiling.

The wine cellar journal
It's an indispensable tool for all lovers who keep wine. In the journal you will record:

The region of origin, the vintage, the name of the winery or the producer, the place, the price and the date of purchase, the number of bottles bought (to be corrected each time you open one), and especially the place where the wine is stored! A wine cellar journal allows you to find bottles quickly. To help even more, use a felt-tip pen to mark your shelves or racks. For example, Burgundy on B4, Languedoc on B5, Bordeaux to drink young on C1, etc.

CHEAT SHEETS

TO MEMORIZE IN THE BLINK OF AN EYE

CHEAT SHEET
Juliette plans a party

CHEAT SHEET
Jack learns to taste wine

CHEAT SHEET
Henry participates in the harvest

CHEAT SHEET Caroline
visits the vineyards

CHEAT SHEET Elizabeth
becomes an apprentice sommelier

CHEAT SHEET
Paul buys wine

In a suitable glass, wine gives off more aromas and feels better in the mouth.

Open a powerful wine three hours before the meal.

To open a bottle of Champagne, don't pull the cork, turn the bottle!

Carafe a young wine to let it breathe. Decant an old wine to separate it from the deposits.

For a romantic dinner, avoid red wine. It stains the teeth.

The best way to chill wine quickly: a bucket filled with water and ice cubes plus a pinch of salt.

A white wine must be served between 46° and 55°F, a red between 55° and 64°F.

Serve bottles in this order: from lightest to most powerful.

CHEAT SHEET
Juliette plans a party

To avoid a hangover, you should drink as much water as possible before going to bed.

Cold masks the aromas and hardens the tannins. Heat makes wine heavy and pasty.

Don't fill a glass more than one-third full.

After opening, a bottle that is mostly full keeps better than an almost empty bottle.

White wine is effective in getting rid of red-wine stains.

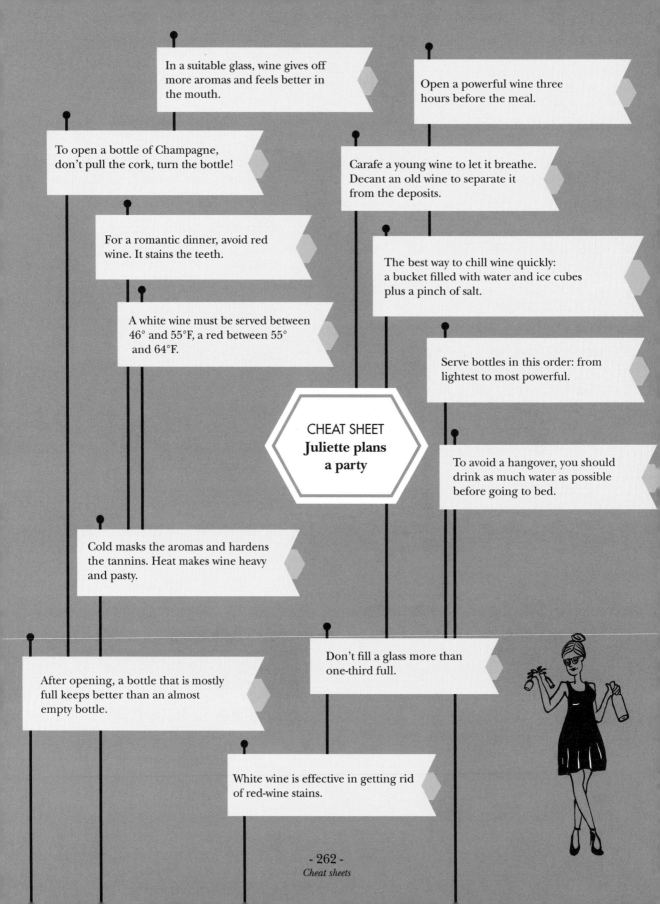

The color of a red wine is a testimony to its age and its origin.

Rosé is not made by mixing red and white wines.

The tears in the glass indicate the quantity of alcohol and sugar in the wine.

The primary aromas are contained in the base of the grape while the tertiary aromas are created from the aging.

A young wine has springtime aromas, an old wine an autumnal bouquet.

The number of bubbles in a sparkling wine depends on how clean the glass is.

A reductive odor is due to a lack of oxygen in the wine.

To "trill" the wine means to taste it while breathing in to help the wine express itself inside your mouth.

CHEAT SHEET
Jack learns to taste wine

Acidity is the backbone of wine, essential to its future.

A fresh or lively wine is a wine that has a lot of acidity and not much fat.

A heavy or heady wine is a wine that has a lot of fat or alcohol and little acidity.

Retro-olfaction allows you to smell with your mouth.

The tannins in wine dry the tongue and give structure to the wine. They are rough, silky, or velvety, depending on their quality.

Aromas are perceived by both the nose and the mouth.

Naturally sweet wine is a wine muted by the addition of alcohol during fermentation.

During the slow maturing of the fruit, the grape changes color: from green, it becomes yellow or red depending on the varietal.

A grape's varietal name designates the variety of vine cultivated to produce a wine.

Malolactic fermentation is part of the normal fermentation process for red wines; it's rare for whites and rosés.

Biodynamics is a more intense form of organic agriculture that is mainly based on cycles of the moon.

The skin of the grape gives its color to the wine. It is covered with a "bloom," which contains the yeast for fermentation.

Phylloxera is an American aphid that has forced winegrowers to use resistant rootstocks for vines.

An organic wine is a wine that comes from organic agriculture, which is a farming practice that does not use any chemical treatment.

CHEAT SHEET
Henry participates in the grape harvest

The Jeroboam is a 3-liter bottle, which holds the equivalent four classic 750 mL bottles.

The creation of alcohol is the result of the transformation of sugar by yeast.

Champagne's bubbles are created by a fermentation that happens inside the bottle.

To make a white wine, grapes are pressed right away, but for red wines, the skins are allowed to macerate in the juice.

Goblet pruning is a manner of pruning the vine very short. It is used in vineyards where it's hot.

Late harvest is reserved for sweet wines.

The quality of the vintage depends on the weather during the year where the vine grew.

Wine is better if the vine grows in poor soil.

A wine that simply shows its varietal character doesn't express the *terrior* of the place its grapes came from.

Terroir is the ensemble of natural factors, environmental and human, that give a wine its unique characteristics.

CHEAT SHEET
Caroline visits the vineyards

A chalky soil has a tendency to create wines that are finer and less ample than those grown in a clay soil.

A sweet wine goes well with a spicy Thai meal.

A full-bodied wine goes well with a strong dish, a fine wine with a light or delicate dish.

Deli meats go with a bright white, a rosé, a light red, or a full-bodied red.

Match wines and dishes based on their color or their origin.

Lamb requires a robust wine.

With sushi, serve a Sancerre or another Sauvignon Blanc.

CHEAT SHEET
Elizabeth becomes an apprentice sommelier

A contrasting pairing surprises and reveals new flavors.

A simple wine with a simple dish, a sophisticated wine with a sophisticated dish.

With hamburger, serve a Saint-Joseph or Pic Saint-Loup.

Vinaigrette ruins the taste of wine.

A full-bodied red is supple and invasive. It coats a meal like a sauce.

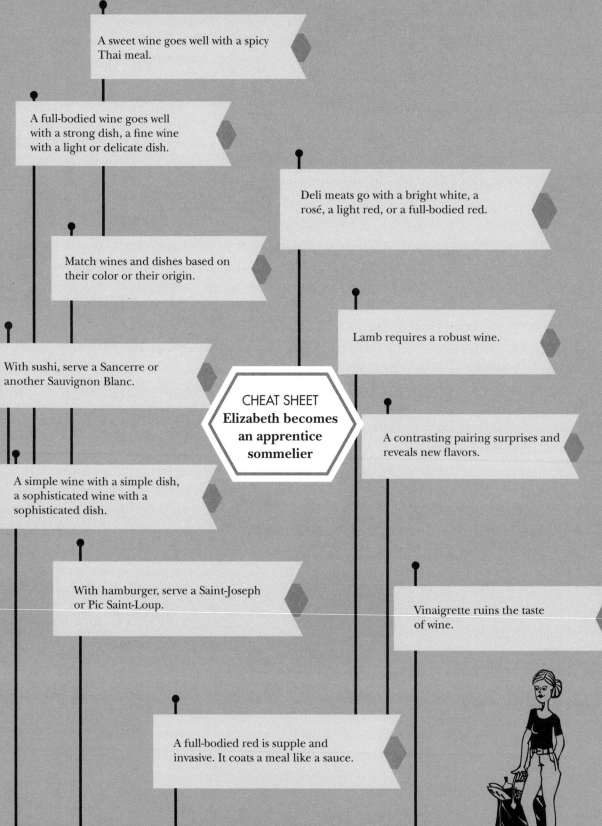

A sommelier is not responsible for a corked bottle, but he must exchange it for you without complaint.

An inoperative fireplace can be used to store wine bottles.

Before aging a wine, ask yourself if it's worth aging.

On the capsule of the bottle, the letters N or E signify that it's a négociant wine. The letter R means that it's a winegrower's wine.

The value of medals on bottles depends on the value of the contest that awarded the medals.

In a grocery store, it's better to buy a young wine with a screwcap.

A good sommelier always makes you taste the wine before he serves it.

You can classify wines according to region or according to vintage.

The back label allows space to add information about the wine and the vineyard.

CHEAT SHEET
Paul buys wine

To age, a wine needs darkness, cool air, humidity, and calm.

It's the airspace in the bottle that allows a wine to age.

It's required to put on the label where the wine was bottled.

The wine cellar notebook is indispensable for managing a wine cellar.

Wine fairs or visits to a winery remain the best way to taste, learn about a wine, and to pay a reasonable price for the wine.

On a Burgundy label, the appellation is in larger print than the name of the winery. The opposite is true for a Bordeaux wine label.

Avoid keeping wine in a place that smells bad.

The term "Grand Vin de Bordeaux" on a label is not regulated and doesn't mean anything.

INDEX